Problem
Solving
in Families

Understanding Families

Series Editors: *Bert N. Adams, University of Wisconsin*
David M. Klein, University of Notre Dame

This book series examines a wide range of subjects relevant to studying families. Topics include, but are not limited to, theory and conceptual design, research methods on the family, racial/ethnic families, mate selection, marriage, family power dynamics, parenthood, divorce and remarriage, custody issues, and aging families.

The series is aimed primarily at scholars working in family studies, sociology, psychology, social work, ethnic studies, gender studies, cultural studies, and related fields as they focus on the family. Volumes will also be useful for graduate and undergraduate courses in sociology of the family, family relations, family and consumer sciences, social work and the family, family psychology, family history, cultural perspectives on the family, and others.

Books appearing in **Understanding Families** are either single- or multiple-authored volumes or concisely edited books of original chapters on focused topics within the broad interdisciplinary field of marriage and family.

The books are reports of significant research, innovations in methodology, treatises on family theory, syntheses of current knowledge in a family subfield, or advanced textbooks. Each volume meets the highest academic standards and makes a substantial contribution to our understanding of marriages and families.

The National Council on Family Relations cosponsors with Sage a book award for students and new professionals. Award-winning manuscripts are published as part of the **Understanding Families** series.

Multiracial Couples: Black and White Voices
Paul C. Rosenblatt, Terri A. Karis, and Richard D. Powell

Understanding Latino Families: Scholarship, Policy, and Practice
Edited by Ruth E. Zambrana

Current Widowhood: Myths & Realities
Helena Znaniecka Lopata

Family Theories: An Introduction
David M. Klein and James M. White

Understanding Differences Between Divorced and Intact Families
Ronald L. Simons and Associates

Adolescents, Work, and Family: An Intergenerational Developmental Analysis
Jeylan T. Mortimer and Michael D. Finch

Families and Time: Keeping Pace in a Hurried Culture
Kerry J. Daly

No More Kin: Exploring Race, Class, and Gender in Family Networks
Anne R. Roschelle

Contemporary Parenting: Challenges and Issues
Edited by Terry Arendell

Families Making Sense of Death
Janice Winchester Nadeau

Black Families in Corporate America
Susan D. Toliver

Reshaping Fatherhood: The Social Construction of Shared Parenting
Anna Dienhart

Problem Solving in Families: Research and Practice
Samuel Vuchinich

African American Children: Socialization and Development in Families
Shirley A. Hill

Samuel Vuchinich

Problem Solving in Families
Research and Practice

UNDERSTANDING FAMILIES

SAGE Publications
International Educational and Professional Publisher
Thousand Oaks   London   New Delhi

For information:

SAGE Publications, Inc.
2455 Teller Road
Thousand Oaks, California 91320
E-mail: order@sagepub.com

SAGE Publications Ltd.
6 Bonhill Street
London EC2A 4PU
United Kingdom

SAGE Publications India Pvt. Ltd.
M-32 Market
Greater Kailash I
New Delhi 110 048 India

Printed in the United States of America

Library of Congress Cataloging-in-Publication Data

This book is printed on acid-free paper.

Vuchinich, Samuel.
    Problem solving in families: Research and practice / by Samuel Vuchinich.
        p.   cm. — (Understanding families; v. 13)
        Includes bibliographical references and index.
        ISBN 0-7619-0877-3 (cloth: alk. paper)
        ISBN 0-7619-0878-1 (pbk.: alk. paper)
        1. Family. 2. Problem solving. 3. Family psychotherapy. I. Title.
    II. Series.
        HQ728.V83   1998
        306.85—ddc21   98-25540

99   00   01   02   03   04   05   7   6   5   4   3   2   1

Acquiring Editor:	Jim Nageotte
Editorial Assistant:	Heidi Van Middlesworth
Production Editor:	Denise Santoyo
Production Assistant:	Stephanie Allen
Typesetters:	Rose Tylak/Christina Hill
Indexer:	Jean Casalegno

For my favorite family problem solvers:
Donna, Michelle, and Amy

Contents

Preface   ix

1. Introducing Family Problem Solving   1

   A Brief History   1
   Seeking an Integrative Synthesis   7
   What Is Family Problem Solving?   10
   The Distinctive Features of Family Problem Solving   17
   Plan of the Book   21

2. The Origins of a Science of Family Problem Solving   23

   Dewey, Thinking, and Problem Solving   25
   Freud, the Family, and Irrational Problem Solving   30
   Problem Solving as Instinct: A Legacy of William James   34
   Problem Solving Paradigms: 1920 to 1950   37
   Summary   42

3. Family Problem Solving Comes of Age   43

   The Dissection of the Small Group and the Family   44
   Social Class, Culture, and Family Problem Solving   53
   The Birth of Family Therapy: "We've Got a Problem!"   57
   Social Learning Theory, Mental Health, and Problem Solving   65
   Family Paradigms and Problem Solving   68
   Cognitive Problem Solving Skills: Thinking and Solving   71
   Cognitive–Behavioral Family Therapy and Counseling   77
   Family Conflict and Family Problem Solving   79
   Toward a Theory of Family Problem Solving   82
   Summary   84

4. Families, Problems, and Solutions   92

   The Social Construction of Family Problems   95
   The Social Nature of Problems   98
   Crime and Punishment at the Dinner Table   103
   What Makes Something a Family Problem?   105
   Constructing a Family Problem   107
   Solutions as Social Constructions   116
   Cohesion and Social Skills in Family Problem Solving   118
   Ritual in Family Problem Solving   122
   Summary   129

5. The Rational Model and Beyond   130

   Human Groups, Families, and the Rational Model   133
   The Scope of the Rational Model of Family Problem Solving   136
   The Tyranny of 20-Minute Problem Solving   137
   In Search of Family Problem Solving in the Home   139
   The Existential Status of Family Problems   142
   Phases and Sequences in Family Problem Solving   144
   Summary   151

6. Applications in Family Problem Solving   152

   Unmet Needs, Negative Emotions, and Troubled Family Systems   152
   The Logic of Family Problem Solving Applications   155
   The Context of Training in Family Problem Solving   156
   Why Training in Family Problem Solving Works   158
   Family Problem Solving and Mental Health Disorders   161
   Family Problem Solving in Prevention Programs   174
   Family Problem Solving in Parent Education   180
   Summary   182

7. Recent Advances in Family Problem Solving   184

   The Natural Course of Development of Family Problem Solving   185
   Taking the Social Construction of Family
        Problem Solving Seriously   196
   Technology and Family Problem Solving   198
   Summary   205

   Appendixes   208

   References   218

   Index   231

   About the Author   238

Preface

Years ago I was watching a videotape a family had made of one of their dinners at home. Things were going smoothly enough, with food being passed and people busy eating. After about 10 minutes, the seemingly idle talk was shattered by a teenage daughter's shriek of outrage at something her younger sister announced she had done that day. The other siblings quickly joined in the teenager's complaint as the accused sister quickly went on the defensive, trying to sidestep the attacks. It seems that she had taken some money out of the mother's purse without permission, and then used it for lunch with her friends at a nice restaurant. The father gruffly intervened. After discovering what had happened, he chastised the younger sister and withdrew her privilege of having lunch with her friends. She briefly protested the punishment. But her bowed head and crestfallen demeanor betrayed a resigned acceptance of the punishment. The tense silence after this skirmish soon gave way to a nervous little joke between two siblings that was not really funny. Then the teenage daughter asked "What's for dessert?" The other two siblings then chimed in unison, "Yeah, what's for dessert?" As the punished sister chimed in, she raised her head, smiled, and looked at her sisters. This little ritual apparently brought her back into the fold as all was forgiven. The dinner continued and the seemingly idle talk returned.

Any sequence of events is open to many interpretations. When I first observed this one, what struck me most was how quickly a fairly boring dinner was transformed into a dramatic arena of emotional expression. And then just as quickly, how the matter was apparently resolved and they were back to dinner as usual. The entire episode lasted less than 60 seconds. I had to watch it carefully several times to discern what each person had said, and just what all the fuss was about. Slowly I began to realize that there was much more going on than emotional expression. This family was solving a problem. It was not a major problem that had survival consequences for anyone. But it was a real problem that was acknowledged, dealt with, and resolved. This episode changed the way I looked at families, problems, and solutions.

I was fascinated at how readily raw outrage, accusation, denial, coalitions, retribution, remorse, and reconciliation appeared. I got the sense that their appearance was subtly orchestrated and was not merely a series of chaotic events. I began asking myself the question, "How did they do that?" I have spent the better part of 10 years asking that same question. There have been hundreds more videotapes of families since that one—along with countless interviews, discussions, and debates. I have seen families do truly amazing things and participated in some of these actions myself. My quest has been to find out how families solve their problems. It has been an enlightening quest and I have found not only answers but a new appreciation for the glorious nature of family life.

I have learned that family problem solving is not just a discrete set of behaviors that is activated when a problem is confronted. It is a process through which the family continuously adapts to its environment and defines what it is, as well as where it is going. It is not a highly specialized part of family life that is only occasionally triggered into action. Instead, it represents part of the fundamental core of what a family is. It governs essential parts of family behavior on a daily basis. This book explains the key elements of this process and discusses how knowledge about it can be used to help families.

I want to acknowledge some of the colleagues and acquaintances who provided encouragement, insight, inspiration, and other intangibles to the stream of ideas that ultimately led to this book: Alan Acock, Bert Adams, Peter Burke, Barbara DeBaryshe, Marion Forgatch, Charles Goodwin, Marjorie Goodwin, John Gottman, Alan Grimshaw, Mavis Hetherington, David Klein, Gerald Patterson, John Reid, Fred Strodtbeck, and Regina Vuchinich. Several organizations provided support for phases of this endeavor: National Institute of Mental Health, Family Research Consortium; Department of Human Development and Family Sciences, Oregon State University; Oregon Social Learning Center; Department of Psychology, University of Virginia. Finally I thank all the families over the years who graciously allowed our research teams into their homes. They have shown all of us what it means to be a family.

1

Introducing Family
Problem Solving

How do families solve their problems? That is the primary question this book seeks to answer. Family groups have had their problems since the beginning. Some problems have been inconsequential and easily solved. Others have been daunting and ultimately led to the demise of individuals and families. Efforts to understand these phenomena raise a host of questions. What are the internal processes that allow some families to resolve their difficulties while others struggle and fail? Are family problems different from other kinds of problems? What factors promote effective family problem solving? The list of such relevant questions is a lengthy one, and answers to the questions are often complex. But an expanding body of theory and research in the twentieth century has yielded some answers. It is there that a scientific understanding of family problem solving must begin.

A Brief History

A science of any set of phenomena does not develop in a social, cultural, and historical vacuum. A full understanding of any scientific topic requires attention to its cultural background. Thus I begin with a brief history of family problem solving in western culture. Even though families have been solving their problems for thousands of years, the concept of family problem solving has received scant attention in recorded history. The prominence of family problems and conflicts, however, has been well documented from early writings such as the Bible, biographies, anthropology, drama, literature, and personal histories. Such writings provide often elaborate details on a wide variety of family troubles. The way family problems have been depicted in the past created a context for conceptualizing how they can be solved. The biblical story

1

of the brothers Cain and Abel, for example, captures the strain of sibling rivalry as succinctly as anything ever written (Genesis 4:2–6, 8–13).

> And Abel was a keeper of sheep, but Cain was a tiller of the ground. And in process of time it came to pass, that Cain brought of the fruit of the ground an offering unto the LORD. And Abel, he also brought of the firstlings of his flock and of the fat thereof. And the LORD had respect unto Abel and to his offering. But unto Cain and to his offering he had not respect. And Cain was very wroth and his countenance fell. . . . And Cain talked with Abel his brother: and it came to pass, when they were in the field, that Cain rose up against Abel his brother, and slew him.

The Bible leaves to the imagination the details of the relationship between Cain and Abel, as well as any details about why Cain killed Abel. We do know that the Lord favored Abel's offering because he had previously shown more faith in God than Cain (Hebrews 11:4). But we do not know whether Cain ever tried to resolve whatever problem he had with Abel. Most readers infer that Cain was jealous of Abel being favored by the Lord. But such jealousy would seem to be insufficient grounds for fratricide (Figure 1.1).

Such ambiguity in early literature was not uncommon. The details of the family problems were often missing in the written record. However, later on, the details began to appear. The early Greek play, *Oedipus Rex* (Sophocles, 429 B.C./1960), for example, portrays the social and emotional problems of incest in only thinly veiled terms. Oedipus summarizes his experiences in the following passages:

> Oedipus (Scene II): At a feast, a drunken man maundering in his cups cries out that I am not my father's son. I contained myself that night, though I felt anger and a sinking heart. The next day I visited my mother and father, and questioned them. They stormed, calling it all the slanderous rant of a fool; And this relieved me. Yet the suspicion remained always aching in my mind; I knew there was talk; I could not rest; And finally, saying nothing to my parents, I went to the shrine at Delphi. The god dismissed my question without reply; He spoke of other things. Some were clear, full of wretchedness, dreadful, unbearable: As, that I should lie with my own mother, breed children from whom all men would turn their eyes; And that I should be my father's murderer. . .
>
> Oedipus (Scene IV): Ah God! It was true! All the prophecies! Now, O Light, may I look on you for the last time! I, Oedipus, Damned in his birth, in his marriage damned, damned in the blood he shed with his own hand!

This stunning revelation led to his mother's suicide, and then Oedipus's self-inflicted gouging of his own eyes. Modern readers can readily

Figure 1.1. "Cain Killing Abel." English Thirteenth-Century Psalter. Cambridge, St. John's College Library

understand why his parents sought to keep the dark, incestuous secret from him. But they might also at least consider how the parents could have told him the truth and accepted some responsibility for the situation. That, of course, was unfathomable in 429 B.C.

All indications are that the history of family problems was a long and tortuous one. Available writings tend to emphasize the anguish and

Figure 1.2. Big Daddy and Brick from "Cat on a Hot Tin Roof" (Williams, 1995)

tragedy of family conflicts that were not resolved rather than the positive outcomes from those that were. Reactions to the emotional intensity of family problems are easy to elicit from readers. A reader's own family experiences provide an intimate basis for understanding and sympathizing with those situations.

But describing family problem solving is a somewhat more complex task for a writer, with less opportunity to elicit immediate affective empathy from the reader. Skilled writers, however, have reaped considerable benefits when they are able to overcome such limitations. The playwright Tennessee Williams, for example, was a master at depicting family conflicts. After laying bare the rawest of family emotions, he could induce powerful audience response, and critical acclaim, by subtly resolving those intense conflicts. In *Cat on a Hot Tin Roof* (Williams, 1955), the dialogue sensuously seethes with parent–child, sibling, and in-law conflicts at the birthday celebration of the wealthy family plantation patriarch, Big Daddy Pollitt. But he is the only one not yet informed that he has just been diagnosed with terminal cancer (Figure 1.2).

In a central plotline, Big Daddy confronts his favorite son Brick, demanding to know why he became an alcoholic after the suicide death of his best friend Skipper. Brick explained that the night of the suicide he had hung up the telephone on Skipper. Skipper had called to confess that he had slept with Brick's wife (Maggie the Cat) and asked for Brick's forgiveness. Emotionally distraught after Brick hung up on him, Skipper committed suicide. After an extended conflict between father and son that reveals these facts, the following interchange takes place:

> Big Daddy: Anyhow now!—we have tracked down the lie with which you're disgusted and which you are drinking to kill your disgust with, Brick. You been passing the buck. This disgust with mendacity is disgust with yourself. *You!*—dug the grave of your friend and kicked him in it!—before you'd face the truth with him. [The implied truth here is that Skipper was bisexual.]
>
> Brick: His truth, not mine!
>
> Big Daddy: His truth, okay! But you wouldn't face it with him!
>
> Brick: Who *can* face the truth? Can you?
>
> Big Daddy: Now don't start passin' the rotten buck again, boy!
>
> Brick: How about those birthday congratulations, these many, many happy returns of the day, when everybody knows there won't be any! [Brick suddenly catches his breath as he realizes that he has made a shocking disclosure about Big Daddy's impending death.]

After further conflict and confirmation that the family has been lying to Big Daddy about his condition, the father–son conflict is resolved by Brick.

> Brick: I'm sorry Big Daddy. My head don't work any more and its hard for me to understand how anybody could care if he lived or died or was dying or cared about anything but whether or not there was liquor left in the bottle and so I said what I said without thinking. In some ways I'm no better than the others, in some ways worse because I'm less alive. Maybe it's being alive that makes them lie, and being almost not alive makes me sort of accidentally truthful—I don't know but—anyway—we've been friends—And being friends is telling each other the truth—You told me! I told you! (Williams, 1955, pp. 108–112)

Here Brick apologizes and acknowledges that Big Daddy had forced him to face the truth about Skipper. In turn, Brick exposed Big Daddy to the truth about his impending death from cancer. Framing these revelations as acts of friendship affirms a strong and appropriate bond between an adult-child and his father. Indeed, it resolves a major conflict between Brick and Big Daddy. Though happy endings were hardly Tennessee Williams's forte, such resolutions provided an effective counterpoint to his portrayals of family pathos. The creation—then resolution—of family conflicts has come to be a dramatic device used in books, plays, poetry, films, and television in American culture.

Outside of the western cultural tradition, the anthropological study of surviving members of ancient cultures provides a window on some aspects of the natural history of family disputes and their resolution (e.g., Chagnon, 1983; Frake, 1964). The social structure of the kinship system typically designated one person or a council of leaders as the arbiter of family disputes. In preagrarian cultures, most aspects of life were organized in terms of kinship rights and obligations. Thus the kin domain was involved in most internal conflicts. In some cultures, religious leaders were responsible for dealing with serious family conflicts. The traditional Hawaiian culture had a religious ritual known as *ho'oponopono* (Pukui, Haertig, & Lee, 1972), which involved a family elder or religious leader in a structured home-visit procedure that included some elements of family interaction similar to those used in modern family therapy.

Anthropologists also interpreted aspects of family systems in terms of the function of avoiding conflicts. The incest taboo, for example, was seen as a family rule that provided a way of preventing intrafamily sexual relationships that would prove to be socially destructive (Malinowski, 1927). Although this approach to family structures was not informative about the process of dispute resolution, it suggested that family conflicts were of such importance that systematic ways of avoiding them were firmly embedded in social structure.

There is insufficient data to empirically determine the extent to which these mechanisms effectively "managed" most family conflicts. Even though social structures evolved to prevent them, and kin systems designated official procedures for managing them, it is inevitable that many family conflicts still fell through the structural cracks without being prevented or resolved by official means. In such cases, family members were left to their own devices to cope with the disputes. But virtually nothing is known about how families did this prior to the twentieth century.

This state of affairs began to change as the tools of scientific analysis were turned to the study of human behavior after 1900. Anthropologists were the first to develop sustained objective analyses of human family life (e.g., Malinowski, 1927; Mead, 1928; Morgan, 1877; Westermarck, 1891/1922). It did not take long for the budding sciences of psychology and sociology to begin systematic studies of current family life in Europe and America. Sociologists quickly became concerned with divorce and the sources of marital dissatisfaction problems (Burgess & Cottrell, 1939; Terman, 1938)—topics quite relevant for today's family. Psychology was examining problem solving, though not in the family context, by 1910 (Dewey, 1910/1982). Sigmund Freud's theories placed aspects of family dynamics at the core of some psychological and societal problems (Freud, 1923, 1930). But it would take decades for theory and research methods to develop to a level of sophistication that would permit the beginning of scientific analysis of family problem solving (e.g., Strodtbeck, 1954). Once that began, there was a rapid expansion of research on family problem solving. One purpose of this book is to present an integrated synthesis of that work.

Seeking an Integrative Synthesis

The approach to family problem solving in this book is scientific, integrative, and applied. This is a unique perspective in several ways. As we shall see, theory and research in family problem solving emerged in several fields, usually with little cross-disciplinary interchange. The disciplines include family studies, developmental psychology, sociology, family therapy, communication, social psychology, psychiatry, and clinical psychology. The relative lack of interdisciplinary exchange was in part a result of major paradigmatic differences between some of these fields. For example, family therapy emphasizes clinical technique for treatment results, whereas social psychology focuses on precise measurement and experimental design. Such basic differences inhibit the application of findings from one discipline to another field of inquiry. Substantial differences in the way family problem solving is conceptualized and measured across disciplines forestalls any efforts at systematic meta-analysis or integration based on quantitative criteria. Yet the accumulated research suggests several important points of convergence that have never been recognized because of disciplinary boundaries. This book is integrative in the sense that it draws on theory and research from several disciplines to construct a comprehensive perspective on family problem solving.

We seek an expanded understanding of family problem solving based on systematic theory and empirical studies. In this respect, our analysis takes a scientific approach. Family problem solving could be examined from many viewpoints. For example, a feminist approach might focus on the politically gendered nature of family problems, how that affects the ways they are solved, and how power relations are constructed in family interaction (e.g., Aulette, 1996; Thompson & Walker, 1995). There are several possible valid approaches to this topic, including those based on philosophy, semiotics, or religion.

The choice of an empirical scientific approach reflects my preference and the availability of a large literature that has pursued this approach.

The scientific approach has its limitations. Indeed, we must evaluate the extent to which the complexity of family problem solving can be captured with quantitative measures and statistical analysis. We must also consider whether an "objective" analysis of family problem solving is possible. Certainly considering the research from several disciplines can help minimize the tunnel vision that limits how a concept is understood. Ultimately, our integrative analysis will lead to an evaluation of the strengths and limits of a scientific analysis of family problem solving.

The third element of my approach is a focus on applications of family problem solving in prevention, intervention, and treatment programs for children and families. Beneficial application of research findings is an ultimate goal of most scientific endeavors. In the case of family problem solving, research has already led to useful applications that are expanding. In fact, the extent of applications is relatively large given the lack of scientific consensus on several key aspects of family problem solving. However, it is not uncommon for discoveries to have widespread application *before* a full scientific understanding of how they work is obtained. For example, we enjoyed the analgesic benefits of aspirin decades before anyone knew how it worked. The apparent success of family problem solving applications motivates increased efforts to more completely understand the basis for these benefits. Progress could lead to enhanced benefits or extending the applications to other domains.

Most applications of family problem solving findings thus far have been in the fields of family therapy (e.g., Forgatch & Patterson, 1989; Haley, 1987; Robin & Foster, 1989) and clinical psychology (Kazdin, Siegel, & Bass, 1992). Components using the research have been especially useful in treating child and adolescent disorders (e.g., Hibbs & Jensen, 1996). These successes have led to other applications in prevention (Spoth & Redmond, 1996; Tolan & McKay, 1996) and intervention programs (Henggeler, 1992; Henggeler & Borduin, 1990). Elements of family problem solving have been part of parent education efforts for decades (e.g., Dreikurs, 1948, 1964) and continue to be actively promoted (Dinkmeyer & McKay, 1989). The expanded use of a family preservation approach to child protective services and social welfare has resulted in the implementation of family problem solving concepts in intervention efforts (Henggeler, 1992).

In recent years, parenting and family life have become hotly debated issues of social policy. Though ideologies on these issues have been part of the debate, the primary focus has been on the kinds of government policies and programs that should be funded with tax dollars. Issues such as family leave, abortion, equal treatment of families with diverse ethnic backgrounds, seeking child support from "deadbeat dads," welfare reform, gender equality, and child care for welfare recipients all involve negotiations among family members to achieve certain desired outcomes, usually with major implications for the children involved. The implementation of such policies and programs ultimately involves some form of family problem solving. Indeed, the success of such macrolevel policies depends on how they are applied at the microlevel of the individual family. Any experienced social worker can attest to this. In this realm, there is much potential for application of effective problem solving methods.

Changes in American family life over the past 50 years have been a topic of great interest among policymakers, researchers, and average family members (e.g., Aulette, 1996). One area of special concern has been the increase in the divorce rate. Whether such changes should be promoted or inhibited is open to multiple interpretations. But such changes ultimately create problems that families have to deal with on a personal level. The extent to which families are able to solve these problems on a day-to-day basis can determine whether these changes have a negative impact on them. An increasing divorce rate could mean that married couples are less able to resolve their problems than they have been in the past. It is possible that one of the changes occurring in American family life is a decreased ability or willingness to resolve family problems. Though this possibility is speculative, it suggests an interesting concept. Social systems, such as American society, may have certain patterns of family problem solving built into them. As the society changes, the patterns change. If societal changes occur that erode family problem solving, it may be especially important to promote applications that minimize this erosion. This may minimize the negative effects of family changes that no one can control.

There is, as yet, relatively little accumulated knowledge on the extent to which family problem solving varies systematically across social class, ethnic group, and different family structures (e.g., Brown & Shalett, 1997; Straus, 1968, 1972; Tallman, 1980; Tallman & Miller, 1974). Most available research has sought general principles that should apply across the structural and cultural variations. But the studies that have considered these distinctions have found some significant differences in the way families solve problems (Minuchin, Rosman, & Baker, 1978; Straus, 1968; Strodtbeck, 1954; Vuchinich, Vuchinich, & Wood, 1993). Counselors, therapists, and social workers who work with families across these social boundaries have begun to address these issues from the standpoint of practice (Brown & Shalett, 1997). The emergence of these studies will increase the implications of family problem solving research for family policy.

Another issue for application concerns the role of gender in family problem solving. Feminist scholars who have turned their attention to family life have become interested in how power relations in families are created and maintained (e.g., Thompson & Walker, 1995). One concern is how men seem to obtain a relative power advantage over women in several domains. Of course power is one issue that is often central to family problem solving. Indeed, the early family therapists who examined family problem solving saw hierarchy as one of the primary issues in family problems (Haley, 1987). The role of mother and father during problem solving has been a topic of research for some time (Leik, 1963; Vuchinich, 1987; Vuchinich, Angelelli, & Gatherum, 1996). Thus research on family problem solving may be informative about how gendered power relations form in the family context. However, cautious interpretation will be needed in this area because aspects of feminist ideology are skeptical of empirical research with a positivistic approach. Furthermore, many theorists doubt that any ideology is objective and "value free" (Aulette, 1996).

This book will review the applications of family problem solving findings that are already in place, and consider the implications of recent research for the applications that are emerging. This work represents one of the most exciting aspects of the family problem solving field. The current period of time is especially important because the success of some applications has generated numerous efforts at expansion. It is my hope that this book can contribute to thinking about refinements and testing of those applications in clinical psychology, family therapy, social work, parent education, and family studies.

What Is Family Problem Solving?

On the face of it, the phrase *family problem solving* seems to have a straightforward meaning. In general usage, most people have a notion of what families are, and that families have certain kinds of problems. It would not be uncommon for someone to say, "Tom can't go bowling, he has a family problem to deal with." Even without more contextual detail one might well infer that Tom has some difficulty with a family relationship. That could include a marital problem, parent–child problem, caregiving problem, in-law problem, and so on. Because these relationships involve several domains, the family problem might refer to difficulties with emotions, money, sex, child rearing, pregnancy, illness, or kin obligations.

Although *family problem* is part of the vernacular, the phrase *family problem solving* is not. By inference, one would conclude that the term means the act or process of eliminating the difficulties that create the family problem. That is an accurate interpretation but would depend entirely on context to indicate what was involved. The reason for the lack of distinct meaning is that the phrase *family problem solving* was created by social and behavioral scientists about 30 years ago. It has little meaning to the "person on the street" unless he or she has been exposed to it through some program associated with schools, counseling, parent education, or universities. Most families solve their problems. But they do not talk much about how they do it. There is not a standard cultural vocabulary for that process. Thus most adults in families have a general idea of what the term means, but little else.

Over time, scientific efforts to isolate, explain, and understand family problem solving have revealed an elusive, multilayered phenomenon that does not easily yield to a simple, precise definition. A viable scientific definition has emerged through years of research and practice. But it has been achieved only through negotiating numerous pitfalls and blind alleys. I will present a brief working definition with the caveat that its full meaning unfolds only through special consideration of the terms involved. A definition of family problem solving depends on a definition of *family problems.*

> *Family problems are conditions that block the attainment of individual or family goals. These conditions may include behaviors, rules, expectations, attitudes, relationships, social structures, action patterns, or circumstances external to the family.*

Central to this definition is the concept of a *goal*. In families, roles determine many goals and how they may be pursued. Family roles provide one framework for understanding the organization of emotions, thoughts, and behaviors of family members. These roles (e.g., mother, son, grandfather) entail rights, obligations, identities, and expectations. These structures, as well as the attending processes, help people create order in their lives as families. One element of enacting and creating these structures is the concept of a goal (Sternberg, 1994; Tallman, 1988). A goal is an objective that has not been obtained. A goal is something an individual or group wants, but currently has not attained. Goals come in many shapes and sizes. They may be long term or short term, emotionally intense or mundane. Examples include a parent wanting his daughter to take out the trash, a child wanting her mother's approval, a family seeking to get an uncle out of jail, one sibling wanting another sibling's toy, and so on. When these goals are part of family structures, they may be seen as family-based goals.

When the attainment of one or more family-based goals is blocked, a "family problem" is created. Conditions that block goal attainment typically create a state of negative tension in the individual or family group. Failure to reach the goal is frustrating for humans. Of course some goals are more important than others. Thus some are experienced more negatively, and become more serious family problems, than others. Such distinctions will be addressed later. The primary point is that goals are built into family structures and processes. And when such a goal is blocked, it becomes a family problem. The basic structure of a problem is depicted in Figure 1.3a.

Once family problems are defined in this way, a basic definition of family problem solving becomes straightforward.

Family problem solving is the removal of conditions that block the attainment of a family-based goal.

A primary feature of this definition is that it is reactive, or adaptive, in nature. The solution process is an adaptation to the presence of the family problem. This definition thus places emphasis on the conditions that block goal attainment and how they can be removed. Figure 1.3b schematically depicts the basic definition of a solution.

This basic definition does not include specifications of *how* the blocking conditions are removed. Such an open definition is needed because of the great diversity and complexity in the specific techniques families use to solve their problems. In addition, this definition serves to distinguish family problem solving from different, but related, features of families. For example, cohesion is a family trait that can influence problem solving, but it is not the same thing as problem solving.

Each chapter of the book will provide further specifications on this definition. The family context places limitation on how blocking conditions can be removed. Consider the family problem of the daughter who refuses to do her chore of taking out the trash. According to the definition, this problem is solved if the daughter takes out the trash. But is the trash problem really solved if the daughter is forced to take out the trash at gunpoint? At one level of analysis the answer is yes. The family goal of having the daughter take out the trash was attained. But accomplishing this with a threat of death by gunshot violates other guidelines that typically govern family life. What must be taken into account is that family goals, problems, and solutions do not exist in a vacuum. There are limits on what are appropriate solutions in a family context. In most families, parental threats with guns are not appropriate.

A definition of family problem solving must be transparent to incredible variation across families, individuals, and situations. Because the goal concept is so flexible, this definition is widely applicable. That is one reason why it has become the definition of choice in several disciplines

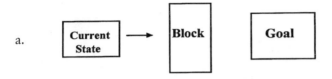

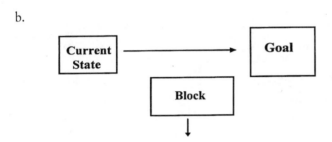

Figure 1.3. a. Diagram of a Family Problem as Blocked Goal Attainment
b. Diagram of a Solution as Removal of the Block to Goal
Attainment

(Tallman, 1988; Tallman, Leik, Gray, & Stafford, 1993) and is showing indications that it will stand the test of time. It is clear that this definition of family problem solving does not include all the important aspects of the phenomenon. But it is equally clear that any definition that attempted to include all those aspects would be hopelessly complex and thus useless. This is an implicit lesson that has emerged through 40 years of scientific inquiry.

The following example of problem solving is provided to show how these definitions can be applied to routine family situations. The example has some special properties. This book seeks to bring a new level of ecological validity (Bronfenbrenner, 1979) to research on family problem solving. I am most interested in problem solving that takes place in a routine ecological niche in normal, day-to-day family life. The appropriateness of this may seem obvious. But as we will see later, most research on family problem solving is based on interactions in laboratories or in structured tasks that may have little ecological validity. To illustrate the approach, I shall present a verbatim transcript of a family discussion that took place in the home.

Family problem solving often does not occur in brief, well-organized, tightly focused, business-like interactions. More typically, it takes time

Figure 1.4. Daughter and Mother Laughing at Father's Comment During Problem Solving

to develop and may ramble from one loosely defined topic to another. Some topics may seem to be trivial or irrelevant. In real-life situations, it may initially seem difficult to clearly identify a goal, the blocks to that goal, and efforts to remove the blocks. But with patience, careful attention to what is said, and how it is said, the underlying problem structures and goals usually emerge. Even problems that may seem to be "much ado about nothing" can reveal the way families deal with their most primal problems. This book includes many unedited transcripts of family interaction. These are considered an important form of raw data on family problem solving that has rarely received sustained attention. Such data provide an important empirical window for understanding the phenomena of interest for both researchers and practitioners.

The first example involves a mother, father, and 12-year-old daughter talking in their living room. The daughter complains about the father infringing on her privacy (Figure 1.4). A verbatim transcript follows.

Daughter: Lots of times, I mean maybe when I have my friends over or something, or just when I'm by myself, I like to have my door shut. And nobody ever knocks, they just come on in, or they just they say "Leave your door open, I don't want you. . ." Dad always wants me to leave my door open 'cause he doesn't want. . . my door to be open.

Mother: I never heard him say that.

Daughter: I HAVE.

Father: I never thought I said that.

Daughter: YOU HAVE! Before. You didn't want me to be cramped up in one room.

Mother: Well, the only time I see you shut the door is when you're talkin' on the telephone. I mean at night the door is wide open and all the lights have to be on. So I don't understand the problem.

Daughter *(to mother):* Well, but like when I have friends over and you're not here Mom.

Father: Well, the only thing is when you have friends over I just think that that's silly to go to your room and shut the door when you could go downstairs and have as much privacy and have a TV down there, you know, the stereo, and Nintendo, and whatever. But you go to your room and just sit in your room with you and a couple of your friends. And I just think that's kind of a boring thing to do.

Daughter: Well, but . . . we talk.

Father: But you could, I just think you could talk downsta—

Daughter: And downstairs, Amy's [an older sibling] down there too.

Father: No. Amy. You know, Amy doesn't hang around your friends if you don't want her to. I mean, it's just a matter of. . . I think that's a better room than to be all cramped up in your little bedroom with two other girls. You oughta' just be downstairs and so they could have ya' know more room to spread out and watch TV or play the piano.

Mother *(to father):* Well, you know. Maybe when they want to do those things they go down there. Maybe they do need their little privacy.

Father: Maybe you're right and I'm wrong. It would be the first time all year long. But that's okay. [Daughter and Mother briefly laugh]

Mother: I mean are there other times you want to be by yourself and feel like we're bothering you?

Daughter: Well, sometimes when I'm just in my room. I'm just. . . sometimes I have the door shut.

Father: But don't we always knock?

Daughter: NO!

Father: I do.

Daughter: No you. . . well, you guys just usually come right in.

Mother: Well, I guess it's just times when . . . you know I don't think it's real important to you to knock on your door.

Daughter: Well maybe . . .

Father: I mean I didn't realize that I mean . . . I mean I will certainly knock because I think you are entitled to some privacy. And I . . . I . . . I always thought that I knocked. You know. I mean I never come into the bathroom when you're in the bathroom do I?

Daughter: No. But when your door's shut I just don't barge in.

Father: Oh no, I know you've [mother and daughter laugh] never done that.

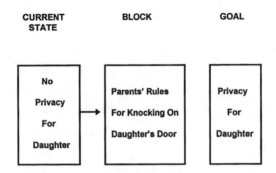

Figure 1.5. Problem Diagram of Daughter's Problem

In terms of our definitions, the blocked goal at issue here, and thus a key element in the "problem," is the daughter's goal of having privacy in her room at home. The parents, and especially the father, have blocked attainment of that goal by "barging in" on her and requiring that her door be open. After some conflict, the father admits that he is wrong and agrees to knock on the daughter's door before entering. Ideally, this should achieve the privacy the daughter was seeking, and thus remove the block to her goal attainment. Thus in our terms a solution has been found and agreed on. Figure 1.5 diagrams the problem in this situation.

Of course there are many complexities in even this simple example. Did the father actually follow through with the solution? Will other privacy rules have to be added? Will the daughter use her privacy responsibly? As we shall see, family problem solving is a process and is usually not completed in one brief episode.

This transcript includes several interesting aspects of family dynamics. For example, the father did not back down until the mother "took sides" with the daughter by suggesting that the daughter needed more privacy. Such coalitions are often important in problem solving. Even in conceding that he was wrong, the father implied that he is usually right—thus saving some face. He was also quick to make it clear that he had never barged into the bathroom when the daughter was in there. This may have been especially relevant because the daughter had earlier indicated that the problem usually happened when the mother was away. Although such interpretations are, of course, speculative, it is likely that both father and daughter are acknowledging the new physical boundaries associated with her puberty. Such complications highlight an important fact: Family problem solving does not occur in a vacuum. Only a simple definition can survive interpretation in the social and psychological context of family life.

The Distinctive Features of Family Problem Solving

There is an extensive scientific literature on how individual humans think and solve problems. This work began with Dewey (1910/1982) and has grown steadily as new discoveries about brain and cognitive functioning have appeared (Pinker, 1997; Sternberg, 1994). Much of this has focused on the basic perceptual and cognitive processes that promote solutions to mathematical problems, or simple problems of logic. A substantial proportion of this work has revolved around the nature of intelligence as an individual characteristic (Sternberg, 1994). Indeed, perhaps the most distinguishing observable indicator of intelligence is the ability to solve problems. The importance of this in human functioning has motivated the vast amount of scientific attention given to the concept. Although important basic principles have been established in this area, it has become apparent that some of the most fundamental features of intelligence are still a mystery (e.g., Pinker, 1997; Sternberg, 1994). Thirty years ago, there was great optimism that enough was known to create "artificial intelligence" with computers. Today, we do have somewhat "smarter" telephones, televisions, cars, household appliances, bombs, computers, and chess games. But what these gadgets can do is much less than what was envisioned, and can only be considered problem solving intelligence in a limited sense of the term. Thus there are still limits to our understanding of the nature of individual intelligence and problem solving. Progress along this line will undoubtedly continue. But a focus on individual problem solving can explain only a relatively small part of family problem solving.

It is known that problem solving is correlated with individual characteristics such as intelligence and creativity (Sternberg, 1994). Other things being equal, families whose members have more intelligence and creativity will solve problems better than those with less of these traits. But other things are never equal. Consider a family whose members are very intelligent and creative, but also have low cohesion, low cooperation, high levels of conflict, and poor conflict resolution skills. Such a family may come up with brilliant ideas but never solve a single problem. As we shall see, when the realm of group problem solving is entered, some different principles come into play. Furthermore, when one enters the realm of family problem solving, yet another different layer of principles must be taken into account. In the psychological realm of individual intelligence, little attention has ever been given to solving the kinds of interpersonal problems so prevalent in family life.

This does not imply that knowledge about individual intelligence and creativity is not important for understanding family problem solving. It

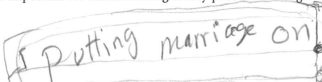

is a necessary part of the overall picture, which is well described elsewhere (e.g., Sternberg, 1994). The focus in this text is on the group and family problem solving principles. One reason for this is the applied orientation of this book. It is difficult to change the intelligence and creativity levels of family members. These are traits that crystallize at a relatively early age. Thus seeking to improve family problem solving by changing the basic intelligence of family members is likely to be a major challenge. On the other hand, changing some behaviors and cognitions of families according to group and family principles may provide a more feasible avenue for effective change.

Several aspects of generic small group processes apply to families, which are clearly one type of small group. But most of what is known about small group problem solving is based on research on artificial small groups, often college students, doing brief, assigned tasks in a laboratory. The extent to which such research applies to family groups is unclear (e.g., Leik, 1963; Steinhauer, 1989; Weick, 1971). Family groups have some distinctive properties that may have a fundamental impact on the way they solve problems (e.g., Steinhauer, 1989; Weick, 1971). A primary goal of this book is to clarify some of the distinctive features of family problem solving.

Two characteristics of family groups that distinguish problem solving in families from problem solving in other groups merit consideration from the outset. They are the emotional intensity of family problems and the long-term nature of family relationships.

First, family relationships have a powerful affective component. Attachment, bonding, love, and devotion are primary features of family roles. Family relationships are typically the most intense that humans experience. Just as "the course of true love never runs smooth," the positive emotions are often matched with equally powerful negative affect such as rebellion, anger, frustration, sadness, abuse, jealousy, betrayal, and resentment. Problem solving in the midst of such intense emotional experience may not be governed by rational principles of logic and reason. The question of how such emotional content enters into the problem solving process must be addressed when dealing with families. Ultimately, problem solving in practice may have different features in families than in the business world—or the world of college experiments (Steinhauer, 1989; Weick, 1971).

Second, in family problem solving the members usually have close emotional contact with each other over many years—often most of their lives. Relationships, and problem solving patterns, once established, may solidify and remain relatively constant over long periods of time. The nature of these relationships can have a substantial impact on problem solving (Steinhauer, 1989). For example, a married couple may have always argued a lot because of unresolved emotional issues (e.g., an extramarital affair early in the marriage) that have plagued their relationship. Similarly, a parent–child relationship may be tainted forever by the parent's physical abuse of the child in preadolescence. These long-standing relationship issues can undermine and disrupt effective family problem solving for years. Similarly, healthy family relationships can facilitate effective problem solving over the long term. In other types of groups, issues can be more easily separated from relationships. There is typically less spillover from relationships into problem solving. Thus the study of family problem solving cannot ignore the long-term nature of family relationships.

Problem solving can occur among family dyads, triads, tetrads, and beyond. The definitive features, regardless of how many family members are involved, are that family-based goals, intense affect, and enduring relationships are involved. The character of a problem varies somewhat across the subsystems *within* a family. The process, for example, in the marital dyad would be expected to differ from that between school-age siblings. However, there is some research suggesting that families have distinctive problem solving styles (e.g., Haley, 1987; Reiss, 1981; Vuchinich et al., 1993), which would constrain the problem solving process in any family subsystem. For example, some families typically argue to try to solve problems, and other families tend to withdraw and hope the problem goes away. Such tendencies are apparent across family subsystems. Family problem solving also varies systematically across the life span. For example, parents typically have more power in families when their children are infants than when their children reach the age of 60.

The point is that family problem solving is not a monolithic entity for all families, or for any specific family. There is variation. All families do not do it the same way. Any one family has some variation in problem solving over time and within its various subgroups. Such variation is quite interesting and will be addressed in this book. But the focus in this book is on the fundamental nature of family problem solving. It is necessary to understand this basic nature before systematic analysis of variation can be done.

The role of the marital dyad in family problem solving requires some special considerations. Marital problem solving is clearly one form of family problem solving. Indeed, there is a large literature on marital conflicts, relationships, and marriage counseling. Much of this work applies to any enduring adult intimate dyad, regardless of whether or not they are married, have children, or are heterosexual. For simplicity, I will refer to all these as adult dyadic relationships. These relationships typically have high emotional content and often endure over time. But without the presence of children or intergenerational relationships, the forms they take are less complex.

The question of whether an adult dyad is a family can be debated. Often the term *family* is reserved for groups that include children, or intergenerational membership in which the socialization function takes place. As the American family changes, such definitions of family are called into question. This issue is relevant as I define the boundaries of this book. Marital or adult dyadic problem solving is certainly a form of family problem solving. But the parameters of a marriage or enduring adult dyad are somewhat different from those of a group with parents and children. The vast literature on marital relations, most of which ignores children, is an indication of this difference. To provide a tighter focus, and to offer some counterbalance to the marital literature, this book will focus on family problem solving that involves both parents and children.

Efforts to understand the nature of family dynamics and family well-being have often led to the consideration of global concepts such as cohesion, adaptability (Olson, 1986), or paradigm (Reiss, 1981). Such concepts seek to represent features of families that have a broad scope. Our approach to family problem solving seeks to understand family characteristics that have a somewhat more narrow scope. It focuses on more specific behavioral, cognitive, and affective patterns that characterize how families come to grips with one circumstance—solving problems. Such patterns are clearly related to the more global family concepts such as adaptability, and they have ample complexity of their own. But this approach is somewhat cautious about assuming the existence of family-level constructs (e.g., that a family has a measurable level of adaptability).

An advantage of studying problem solving is that so much of it occurs through communication and can be observed. The emergence of complaints, conflicts, possible solutions, and so on puts on display the individual goals, roles, power structures, and supportive relations operating in a family. The distinctive way that family members merge their individual needs and goals with the needs and goals of the family group is revealed. In this respect, family problem solving provides a window into the very core of a family. Thus even though examining problem solving focuses on some specific features of family life, those features are linked to more global family characteristics.

All families have problems that they seek to solve. But some families have problems that are much more difficult to solve than others. Some families do not have enough food to keep them alive; some families have members who are physically or sexually abusive; some families lose everything they have through natural disaster. There are some limited connections in research on problem solving, family crisis, and family stress (Klein & Hill, 1997). But little systematic work exists. It is not clear whether the processes involved in solving the "normal" family problems are the same as those involved in solving the more extreme problems. It is not clear how family problem solving may be part of family resiliency to crisis. It is clear, however, that family problem solving concepts are being increasingly used in intervention and treatment programs for families experiencing extreme stress (Henggeler, 1992; Hibbs & Jensen, 1996). These applications, and the potential for more effective preventions and interventions, provide further motivation for a more comprehensive understanding of family problem solving. A goal of this book is to forge closer linkages between research and practical applications that involve family problem solving. Chapter 6 is devoted to this effort.

These guidelines for our analysis of family problem solving should make clear that the goal is not to attempt an exhaustive review of all past work on the topic. In seeking an integration of findings, concepts, and theories, this approach must be selective. Our integrative approach will also be reluctant to accept the presuppositions of any single specific discipline (e.g., social psychology, family therapy, sociology). I seek to build on work done in these diverse disciplines that requires maintaining an objective distance from any one of them. This will inevitably entail raising issues that have may have come under scrutiny by any previous disciplinary paradigm. An example of this is the question of how issues come to be defined as family *problems* for which a solution should be sought. Although some work has addressed this tangentially (Aldous & Ganey, 1989; Haley, 1987; Weick, 1971), it is handled largely through presupposition. Yet how problems arise may largely determine how they are solved. It is inevitable that my analysis will suggest some areas that need further attention if progress is to be made. To motivate the reader, my approach is intended to be an invitation to take a new look at some old territory and to venture forth into some unknown areas.

Plan of the Book

Science often progresses in fits and starts. Decades of empirical and theoretical work have frequently yielded conflicting and confusing re-sults in a given area of study. Occasionally, one definitive experiment, or a new synthesis of previous studies, allows sense to be made of the confusion. Such breakthroughs often become legendary, such as the discovery of the shape of the DNA molecule, the Salk polio vaccine, or

Einstein's $E = mc^2$ equation. In the behavioral sciences such break-throughs are rare, in part because of the complexity of human behavior and the multiple interpretations that can be applied to it. The ongoing search to understand human behavior requires effort to make sense of scientific results. Even though such efforts may not succeed, as in the case of cold fusion or the double bind hypothesis, science requires that they continue.

This book does not announce any dramatic breakthroughs. Instead, it offers a systematic presentation of the main currents of thinking about family problem solving. Perhaps this will stimulate some dramatic break-throughs in the near future. The review also includes a series of personal reflections and insights on family problem solving. These insights are based on personal experience, hundreds of videotapes of families in their homes, as well as efforts to find order in a century's worth of work on a set of complex phenomena. It is hoped that this approach will be useful to those pursuing research and applications in family problem solving. The review and synthesis is organized into seven chapters.

Chapter 1, Introducing Family Problem Solving, has introduced the concept of family problem solving, the purpose of the book, and the approach that will be taken in the analysis. Chapter 2, The Origins of a Science of Family Problem Solving, describes the theories and methods that provide the foundations for scientific work on family problem solving from 1900 through 1950. Chapter 3, Family Problem Solving Comes of Age, reviews the most important research findings on family problem solving in the latter half of the twentieth century. The review traces the emergence of theory and the main strands of empirical research and practice. The chapter summarizes the current state of the art and shows points of integration between diverse theoretical perspectives. Chapter 4, Families, Problems, and Solutions, presents some new frame-works for conceptualizing key components of family problem solving. These frameworks build from the conclusions in chapter 3. Chapter 5, The Rational Model and Beyond, extends chapters 3 and 4 to give an evaluation of the dominant rational paradigm and its elements. Chapter 6, Applications in Family Problem Solving, reviews the applications of family problem solving in prevention and intervention programs for children and families. This includes consideration of the success of applications and suggested directions for improvement. Chapter 7, Recent Advances in Family Problem Solving, describes five specific areas of family problem solving in which significant recent advances have occurred. The implications of these advances for future research and practice are described. The appendixes include details on specific research studies.

2

The Origins of a Science
of Family Problem Solving

How is family problem solving understood in scientific terms? Chapters 2 and 3 describe some answers to that question. The immediate goals of any science are to describe, explain, and predict some observable set of phenomena. These goals are pursued by establishing theories, measurement techniques, designs for collecting data, analysis strategies, and interpretations of results. Family problem solving has emerged as a topic of study in several scientific disciplines. As a result, a variety of scientific theories and methods have been used in examining family problem solving. These disciplines continue to examine this topic from diverse perspectives. There is not yet a unified "science" of family problem solving. Thus the title of this chapter refers to scientific work that has been done in a variety of fields. This book was written, in part, to promote bridges between these fields.

The ultimate goal of scientific work on family problem solving is knowledge that can help individuals and families. Even though aspects of the science may be somewhat abstract, these abstractions are means to an end. Consider a family whose house has just burned down. Such a disaster creates a host of problems for the individuals and the family as a group. What is the best way to describe and explain how families deal with such problems? Is it possible to predict how they will react and how well they will adapt? Because some answers to these questions have already been found, it is currently possible to help families through problems, and even prepare them in advance to manage such situations. Details on these programs are the primary topic of chapter 6. But the current applications may be just the tip of the iceberg. The basic science suggests that more and better applications may be feasible in the near future.

Part of the scientific record is made up of the fascinating results of the specific research studies that have been done. But of equal importance is an understanding of the assumptions, paradigms, and theories that provide the context for the scientific findings. The next two chapters review the most important empirical research results, and also review the history of the ideas that have shaped work on family problem solving. Some of the most prominent current thinking about this topic had its origins around 1900. In tracing the persistent influence of some of these theories, the reader can better grasp not only what the findings mean, but also why certain kinds of research were done in the first place. The review shows that, as in all sciences, some research directions flourished, and others led to dead ends. In approaching the current and future research, it is essential to understand why some previous approaches worked out, whereas others did not.

Chapter 2 begins a scientific odyssey that spans the twentieth century. It starts with three of the most influential early psychologists: John Dewey, Sigmund Freud, and William James. Their work and the work of others through 1950 led to the realization that family problem solving is an arena of human interaction that can and must be explored using scientific methods. Chapter 3 shows how the early work led to a vibrant body of ongoing scientific research and practice as the twentieth century draws to a close. The logic and emotion of family problem solving has been portrayed in a rich and expanding tapestry. One of the most important phases of scientific inquiry is the effort to interpret and make sense of studies that have been done in the past. If successful, this can isolate connections between studies that had never been considered. Ultimately, such connections can be the basis for a new synthesis and a deeper understanding of the phenomena of interest. Chapters 2 and 3 point out some new connections of this nature. The remaining chapters suggest some directions toward a new synthesis of research and practice in family problem solving. Readers with special interests may wish to read sections of chapters 2 or 3 selectively. Figure 2.1 gives the family tree of family problem solving. It includes the theorists, researchers, and practitioners who will be the focus of my review. The figure is ordered in terms of the sequential development of important lines of work and in terms of who influenced whom. Research on family problem solving has several important strands, so the reader may find it useful to refer to this figure throughout these two chapters.

Science uses theories to organize descriptions, explanations, and predictions about observable events or other forms of data (Klein & White, 1996). Theories provide an account of how and why certain things happen. Darwin's theory of evolution, for example, explains how living things change as they adapt to their environments. Theories guide the directions of research. Research, in turn, indicates whether theory is correct and how it might need to change. Ultimately, a theory is accepted if it accurately accounts for the events, or aspects of, the world it is

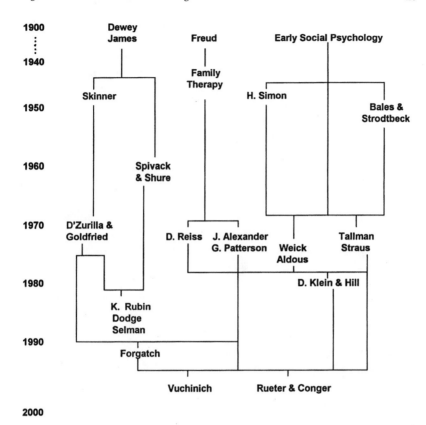

Figure 2.1. The Family Tree of Family Problem Solving

intended to explain. The basis for theories about family problem solving developed over a period of 50 years. Theories must define clearly the basic elements of the events they seek to explain. In the case of family problem solving, such definitions have proven to be somewhat elusive. What is "problem solving" to begin with? This necessarily leads to the question, "What is a problem?"

Dewey, Thinking, and Problem Solving

In 1900, science on human behavior was just getting started. There had been some early theories, but little of what we would consider empirical research on human behavior. Psychology and sociology were in their infancy. Darwin's theory of human evolution (Darwin, 1871) had caused a large public controversy because it conflicted with the Christian view of human origins. People were not sure if it was a good idea to mix science and human behavior. But a hard core group of social and behavioral theorists actively pursued that goal. Among them was John Dewey, an American philosopher, psychologist, and educator (Figure 2.2). He was a prolific scholar who wrote on many topics. But his seminal work on problem solving is the most appropriate place for me to begin.

Dewey wanted to understand how people think. In pursuing that goal he provided the first systematic explanation of what human problem solving is. Dewey was not concerned with families. Accounting for individual thinking was difficult enough. His early theory might well have been just a minor footnote, earned because he was the first to theorize problem solving. But Dewey's explanation of problem solving has come to take on a life of its own. More than 80 years later, research and practice on family problem solving has come to be dominated by his formulation of the problem solving process. Dewey maintained that problem solving proceeds through a series of phases (Dewey, 1910/ 1982). To simplify terminology, I describe them in current terms.

1. Define the problem.
2. Generate alternative possible solutions.
3. Evaluate the alternative solutions.
4. Select one solution to implement.
5. Adjust the solution if necessary.

Dewey did not do empirical research to verify his theory. He presented this as a process that some people used only sometimes in the process of inquiry or rational thought. This represents a "rational" view of problem solving, which assumes a person systematically weighs the costs and benefits of each potential solution and informally calculates which choice will provide maximum benefit. For our purposes, a key question about this is whether families use these phases when they try to solve their problems. Does your family use these phases for rational problem solving?

If Dewey had been entirely correct about individual problem solving, and if the same rational process governs family problem solving, this book would be a very short one indeed. As it turned out, Dewey was not entirely correct, and individual problem solving is not the same as family problem solving. So we must move beyond Dewey's formulation. But he was right about a lot of things, and his ideas have made a lasting contribution, which we will see again and again. One of the most important of these is the way he defined what a "problem" is. Everyone

Figure 2.2 John Dewey

has problems now and again. These are experienced as difficulties, often carry some form of negative feelings (e.g., frustration, stress, anger, sadness) with them, and come in all sizes and shapes. Problems are so varied that we rarely consider their general nature and what they all might have in common. But any understanding of family problem solving requires that we know what the basic nature of problems are. Dewey was the first to address this question directly. His ideas have turned out to be pertinent for current work on family problem solving.

Dewey conceptualized a problem as a "disturbance" or "imbalance in organic–environmental interaction" (Dewey, 1938). Such a disturbance creates a tension or state of disequilibrium that draws the attention of the person. The recognition of an imbalance was a precondition for critical thought or inquiry. Indeed, the perception of a disturbance stimulated the initiation of thought or inquiry. Dewey assumed that this tension was often vague and not clearly focused. In fact, his first stage of thought was a "search" of the environment for information that would clarify the source of tension. Furthermore, he defined *inquiry* as a process that "transforms an indeterminate situation to a determinate one." In Dewey's terms, a basic part of problem solving is making sense out of perceived stresses that result from misalignments between organism and environment.

This formulation is consistent with the idea that problems are situations of blocked goal attainment (e.g., Tallman, 1988), because blocked goals create a tension or imbalance. But Dewey's view of the nature of problems is based on Darwin's theory of adaptation between organism and environment. The fundamental goal of the organism was survival, which was sought by meeting needs. Adaptation created a state of equilibrium in which the organism's needs are met through interaction with the environment. From this perspective, perceived goals and complex "goal" structures of the organism are secondary to the more basic adaptation process.

Dewey's position on the nature of problems is especially relevant for family problem solving for three reasons. First, family problems are often emotionally intense and involve organic arousal that accompanies the conflict, bonding, and other affect-laden aspects of family life. Such problems are easy to conceptualize in terms of Dewey's organic–adaptation view of what problems are. Affect-laden family problems are not so easily subsumed in a pure rational model that assumes that family members behave rationally.

Second, family problems are often vague and ill-defined, often with little consensus on whether a problem even exists. Most research on family problem solving has either defined the problem to be solved (Leik, 1963; Reiss, 1981; Straus, 1968) or required a family to select a specific problem from a list (Forgatch, 1989; Vuchinich et al., 1993), and then mandated that the family do a "problem solving" task within a limited time span. Only a few preliminary studies have explored the way families come to define a problem (e.g., Aldous & Ganey, 1989). Some studies evaluate how clearly families define a problem to be discussed (Forgatch, 1989). But little is known about how families define or conceptualize their problems. From the standpoint of Dewey's model, the scarcity of work on defining a problem creates a fundamental gap in knowledge about family problem solving. Work in family therapy includes important insights on the nature of family problems, how they are defined and negotiated (e.g., Haley, 1987; Madanes, 1981). Because they are oriented toward treatment of troubled families, these insights have not yet been integrated into more general models of family problem solving. That task will be taken up in chapter 3.

Third, in Dewey's view of problems, they represent an imbalance or disequilibrium in the organism–environment interaction. Problems are not just tensions resulting from unmet needs. They signal a flaw or fault in the way the organism links up with the environment. In the family context, an important part of the environment is the other family members. Dewey was not a systems theorist. However, his equilibrium is one step away from a system that organizes behavior so that needs are routinely met through interactions with the environment. Applied to the modern concept of a family system, Dewey's view means that family problems are based on flaws in the family system. Thus family problems are not typically matters of simple, short-term need fulfillment. Instead, they signal faults in a complex system that provides for more long-term need fulfillment.

A systemic view of problems is well established in family therapy (Haley, 1987; Madanes, 1981; Steinhauer, 1989). But much of the research on family problem solving has treated problems as short-term puzzles. It is certainly useful to know how families solve short-term puzzles. But it is essential to recognize that many family problems are not short-term puzzles. Families may use very different problem solving methods when dealing with small puzzles than when dealing with flaws in the family system. Dewey's adaptation model would require attention to the latter methods.

This retrospective interpretation of Dewey's theory of thought and inquiry is intended to draw attention to a fundamental yet neglected area of family problem solving: the nature of family problems. Implications of this are developed in chapter 4. Most research on family problem solving begs an essential question: How do families define their problems? Dewey provided insights that can be useful in addressing that question. The history of scientific work on family problem solving has favored the rational components of Dewey's model, such as generating alternate solutions, evaluating the alternatives, and testing the solution. Although these are truly fundamental, they are nonetheless secondary phases in Dewey's model, which begins with defining the problem.

Dewey's adaptational model of problems does have a legacy that is not as well-known as the legacy of his stage model. For example, Tallman acknowledges Dewey's work as a basis for his adaptational work on child problem solving and adjustment (Tallman, 1961), and later in his influential goal-based model of family problem solving (Tallman, 1988, 1993). The seminal work of D'Zurilla and Goldfried (1971) on problem solving treatments for depression and anxiety is based on the principle that the individual uses problem solving to achieve a better adaptation to the environment. That approach has led to applications in family problem solving (Forgatch & Patterson, 1989).

Dewey's work may also be seen as a beginning point in efforts to teach families and individuals how to do better family problem solving. Dewey's famous volume, *How We Think* (1910/1982), was written for educators to promote the teaching of critical thinking—and his problem solving model—in schools. Dewey believed that better thinking in society would help alleviate social problems, and that this could be achieved through schools. Thus Dewey was not just interested in what problems are and how people try to solve them. He also was interested in improving the human condition by teaching people how to solve their problems. The current prevention and intervention programs that teach problem solving skills share this strategy.

Even though Dewey rarely mentioned families, his work has had a tremendous impact on research in family problem solving. In chapter 3, I will demonstrate that there have been benefits and liabilities in the way this impact has taken shape. Dewey may be viewed as a primary ancestor of the "Rational School" of family problem solving. At the same time he was developing his model, another important individual was creating a set of theories that provide a very different perspective on families and family problem solving: Sigmund Freud.

Freud, the Family, and Irrational Problem Solving

Freud (1856–1939) sought treatments for some forms of mental illness (Figure 2.3). He developed theories about human behavior that led to new approaches to treatment—and to understanding the nature of humans. He is not typically acknowledged as making any contribution to research on family problem solving. Yet his ideas about the role of family members in the development of emotional problems have important implications for understanding family problem solving. Whereas Dewey emphasized the rational, Freud plumbed the depths of the irrational. Unlike Dewey, for Freud the family was at the core of individual problems.

This book seeks to integrate diverse approaches to family problem solving. Family therapy, for example, provides primary models for understanding family problems and what to do about them. As maintained previously, research on family problem solving has tended to overlook the nature of family problems and how they function in the family. This oversight is in part a result of the dominance of the rational paradigm in research in this area. The solving of more "serious" family problems involving mental health, abuse, crime, and other dysfunctions does not easily fit into the rational paradigm. Family members involved in such behaviors are considered to be patently irrational. Problem solving in such families is typically relegated to other disciplines, and paradigms, such as family therapy, psychiatry, or clinical psychology.

Figure 2.3 Sigmund Freud

This state of affairs is understandable given the nature of scientific paradigms and professions. But the result is two or more parallel paradigms for family problem solving that rarely contribute to each other. My position is that cross-pollination would promote better models of family problem solving. Thus irrational family situations and irrational efforts at family problem solving should be considered in an integrative approach.

This brings us back to Freud. He placed irrational individual problems squarely in the context of the family. I will review a few of his key ideas that are important for research on family problem solving. In acknowledging Freud's contributions, it is useful to begin with perhaps the most important one. Freud's elaborate theories always placed family members and family relationships at the core of individual problems. His treatment method of psychoanalysis revolved around talk about family members and family relationships. Thus it should not be surprising that some practitioners trained in this model would ultimately consider treating the family as a unit or system. Indeed, most of the founders of family therapy were psychiatrists.

But Freud's technique strictly required that the therapist must treat only one individual patient. Freud had a good explanation for why psychoanalysis should not treat more than one family member at a time. This involves the *transference* process in which the therapist creates an intimate trust and context that allows the patient to express often troubling dreams, subconscious feelings, and perceptions that ultimately involve other family members. The presence of other family members, who might be involved in these expressions in sexual or aggressive ways, would inhibit such expressions and thus short circuit the treatment (Rosenbaum & Beebe, 1975). Thus even though Freud conceptualized the family as a locus of serious interpersonal problems, his method of dealing with such problems could focus only on the individual.

Because Freud's theories are so complex, widely disseminated, and controversial, the discussion here can focus only on a few points most relevant to family problem solving. Freud advanced a theory of the psychosexual development that maintained that needs for sex and aggression, conceptualized as the Id, provided the motivation for much of human behavior. These drives were organismic and not fundamentally governed by a rational logic (Freud, 1923). Thus from first principles, rationality was not a basic process in Freud's model.

A semblance of rationality did enter Freud's model as the Ego, which sought to balance the organic needs of the Id with the moral standards of social life embodied in the Superego. Logical processes, as well as other devices (e.g., defense mechanisms), are used in seeking to achieve this balance. But perhaps most pertinent is the fact that conscious life itself was viewed as a "problem" of getting primal needs met within the limits of moral standards. The Ego had the ongoing task of solving this problem. If solutions were obtained, life progressed with needs being fulfilled in socially prescribed ways. But if solutions were not obtained, dominance by the Id or Superego produced abnormal experiences and behavior patterns. Even without considering the family context, Freud saw people in a virtually constant balancing–problem solving task. The consequences of not dealing with this task were dire indeed. Current problem solving treatments for depression, anxiety, and antisocial behavior focus on the importance of thinking about life situations as problems to be solved (e.g., D'Zurilla & Goldfried, 1971; Haley, 1987; Kendall, 1991).

Freud maintained that people were only conscious of the Ego, and that the basic conflicts between the Id and Superego were largely unconscious (Freud, 1923). Thus people were not even aware of their most serious problems, which were ultimately causing their symptoms. Psychoanalysis was a procedure that began with the patient's "presenting" complaints or problems and worked toward finding and resolving the true unconscious problems. Freud's theory of the unconscious adds an interesting twist to family problem solving. Family members will inevitably have perceived problems. But those may *not* be the true problem. Thus solving the perceived problems may not solve the true problem at all. It is important to note that Freud's view was that this unconscious nature of true problems held for everyone, not just those with psychological problems.

The family was a key part of Freud's theories. The birth of the Superego, which limited the Id's primal drives, occurred through the process of identification. The child ultimately seeks to emulate the same-sex parent and adopts his or her behavior patterns and moral standards. Once this happens, there is a foundation for consensus between parent and child that facilitates resolution of perceived problems that arise. Before that, parent–child interaction is fraught with difficulties as the parents must impose their will on the child who is governed by organismic drives. But even identification has unique family entanglements of its own. The Oedipal complex, as defined by Freud, is based on the adolescent male's unconscious sexual desires for the mother, which put him in direct competition with the father. This creates serious conflict between son and father. No amount of rational problem solving can alleviate this problem, which has roots in the unconscious. Rational logic does not apply—only the irrational logic of Freud's theory can resolve this issue.

Freud's theories and methods have made lasting contributions to many domains of the science of human behavior and mental illness. In terms of family problem solving, Freud's views offer an important counterpoint to the rational models. It suggests that what family members perceive and verbalize as their problems may be only a transformation of the problems that need to be solved. Effectively "solving" perceived family problems may not even begin to deal with more important unconscious problems. This is a complex issue, which will be taken up in chapter 3.

For now, we must acknowledge Freud as contributing a compelling set of theories with implications for the nature of family process, family problems, and how they can be solved. Freud was among the first to propose *any* model of interpersonal family dynamics. His theoretical formulation and extension to an applied method of treatment is a monumental achievement. Many of his theories were wrong at least as much as they were right. But they stimulated the development of better theories, methods, and practices that are producing beneficial results today.

Figure 2.4 William James

Problem Solving as Instinct:
A Legacy of William James

The dichotomy between Dewey's rational view of problems and Freud's irrational view is not easily reconciled. It ultimately led to two separate approaches to understanding family problem solving. But a contemporary of Dewey and Freud's provided a basis for building a link between the opposing theories. William James was one of the founders of American psychology (James, 1890). Like Dewey, he was influenced by Darwin's theory of evolution by natural selection, and was interested in how humans think. But for our concerns, his ideas about instincts are most significant (Figure 2.4).

Instincts are capabilities with which organisms are born. They are inherited and have a basis in some physical, biological forms, such as genes, biochemicals, neurons, and so on. Instincts produce specific kinds of reactions to stimulation from the environment, or conditions of the organism. For example, removing one's hand from a burning flame is based on instinct. James was interested in how much of human behavior was determined by instincts and how much was learned. At that time, as now, it was generally believed that most animal behavior was based on instincts, whereas most human behavior was learned rather than instinctive. James proposed just the opposite. He argued that human intelligence is based on humans having many more instincts than animals. These more complex instincts allow humans to do many things automatically and then extend these capabilities with learning. James raised the possibility that basic components for learning, thinking, and other complex processes may be instinctive in nature.

Neither Dewey, nor anyone since, has been able to adequately explain where the basic phases in his theory of human problem solving come from. Why do—or how did—humans come to define a problem, generate alternative solutions, and select the best option? Though James never studied family problem solving, he may have provided the basis for explaining how it happens. In a nutshell, James's theory suggests that the phases of problem solving may have their basis in human instincts. This is a somewhat radical idea because it implies that a key element of human rationality has a physical, and thus limited, foundation. This runs counter to much of western philosophy, religion, and human science, which views rationality and other "higher" human characteristics as being generated by various thought processes, not deterministic instincts.

In recent years, aspects of James's ideas have been pursued with great vigor as new discoveries have been made about how genetics is related to human behavior and what physical processes operate within the human brain. For example, it was once believed that human language was based almost entirely on learning processes. But research is suggesting that much of it is instinctual (e.g., Pinker, 1994). The fields of cognitive science, evolutionary psychology, neuroscience, and behavioral genetics are producing impressive theory and research suggesting that there is a genetic, instinctive basis for many human behaviors usually thought to be learned (e.g., Barkow, Cosmides, & Tooby, 1992; Pinker, 1997; Tooby & Cosmides, 1997). This has been extended to include social exchange in small and large human groups (Barkow et al., 1992).

At the core of much of this work is the notion that neural structures, which govern thought and action within the brain, evolved to solve the problems that humans were confronted with in their day-to-day activities. Those individuals and groups with more effective neural structures tended to survive. Thus effective problem solving itself is placed at the crux of determining which neural structures are passed down to succeeding generations in the genetic code and which are not. This is reasonable in general terms, but the nature of problem solving itself has not been detailed in terms of the specific neural networks or genes involved. At present, the idea that certain neural structures provide specialized capabilities that are the basis for solving problems is simply an interesting hypothesis. Thus evolutionary psychology does not yet provide conclusive conceptual or empirical evidence that Dewey's elements of problem solving (or some variation of them) can be found in human instincts produced by genetic evolution. There is, however, some pertinent evidence on social problem solving in some of our close genetic relatives.

Recent studies of social behavior, conflict, cooperation, and altruism in chimpanzees and other primates have found some group problem solving patterns similar to those observed in humans (de Waal, 1989, 1996). Sociobiology has long maintained that complex behaviors such as altruism can be explained without reference to unique "higher-order" human capabilities such as morality (e.g., Wilson, 1975). Instead, the sociobiologists argue that much simpler genetic structures can produce the same observed behavior. It is generally acknowledged that humans and chimpanzees have more than 90% of the same genetic structures. Thus it is certainly plausible that some of those genetic structures promote specific problem solving patterns that should be observable in humans and in chimpanzees. The chimpanzee studies do not provide conclusive evidence. However, similar problem solving patterns in the two species is certainly consistent with the position of evolutionary psychology. Though somewhat speculative, this approach may offer the best available explanation of why humans try to solve problems the way they do.

Most pertinent is the fact that evolutionary psychology provides a link between the rational and irrational elements of family problem solving. Freud implied that the human instincts of sex and aggression were the source of most psychopathology and family problems. Dewey said problem solving should follow a rational procedure. Evolutionary psychology suggests that there are instincts for rationality, as well as sex and aggression. Furthermore, these instincts evolved through a process of selection based on successful solutions to problems. Thus family rationality and irrationality are conceptualized in the same terms: They are both based on instincts. They are both thus posited to have a physical basis that ultimately may be isolated and studied empirically. Furthermore, this approach suggests that basic family processes can be understood in terms of social exchange principles (Klein & White, 1996).

These extensions of James's concepts have conceptual advantages for coming to grips with the origins of family problem solving. But they also have weaknesses. One of the easiest ways of explaining any human behavior has always been to say that it is based on instincts—that it is the nature of the beast. But proving that a behavior, especially those involving complex group processes, is based on instinct has never been easy to do. Thus this notion can be considered only as an interesting possibility at this point. But as we see the separate development of the rational and irrational approaches to family problem solving, it is important to realize that these models are not theoretically incompatible. The next section describes how the maturation of behavioral science made possible a rigorous empirical analysis of family problem solving.

Problem Solving Paradigms: 1920 to 1950

The ideas of Dewey and Freud did not lead to immediate research on family problem solving. However, the 1920s, 1930s, and 1940s saw unprecedented progress in the scientific approach to examining human behavior. This took place as psychology, sociology, social psychology, anthropology, and psychiatry became established as active scientific disciplines. All of these fields developed and refined theories about many aspects of human behavior. Innovative research methods of collecting data on behavior emerged. These included surveys, small group experiments, fieldwork, extensions of psychoanalytic interviews, quasi-experiments, and others. By the 1950s, these advances had reached a level of analytic power that allowed the complex processes of family problem solving to be examined. The work prior to 1950 created some important paradigms that largely determined how science has conceptualized family problem solving up to the present.

INDIVIDUAL AND GROUP
PROBLEM SOLVING IN EXPERIMENTS

Perhaps most influential for family problem solving was the work on small groups that came to be a primary focus of social psychology. Early psychologists were fascinated by the differences between a person's behavior when alone and when in a group situation (e.g., Triplett, 1898). By 1935, there was already a substantial literature comparing individual problem solving with group problem solving (Dashiell, 1935). Most of the early studies found that groups solved problems better than individuals as a result of several processes. These included the summation of individual ideas ("two cabbage heads are better than one"), the stimulation of ideas as a result of another's thinking, increased motivation when working with others, corrections others can provide when a person makes an error, and communication of ideas to others to refine and sharpen them. Later studies showed that group effects were more complex than this and often inhibited good problem solving (Jones & Gerard, 1967, pp. 591–600). But perhaps more significant than the findings of the early problem solving studies was the application of experimental designs and procedures for studying small groups. They showed that some aspects of small group processes could be measured, and that an understanding of them could be systematically pursued with theories and hypothesis testing. By 1950, an experimental paradigm for studying group problem solving was well in place.

THE HAWTHORNE STUDY AND
AFFECT IN THE SMALL GROUP

From 1927 until 1932, a team of researchers studied workers and managers in the Hawthorne telephone assembly plant in Chicago (Roethlisberger & Dickson, 1939). The research examined a vast array of variables that might be related to productivity. One finding, however, forever etched this study into the annals of behavioral science. The researchers found that some work groups established informal standards for production that were *different* from, and usually lower than, those established by management. More important, the workers followed the informal production quotas more closely than the management standards. This was not news to most workers in industries and bureaucracies. But it was a stunning lightning bolt to corporate America and the predominant paradigm of scientific management (Taylor, 1911), which assumed that production was controlled by rational processes.

There are many reasons for the attention this finding has received over the past 60 years. But at the core of the interest has always been the reduction in productivity that was found. The finding that informal small group processes, which had until that time been a rather obscure subfield of psychology, could lower industrial production provided practical justification for more research in that area. Research on small group processes in bureaucratic or industrial settings virtually exploded.

This work influenced research on family problem solving in two ways. First, it showed that strict rational models of small group behavior are inadequate and that nonrational processes must be taken into account. The Hawthorne studies demonstrated that such nonrational factors as who liked whom, who did not like whom, who had informal status, and who could coerce whom were as important as rational factors such as job descriptions, supervisory authority, and pay rates in determining productivity. When considering problem solving in such a small group context, it became apparent that Dewey's rational model would have to be adjusted in some important ways. In the family context, affect and power differentials are perhaps even more prominent than in formal organizations. Thus nonrational processes could well be expected to be primary in family problem solving. This issue was taken up after 1950 as the small group paradigm began to be applied to family groups.

The role of nonrational processes in small groups was a primary theme in further work on organizational behavior (e.g., Barnard, 1938). Herbert Simon's *Administrative Behavior* (1945) focused on variations to rational behavior. Simon claimed that people cannot really be rational because rational decisions require information that allows systematic evaluation of potential outcomes. Such information is often not available. Thus people can only be "intendedly rational." Gary Becker (1981) extended this approach to show how a version of rationality applies to family life. Both Simon and Becker won Nobel prizes, in part for their efforts to adapt rational models of behavior to the realities of human behavior. The Hawthorne study was the first to stimulate widespread interest in this problem. It is one that is still at the core of efforts to understand family problem solving.

Second, the Hawthorne study affected family problem solving with the sheer volume of studies it stimulated on problem solving in bureaucratic and industrial situations. In these settings, the problem is clearly defined by the authority. Furthermore, it must be solved in a short time span during a group meeting. This setting has clear external validity for formal organizations. This research paradigm dominated the way a generation of researchers thought about group problem solving. Thus it was only natural that this paradigm would be applied to initial efforts to examine family problem solving. But the relevance of this approach may be questioned. It raises the possibility that much of the experimental research on group problem solving is of limited value in the family context (e.g., Steinhauer, 1989; Weick, 1971). This issue will be pursued in chapter 5.

OTHER PARADIGMS IN THE 1920S, 1930S, AND 1940S

During the 1920s through the 1940s, there was a slow emergence of a concept of the family as a functioning social unit in American sociology (e.g., Burgess, 1916). It was generally acknowledged that the "socialization" of children into society was essential for understanding social behavior. Anthropologists were already providing penetrating analyses of what happens in family groups (Malinowski, 1927; Mead, 1928), as well as theories about the nature of family systems and their functioning (Murdock, 1949).

THE FAMILY AS A SOCIAL STRUCTURE

The idea that families are distinct social structures with specific functions to perform came to be fully developed in Parsons's structural-functionalism (Parsons, 1951; Parsons & Bales, 1955).

Structural–functionalism holds that the behavior of family members is constrained by roles (e.g., mother, father, son, daughter) that are part of larger social structures. The roles organize behavior so that essential survival functions (e.g., nurturance, social order, acquiring food and shelter) can be accomplished in day-to-day family life. Although Parsons never discussed family problem solving, his theory established a paradigm for understanding what family problems are, and how family members would approach solving them. His collaboration with Bales established an enduring link between small group research and family process (Parsons & Bales, 1955). It was in this context that the first detailed studies of family problem solving were done (e.g., Strodtbeck, 1954). Of equal importance is the location of family interaction processes within a context of social structure. The stratification that cuts across all aspects of a societal system establishes constraints and resources that are available for families. Clearly, this affects the nature of the problems they have and the resources they have available to solve them. In addition, age and sex stratification influences how interaction in families takes place (status, power, nurturance, roles).

THE EARLY YEARS OF PARENT EDUCATION

These early years witnessed several disciplines grappling with the challenges of using science to examine the nature of group problem solving and of families. During this same time period, another strand of work focused on a somewhat more practical matter: instructing parents in child rearing. Some physicians, psychiatrists, psychologists, and others focused on providing parents with information about what was currently known about the best practices of child rearing (e.g., Spock, 1946; Watson, 1928). Since 1914, the federal government's Children's Bureau has published the serial, *Infant Care*, which gives concise instruction to parents. Spock's book (1946) became the most well-known baby care book, and has influenced generations of American parents. The early history of the parent education movement has been documented by Brim (1959). This early work established a paradigm for prevention of family problems through parent education. Though most of it had little to do with family problem solving, it created a culturally accepted channel of communication to parents that has continued to expand as evidenced in the popularity of the current genre of "self-help" family books.

Some of this early work did make a direct contribution to applications in family problem solving. Rudolf Dreikurs, in 1948, introduced the concept of the family council. This influential parent education book advanced the democratic, as opposed to the authoritarian, model of parent–child relations. As part of his recommendations to parents, he suggested that families should have regular family meetings at which grievances were aired and constructive group efforts made to achieve solutions. Specific guidelines for these meetings were detailed. Children were to be encouraged to participate with the parents as equals in order to train them for a democratic society. Dreikurs's democratic parenting model and his family council program are still widely used in the parent education field (Dinkmeyer & McKay, 1989). Dreikurs was a psychiatrist who had experience in working with families, but provided little empirical evidence that family councils were effective. Indeed, his democratic parenting model may have been based largely on his desire to promote the socialization of democracy and eliminate fascist ideology, to which he had been exposed in Europe. In any event, the idea of family meetings as a regular forum for family problem solving in normal families was a new one. This ecological niche for family problem solving places it in the routine context of day-to-day family life. This is quite different from the contexts of family problem solving that would soon emerge in the social psychology laboratory, or in the family therapist's office.

THE SEEDS OF FAMILY THERAPY

Even though Freud's theory was laden with intense family relationships, psychotherapists were slow to begin working with families. The primary reason for this was Freud's view of how psychoanalysis worked, and how it should be conducted. As discussed previously, a key to psychoanalysis was transference, through which the patient made unconscious attributions to the therapist of repressed feelings, drives, attitudes, or fantasies from the patient's childhood. The traditional psychoanalyst often became "a blank screen so that the patient's transference projections could be seen quite clearly" (Rosenbaum & Beebe, 1975, p. 229). It was on this screen that the true nature of the patient's problems would be revealed. The open expression of intense personal emotions, often with sexual or aggressive content, was essential for the therapy to succeed. Freud and generations of psychiatrists held that the presence of anyone else in the room, especially family members, would inhibit this process, violate privacy, and contaminate the transference. Indeed, that is probably true. Psychoanalysis became accepted in the medical model as the primary mode of treatment for most psychological problems. In this milieu, working with more than one family member was considered ill-advised. When a person was in psychoanalysis, other family members were not part of the treatment but could be counseled on practical matters associated with the treatment by social workers.

As psychiatry expanded, variations in the treatment emerged. After 1930, reports of psychoanalysis with more than one family member, and theories supportive of that approach, began to surface (e.g., Ackerman, 1937; Adler, 1930; Fromm-Reichmann, 1948). Because such work deviated from the dominant psychoanalytic model, it is likely that much more of it was being done that never saw the light of publication. But it was becoming apparent that psychoanalysis had limits and was especially ineffective in treating some prevalent disorders, including schizophrenia and serious child behavior problems (Guerin, 1976). This set the stage for new, family-based approaches in the 1950s.

Summary

This chapter offers a new interpretation of the theoretical and historical origins of research and practice in family problem solving. Current research and practice has been heavily influenced by these origins even though they are rarely acknowledged. This approach provides insights into why there has been so much research on some aspects of family problem solving (e.g., the rational) and so little on others (e.g., the emotional). Paradigmatic diversity made a straightforward, linear accumulation of findings on family problem solving impossible. That would come later. Although systematic accumulation of results is scientifically desirable, it can be misleading if the paradigm being used is seriously flawed. In that sense, these diverse paradigmatic origins contributed to what could ultimately become a more accurate and comprehensive understanding of family problem solving. This potential has not yet been fully realized. But the last half of the century witnessed spectacular progress toward that end. That progress is the focus of chapter 3.

3

Family Problem Solving
Comes of Age

The term *family problem solving* never appeared in the scientific literature prior to 1950. But by mid-century, all the necessary ingredients were in place to produce the scientific "discovery" of family problem solving. Small group research was well established with a good record of theory and experimental findings. Family sociology was maturing and began to consider the internal dynamics of how families functioned. The Great Depression and World War II had disrupted many American families, and during this period there were some apparent successes in "social engineering," such as Franklin Roosevelt's New Deal program and innovative training programs in the military. The prestige of social science was on the rise. The family had traditionally been a private, even sacred domain that was not a suitable subject for public policy or scientific examination. But awareness of family problems in America increased in literature and popular culture. The demise of the migrating family from Oklahoma in John Steinbeck's *Grapes of Wrath,* for example, reflected the family traumas experienced by many during the Depression. Seemingly every military husband in World War II feared receiving a "Dear John" letter that said his wife wanted a divorce and had a new boyfriend. This awareness was coupled with an increasing confidence in science of any kind. After all, science had helped us win the war. Social and behavioral sciences prospered in the wake of these conditions. In this milieu, scientific analysis of families could claim a new legitimacy. As an indirect by-product of these trends, research and practice in family problem solving began in earnest after 1950. This chapter examines the main currents of that work between 1950 and the present. That research produced the substance of what we currently know about family problem solving.

The Dissection of the
Small Group and the Family

The early psychological work on small group processes used experimental designs to identify social contexts that promoted better problem solving or performance (Dashiell, 1935). This research, for example, considered whether people performed various tasks better when they were alone, when they were watched by others, or when others were doing the same thing. This approach became quite sophisticated in testing complex hypotheses, and will be reviewed in the next section. However, in 1950, Robert Bales presented an innovative technique for examining small group behavior that moved beyond simple experimental manipulations: Interaction Process Analysis (IPA). Because variations of it were widely applied to family problem solving, we consider his work first.

Bales was using the experimental paradigm to study how small groups solved problems. But he measured more than just final performance scores of the research participants. Moving beyond the current small group paradigm, he was interested in the give and take of each participant's behavior, and how behavior patterns emerged during the group's interaction. He viewed problem solving as fundamentally a group process.

> What we usually regard as individual problem solving, or the process of individual thought, is essentially in form and in genesis a social process; thinking is a re-enactment by the individual of the problem-solving process as he originally went through it with other individuals. It can probably be maintained with considerable success that the best model we have for what goes on *inside* the individual personality is the model of what goes on *between* individuals in the problem-solving process. (Bales, 1950, p. 62)

The idea that many thought processes had a social origin was certainly not new. It had been derived from a number of theories, most notably the symbolic interactionism (originally known as social behaviorism) of G. H. Mead (1934) and C. H. Cooley (1902). However, Bales's application of this idea to problem solving was innovative and provided further implications for studies of small group processes. The nature of the social origins of individual problem solving was not destined to be taken seriously until more than 30 years later. Although Bales's theoretical foundation was of considerable interest, it was his empirical work that made a more lasting impact. It opened the door to a new view of group problem solving that established a baseline for research on family problem solving.

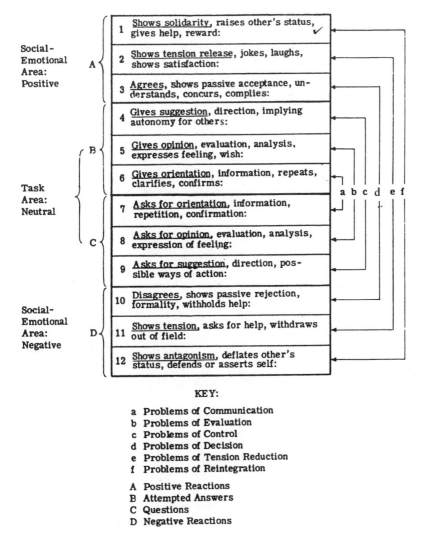

Figure 3.1. Bales's Interaction Process Analysis Codes (Bales, 1950)

Bales's Interaction Process Analysis (IPA) required a coder to apply a categorical rating (e.g., *agrees, disagrees*) to every statement made by each group participant. Bales sought to understand complex small group processes by creating a new, more basic, molecular level of analysis. He coded each statement as a type of "speech act," such as *shows solidarity, agrees, disagrees, asks for clarification.* See Figure 3.1 for a summary of the IPA code. The codes of the IPA had affective or emotional content as well as functional purpose, either positive, negative, or neutral. These codes were designed to capture the key dimensions of the small decision-making group. The previous small group research had suggested that patterns of interpersonal support, conflict, influence, and participation could affect the course of problem solving, but such processes had been difficult to study using available techniques. The IPA provided a new, more descriptive, empirical technique for examining these phenomena.

The small group research was also becoming more interested in "leadership" as a factor that could influence the quality of solutions and group process. The general idea was that good leaders could facilitate better solutions. The emergence of status structures and power relations in the small group had been of concern since the Hawthorne studies. It had become clear that getting the best solutions and productivity from a small group involved much more than merely assigning a supervisor or manager as "leader" with bureaucratic authority and power. Bales's association with Parsons and other sociologists gave him a broader view of the nature of the small group. Structural–functionalism, role theory, and concern with a general theory of action provided a valuable perspective that was quite different from the psychological approach used in most previous small group studies.

Bales began conceptualizing the small group as a social unit that had requisites or system requirements of its own. The behavior of group members was constrained so that these group requirements were met. Prominent among these requirements was the need for a task leader and a social–emotional leader (Bales & Slater, 1955). The task leader was active in initiating, eliciting, and controlling group behavior, which promoted progress on the assigned task. This task was imposed on the group by a higher-level social structure that had the authority to constrain the group's work in that way. Pursuing the task allowed the group to provide a function for the benefit of the external social system. In the Bales experimental procedure this system was a hypothetical bureaucratic organization (e.g., business, industry, or government).

But in order to maintain the functioning of the internal small group system, a social–emotional leader was also needed. This person sought to manage the affective processes within the group. These informal processes had to be managed or else productivity and effectiveness would decline. Such an outcome could result from either too much anger and conflict or from so much cohesion and bonding that little progress would be made on the official tasks at hand. Social–emotional leaders had special "people skills" and were sensitive to the emotional climate of the group. They would take it on themselves to intervene when emotional issues threatened the effectiveness of the group. For example, they would offer encouragement or jokes to foster positive attitudes or break tension. They might make efforts to head off conflicts and anger before they had a negative impact, by offering compromises and other actions intended to smooth ruffled feathers. When the social–emotional leader and task leader were effective, the group should make steady progress on the problem without getting bogged down with internal conflict, unproductive sidetracks, or frustration.

The emergence of two such leaders in small groups was called *role differentiation* (Bales & Slater, 1955). The concept of a social-emotional leader brought the affective, nonrational element of human behavior into the core of all small decision-making groups. The theory of role differentiation provided a way of overcoming the inherent limits of rational models, which were so apparent in the Hawthorne studies and the early small group experiments. It did so in a way that did not require detailing all the affective processes that go on in small groups. Whatever those processes were, the social–emotional leader managed them. This concept is relevant for family groups because it was later proposed that mothers tended to be the social–emotional leaders in families, whereas fathers were the task leaders. I will trace the fate of that hypothesis later in this chapter.

The IPA was used to test the role differentiation concept. One subset of the codes was more task oriented *(gives suggestion, asks for clarification)*, whereas another set was social–emotional *(shows tension release, disagrees, shows tension)*. Bales's research designs typically did *not* assign one member of the group as the leader. The group was given the problem and asked to work on it. It was posited that if role differentiation was a fundamental process, it should emerge quickly and organize the behavior of the group members. The IPA also allowed the amount of participation of each group member to be precisely assessed. It was posited that leaders would have the highest amount of participation.

Several studies using the IPA found evidence of role differentiation and high levels of participation among leaders (e.g., Bales & Slater, 1955). The discovery of the social–emotional leader was influential in further work on small group leadership. The technique of observing (and often recording) a small group trying to solve a problem then coding their behavior has been a mainstay of 40 years of research on all kinds of small groups in psychology, family studies, developmental psychology, family therapy, and communication research.

As impressive as the IPA work was, concerns have been raised about the external validity of the procedures and whether Bales's findings generalized to small groups other than college students in a laboratory setting (e.g., Weick, 1971). Bales's initial sample was made up of 22 groups, half of which were discussions among members of a university

Figure 3.2. Observers' View of Group Discussion in Bales's Laboratory (Bales, 1950)

chess club talking about an assigned chess problem. The rest were largely university committee meetings. All the groups met in a laboratory with a one-way mirror (see Figure 3.2).

Bales quickly became aware that such factors as the number of people in the group, the kind of problem discussed, and the past history of the group could influence what happened during group discussions, and thus affect the scores from his IPA code. He became clear in focusing his attention on groups that met specific conditions (e.g., Bales & Strodtbeck, 1951). It became apparent that extraneous contextual variables would compromise any efforts to rigorously test research hypotheses. To avoid this difficulty, work in the Bales tradition began using a standard task for group discussion (see Appendix A for an example). This decision was scientifically necessary at that stage of the research, and proved to be quite effective in generating systematic results. However, the external validity of these procedures has never been adequately proven. This is an issue to be examined later in chapter 4.

To Bales's credit, his initial book (Bales, 1950) included descriptive summaries and analyses of behavior patterns in several different types of groups, including some groups of children (see Appendix B for sample behavior profiles). Indeed, Bales's group tasks had more external validity than most social–psychological research. Thus any critique of Bales based on external validity must be tempered by the acknowledgment that no research program can meet all desired criteria. But, for our concerns, we must be interested in whether Bales's studies can be applied to family problem solving.

Parsons's sociological theorizing gave primary importance to the family, and it was therefore natural to consider whether the new small group findings applied to the family (Parsons & Bales, 1955). The traditional view of family roles prevalent in the 1950s, as well as Parsons's structural–functional theory of the family, seemed to fit the role differentiation concept, with fathers being the task leaders and mothers being the social–emotional leaders. Pursuing tests of this hypothesis, several researchers used the Bales experimental procedures with family groups (Leik, 1963; Strodtbeck, 1954). These studies can rightly be considered the first empirical examinations of family problem solving.

Strodtbeck's study was noteworthy in part because he applied Bales's IPA coding to audiotape recordings of family members in their own homes. Family members (mother, father, adolescent son) individually indicated their decision on 47 forced-choice written vignettes involving parent–adolescent issues (see Appendix C). Nine of these were chosen for the family to discuss and to try to arrive at the alternative that best represented the thinking of the family (Strodtbeck, 1954). Strodtbeck's team selected the nine vignettes that involved specific patterns of disagreements among family members useful for studying coalitions (two family members chose one option, the third chose the other option). In that sense it was a revealed-difference task. The analysis focused on testing a hypothesis originally advanced by Simmel on the nature of three-person groups. Simmel proposed that in three-person groups, two of the members tend to become more closely affiliated and essentially form a coalition against the third party. Using the IPA, some researchers found evidence for this hypothesis in groups of three college students. Strodtbeck sought to replicate this result in family groups at home. The result did not replicate in family groups, however. This study marked the beginning of a long and often perplexing series of studies on families doing structured interaction tasks.

The results of the early work in this series were decidedly mixed. Some studies found little evidence of the predicted role differentiation between mother and father or related patterns (Leik, 1963; Strodtbeck, 1954). Other studies found some evidence consistent with it (e.g., Kenkel, 1959; Scott, 1962). Over time, researchers were not able to reconcile the conflicting results. Thus the conclusion emerged that families, in the Bales-type situation, have neither a clear task nor a social–emotional leader. Apparently there are not structurally prescribed roles for mother and father in family problem solving tasks. Parents did participate more

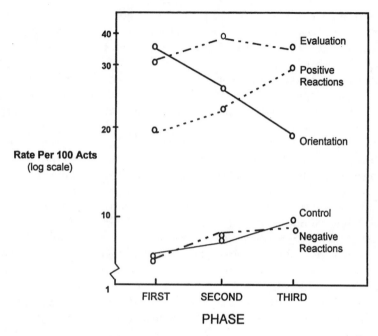

Figure 3.3. Rate of Act Type by Phase of Problem Solving Interaction (Bales & Strodtbeck, 1951)

than children in these settings, indicating that parents were leaders in Bales's sense. But the kinds of behavior mothers and fathers exhibited was quite diverse.

Bales's IPA allowed tests of other fundamental processes at work in group problem solving. Foremost among these was the idea that problem solving proceeded through a series of distinct phases. This general concept was not new, of course; Dewey had proposed a series of phases in critical thinking decades earlier (Dewey, 1910/1982). But the application of it to group problem solving was new. Bales and Strodtbeck (1951) proposed that group problem solving began with an *orientation phase,* when group members collected information about the problem and defined its characteristics. This gave way to an *evaluation phase* as alternative solutions were considered and ranked. Finally, a *control phase* occurred as group members sought to get agreement from group members and curtail further discussion. Different IPA codes would be expected more frequently in each of these stages. For example, the *asks for orientation* code would be expected more often in the orientation phase and less often in the control phase. Figure 3.3 shows a graph from Bales and Strodbeck's (1951) classic paper on the phases of group problem solving in groups of college students. As expected, the frequency of orientation acts was lower in the control (third) phase than in the orientation (first) phase. The frequencies of control, positive, and negative reactions also increased from the orientation to the control phases. This provided initial descriptive evidence in favor of the phase concept. But difficulties with statistical tests, replications, and generalizations to family groups raised questions about the viability of the phase concept for family problem solving (Gottman, 1979; Kieren, Maguire, & Hurlbut, 1996; Klein & Hill, 1979). This issue will be pursued in chapter 5.

Although these experimental studies of family problem solving did not confirm the Parsons–Bales view of the family, the methods captured the imagination of a generation of researchers interested in family dynamics. Much of the best work on family problem solving since Bales may be seen as variations on his research techniques. The challenge has been to find a theory of family problem solving that works.

One approach to explaining the mixed results from the Bales-group family studies has been based on methodological critique. Some have suggested that Bales's IPA is not applicable to families (Gottman, 1979). After all, the IPA was designed for the bureaucratic small group context. The codes relevant for family life may be quite different. Families may function according to a somewhat different logic. Gottman and others have proposed new coding systems that have proven useful (Gottman, 1979, 1993; Kurdek, 1995; Rueter & Conger, 1995; Vuchinich et al., 1996). In addition, the structured problem solving situation in the Bales procedure may have marginal relevance for family life, where "problems" are typically not assigned to the family for solution in a limited time span (Weick, 1971). More recent research has had families choose their own problems for solution (e.g., Forgatch, 1989; Rueter & Conger, 1995; Vuchinich et al., 1993).

The experimental research on non–family-group problem solving continued and found that the processes involved were more complex than initially thought. The early studies that found benefits in the group situation had to be qualified. Later studies showed that group problem solving was not always superior (e.g., Taylor, Berry, & Block, 1958). As it turned out, the relative advantage of group problem solving depended on several factors, including the type of problem that was being solved (Hoffman & Smith, 1961; Jones & Gerard, 1967), the similarity of group members (Hoffman & Maier, 1961), and whether the group leader had the best solution (Riecken, 1958; Torrance, 1955). Interaction among group members can create conflict, pressure to conform, and other processes that impede good problem solving. Indeed, one review concluded that "under most circumstances, groups are less efficient than individuals working alone. Group members distract, inhibit, and generally tend to interfere with one another" (Freedman, Carlsmith, & Sears, 1970, p. 193). These studies exquisitely demonstrated that social and contextual variables influence the course of problem solving in small groups. Although fascinating, this body of studies was more concerned with finding new factors that influenced problem solving than pursuing a systematic research program. As a result, the most complete review of the studies in that era concluded that "the literature on group problem solving [is] a large conglomeration of unrelated experiments, with only the faintest suggestion of commonality" (Hoffman, 1965, p. 127).

Unfortunately, this indictment is almost as true today as it was more than 30 years ago. The various findings on group problem solving have proven to be resistant to systematic integration. The pieces of the puzzle do not seem to fit. Because of this state of affairs, interest in such studies in disciplines such as social psychology has waned. Various conclusions could be drawn from this. Perhaps the most important causal variables have never been assessed. It is also possible that the experimental group tasks create artificial social systems that are *not* coherently organized, because they are not true social systems. If that is correct, then such studies would have limited implications for family groups (Steinhauer, 1989; Weick, 1971). Nevertheless, the basic findings from such studies can be replicated and provide a beginning point or baseline for considering family problem solving.

Most of the small group studies of problem solving used similar experimental procedures. Research participants were brought into a laboratory room, given a specific problem, or series of problems, and then given instructions to solve the problem within a certain amount of time. This procedure yielded quantifiable data, in a short period of time, on a sample of groups large enough for statistical analysis. The context could be controlled so that all the groups experienced approximately the same situation. The experimental designs often allowed for random assignment to groups and blocking to eliminate alternative explanations for results. The scientific method was applied to the fullest extent.

Although impressive in experimental rigor, the issue of external validity looms large over this entire paradigm. Do people behave in real life the way college students do in such artificial tasks? In terms of formal organizations, there is some evidence that they do. A few studies have been done in corporations (e.g., Dunnette, Campbell, & Jaastad, 1963) and the military (Torrance, 1955). But the demands of the workplace do not fit well with experimental procedures. The fields of organizational behavior and management consulting have blossomed in recent years. These tend to focus on management techniques and limited measures of productivity rather than the underlying processes that produce the results. The question of whether experimental findings apply to families is still an unanswered one.

Social Class, Culture, and Family Problem Solving

Another approach to explaining the mixed results in family groups was to raise the possibility that certain social characteristics of families, not yet considered in the Bales-type studies, were important in determining basic aspects of the problem solving process. The social class, or the cultural–ethnic background of the families might largely determine the way they approach their problems. For example, in paternalistic cultures the father might make all the important decisions and the rest of the family would have to go along. If such influences were strong enough, they would wash out the effects found in groups of unacquainted college students. Strodtbeck's initial effort to apply the small group paradigm to the family included diversity in culture and class, but only to improve generalizability of his findings (Strodtbeck, 1954). The presence of class or cultural influences was consistent with Parsons's theory of the family, which embedded the family within a social structural context (Parsons & Bales, 1955).

With these issues as a backdrop, some sociologists took up the question of whether family problem solving is influenced by social class and culture (Straus, 1968, 1972; Tallman, 1980; Tallman & Miller, 1974). The social class issue added a new relevance to family problem solving. Sociology then, as now, was grappling with the problems of unemployment, urban decay, crime, and social change. Of course, these problems were always more prevalent in the lower class. Straus suggested that some of these problems were linked to the "ability of family groups to deal with the kind of novel and problematic situations characteristic of a rapidly changing urban–industrial society" (Straus, 1968, p. 417). Straus predicted that working-class families would have less effective family problem solving abilities than middle-class families. He further posited that this difference would be a result of more open communication in middle-class families. Some relevant class differences in communication had already been demonstrated in sociolinguistic studies (Bernstein, 1960, 1961). The idea was that if families do not communicate with each other openly and effectively, then they will not be able to solve their problems very well. Straus did confirm his hypotheses.

Although his methods warrant further comment, the theory itself is perhaps more important. In one stroke, Straus placed family problem solving at the core of the most prominent sociological issue of the period, and the raging national debate on urban violence. Furthermore, if Straus was correct, a potential avenue for preventing or reducing the social class difficulties would be opened up: improving problem solving in lower-class families. Although he did not pursue this implication, his theorizing represents a way of thinking about the origins of societal problems that is still influential. According to this theory, poor people are poor in part because they make bad decisions. Dewey's early work on the societal benefits of education in problem solving is perfectly applicable. As we shall see, teaching children and parents to do better problem solving is a key to some of the best current school-based programs for preventing negative child outcomes prevalent in the lower class (Brasswell & Bloomquist, 1991; Hughes & Hall, 1989; Spivack, Platt, & Shure, 1976; Tolan & McKay, 1996).

Straus did not provide a detailed explanation for why problem solving in the family unit was distinctly important, nor did he offer any prior evidence that families even had enduring problem solving strategies or styles. Nonetheless, people were ready to entertain his hypothesis linking social class, problem solving, and social problems. Moynihan had already made the case that family characteristics contribute to poverty (1965). Straus's reasoning extended the family contribution toward class difficulties to include communication patterns. In addition, Parsons's work on the links between family and economic development was still influential (Parsons, 1951). The primacy of family responsibilities and values in traditional societies was seen as an inhibiting factor in modern economic development (Straus, 1972; Tallman, 1980). The idea that family characteristics such as problem solving methods could similarly inhibit economic development of the lower class was but one step removed from that position. In modern terms, both Moynihan and Straus can be taken to task for oversimplifying the nature of lower-class families and promoting a "deficit" model of social class. Be that as it may, Straus and Tallman introduced a new variable into the social problem arena. They raised the ante for research on family problem solving. That research would no longer be simply efforts to test the external validity of some experimental studies of abstract principles about the nature of small groups (Strodtbeck, 1954). It was now something that had relevance for major social issues confronting American society.

Although the implications were grand, the actual experiments of Straus and Tallman were rather modest. Creating a family problem solving procedure that minimized class and cultural biases involved formidable methodological challenges. An entirely verbal task in the Bales tradition was ill-advised in the light of Bernstein's sociolinguistic work on class and variation across culture. Straus and Tallman settled on a SIMFAM (SIMulated FAMily) game (Straus, 1968) played on a 9- by

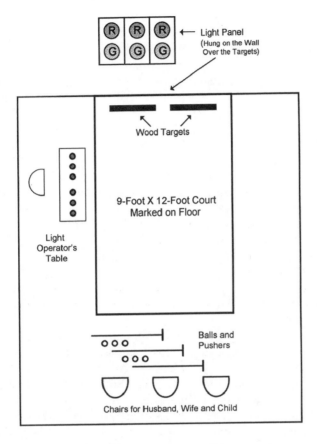

Figure 3.4. Diagram of the Layout of Straus's SIMFAM Family Interaction Task (Straus, 1968). Reprinted by permission of The University of Chicago Press.

12-ft court with mother, father, and child seated at one end, and two wooden targets at the floor at the other end (see Figure 3.4).

This research was conducted in Puerto Rico, Minnesota, and India. Each person had a colored wooden "pusher" stick that was used to push colored balls across the court to try to hit the wooden targets. Points were scored only under certain conditions—for example, if the color of the stick matched the color of the ball, if the ball hit a target, if family members rolled the balls in a certain order. Families were not told, however, the conditions necessary to score. Instead, they were told to begin playing and a green light would be turned on every time they scored a point, and a red light would flash for an incorrect move. "Each family was told that the problem was to figure out how to play the game" and instructed to try to get more points than "other families who have played this game" (Straus, 1968, p. 420).

This task avoided total reliance on verbal behavior, required coordination and communication among family members, had an objective solution, and provided for quantification of success through counting the number of points the family scored. Verbal communication during the task could be measured in terms of how many statements each family member made. Of course, one disadvantage of this design was uncertainty about external validity. Would this task elicit behavior that reflected the way the family solved their real problems at home? Straus did not test this. It was not considered necessary at that time because gaming studies were very popular and many scientists were willing to assume at least a minimal level of external validity in such tasks. Such assumptions are less acceptable today. But Straus's study was still important because it offered an approach to family problem solving outside of the Bales task. Although useful, the Bales task afforded no objectively quantifiable measure of how well a family solved the problem the members discussed (Blechman & McEnroe, 1985; Reiss, 1981). In addition, the initial results of applying the Bales task to family groups were confusing (Leik, 1963; Strodtbeck, 1954).

Straus was open about some of the difficulties with the SIMFAM task, conducted in university or community centers around the world. Indeed, the lower-class families in India were apparently unable to determine what they were supposed to do (Straus, 1968). However, task engagement was better in Puerto Rico and Minneapolis. Substantial class differences were found as predicted. Tallman and Miller (1974) adapted the experiment for use in homes by using beanbags instead of balls. They proposed that communication differences were only relevant in some circumstances and that the class differences Straus found may have been a result instead of the way fathers reacted to the new task situation.

Based on expectation states theory (Berger, Cohen, & Zelditch, 1972), it was suggested that, because of expectations created by the social system, "middle-class families function better in egalitarian structures and blue-collar families function better in father-dominant structures" (Tallman & Miller, 1974, p. 19). If lower-class fathers did not assume a dominant role, "strains may develop making it difficult for the family to organize itself to deal effectively when faced with emergent problems." However, if those fathers assumed their "normal" leadership role, consistent with the hierarchical expectations of lower-class families, lower-class problem solving should be as good as middle-class problem solving. Although this hypothesis is perhaps repugnant from a feminist perspective, it was clearly confirmed (Tallman & Miller, 1974). This study countered Straus's results, and further research has not settled the question of whether or not social class influences family problem solving. Drawing attention to weaknesses in low-income families has fallen into disfavor since the scathing critiques of Moynihan's work on black families (Billingsley, 1968) and efforts to build on family strengths in all social classes. Tallman and Miller's position is based on the assumption that family organization in lower class families is sexist and paternalistic. This has not been proven, and such positions have fallen into disfavor with the rise of feminist theories of the family (Thompson & Walker, 1995) and more detailed research on lower-class families (e.g., Stack, 1974). Researchers today are less willing to simply assume that lower-class mothers have less power in the family than fathers. This stereotype has gone the way of the assumption that mothers are always the social–emotional leaders in American families. Overall, the question of whether social class and family problem solving are linked came to be mired in a labyrinth of class, racial, and sexual politics. It has yet to emerge from that labyrinth. But the research and the ensuing critiques have performed the important service of helping to debunk some stereotypes about how mothers and fathers are involved in family problem solving. Perhaps more important, this work greatly expanded the scope of research on family problem solving. It would no longer be sufficient to assume that all families function in the same way as a result of universal principles of small group behavior. Such principles do constrain problem solving. But it is likely that social structures outside of the family that organize behavior in terms of gender, class, and ethnicity will have their impact in the arena of family problem solving.

The Birth of Family Therapy: "We've Got a Problem!"

By the 1950s, a group of therapists and researchers had developed an understanding of problems of individual adjustment and mental illness in terms of *family processes* (e.g., Ackerman, 1958; Bateson, Jackson, Haley, & Weakland, 1956; Bowen, 1960). They developed entirely new models for several disorders and innovative family-based techniques for treatment. They created a completely original paradigm for conceptualizing family problems and how to solve them.

As is often the case, the new paradigm was not welcomed with open arms by those comfortable with the established paradigms prevalent in experimental social psychology, sociology, psychiatry, or clinical psychology. But over time, family therapy has proven itself to be a useful approach to the treatment of individual and family problems. However, other branches of academic research on family problem solving have not yet assimilated the contributions of family therapy to its subject matter. One reason for this is that the mainstream has been quite occupied grappling with the basic processes of problem solving in "normal" families. Work on families that have some "abnormal" problems could add an insurmountable layer of complexity to an already difficult challenge. The early attention given to the wing of family therapy that focused on schizophrenia (Bateson et al., 1956), a serious psychotic mental disorder, contributed to the perception that such work would not be relevant to normal family processes. In fact, most early work in family therapy did not deal with such extreme disorders. Ackerman sought to set the record straight in 1967: "The family approach arose in the study of nonpsychotic disorders in children as related to the family environment. The relative prominence of recent reports on schizophrenia and family has somewhat obscured this fact" (Guerin, 1976).

But even for less serious disorders and problems, families that seek treatment are often considered to be "different" from other families. It would certainly be ill-advised to build a general model of family functioning based only on families seeking treatment. This was an issue for theories of marriage because, at one time, most of the available research was based on couples in marital counseling for troubled marriages. But the family problem solving field should be cautious not to "throw the baby out with the bathwater."

The problems that bring families into therapy are real. Over the years, family therapy has become the treatment of choice for a broad range of individual and family problems (Gurman & Kniskern, 1991). The vast majority of these do not involve major mental disorders. Most families who have been involved in family therapy, and family therapy research, are not noticeably different from other families. They are families in which a problem has been acknowledged. And the problem is considered, by someone at least, as something that needs professional attention. Any general model of family problem solving must take this type of family into account. Indeed, if research on family problem solving is ever to have any useful application, it is precisely this type of family that will be a primary target for those efforts. Thus it is essential to begin integrating the family therapy work on such families with the research on nonclinical families.

The work in family therapy through 1980 had an important scientific advantage over the research based on other paradigms: external validity. Most of the experimental research on family problem solving up to 1980 involved families trying to solve artificial problems of one sort or another. Virtually all of this research used either a game format (Blechman & McEnroe, 1985; Reiss, 1981; Straus, 1968; Tallman, 1980), or a vignette format in which a family situation was described and the family participants were instructed to discuss that situation (Strodtbeck, 1954). These studies produced interesting, but often mixed results. A fundamental issue, which was rarely addressed during this time, was the external validity of these experimental procedures.

There was a tacit, but untested, assumption on which the validity of all these studies rested. It was assumed that the problem solving of families in these artificial situations would be similar to problem solving in real life situations. This assumption had been a basis for most work in experimental social psychology for decades. So it was considered quite acceptable to apply it to family groups. However, since the Hawthorne studies, the small group research had included a steady stream of field studies and quasi-experiments in business, industry, and military settings (e.g., Dunnette et al.,1963; Torrance, 1955). This work provided important checks of the external validity of laboratory studies. Despite Strodtbeck's early landmark study (1954), and a few notable exceptions (e.g., O'Rourke, 1963; Tallman & Miller, 1974), a corresponding set of field studies for family problem solving has not materialized. Thus the experimental family problem solving work through 1980 was left without much defense to the challenge that its findings held only for experimental tasks, and may have little applicability to real family problem solving (e.g., Aldous, 1971, 1975; Weick, 1971). In light of this fundamental weakness, the family therapy approach to problems, possessed of almost irrefutable external validity, can offer a useful balance to the experimental paradigm.

The history of family therapy, as with any applied science, is filled with its share of brilliant insights, breakthroughs, blind alleys, doctrinaire in-fighting, and controversy. Because of this complexity, only key fragments pertinent to family problem solving can be addressed. Special care is needed in pulling conceptual fragments from one paradigm (e.g., family therapy), and comparing them with fragments of another paradigm (e.g., experimental social psychology). It must be acknowledged that family therapy is oriented primarily toward treatment, whereas other disciplines are oriented toward explanation and prediction. However, much of family therapy is based on general theories of how families function. Productive integrations of the paradigms have already been started (e.g., Steinhauer, 1989). With appropriate cautions in mind, we consider family problem solving in the context of family therapy.

From its beginnings, family therapy has had more than one school of thought. Although these schools share some important core concepts, they emphasize different aspects of family systems and, in turn, different tactics for treatment. One of these schools, often known as strategic family therapy, has a focus that is most relevant for general theories of family problem solving (Guerin, 1976; Haley, 1987; Madanes, 1981; Weakland, 1976). That focus is on interpreting, defining, and solving the specific problem that caused the family to seek treatment. This may seem, at first, to be trite and obvious. But in fact it represents a major, and much needed, contribution in conceptualizing and treating family problems. It has also come to be influential in current prevention and intervention programs that use family problem solving (e.g., Brasswell & Bloomquist, 1991; Forgatch & Patterson, 1989; Spoth & Redmond, 1996; Tolan & McKay, 1996).

Strategic family therapy offers a refreshing counterpoint to experimental studies of artificial problems and games. What about real family problems about which family members had intense concerns, emotions (e.g., anger, sadness, resentment, frustrations), and worries? How do families try to solve these? Do they do it the same way they do in dealing with vignettes or game points? Strategic family therapists placed the family's problem squarely at the center of their theory and practice. They provided the most thorough, penetrating analysis of what a family problem is.

Freud's psychoanalysis introduced the idea that a person's definition of his or her problem is not the real problem at all. In psychoanalysis, the real problem was usually to be found in repressed psychosexual issues from childhood. This led generations of therapists, of all persuasions, to tend to discount the "presenting problem" and look much deeper. In the medical and other models, this often meant a diagnosis of one family member as having a specific "disorder," such as depression, alcoholism, attention deficit disorder, neurosis, borderline personality, schizophrenia, and so on. The identified disorder in one person was the source of the problem. Therapy for the individual with the disorder was the treatment of choice. The presenting problem was seen as "irrational" behavior that would lead to locating the disorder in the "problem" person. Although this approach is appropriate in some circumstances, strategic family therapy suggested that it is not useful for many cases. An entirely different conceptualization of the nature of the "problem" was proposed. Four ideas were central to this reconceptualization.

First, the family's "presenting problem" was seen as a basic part of their "true problem," not as just an overt symptom of an underlying disorder in one family member. Second, the presenting problem was seen as only one undesired behavior in a sequence of actions involving other family members that was repeated again and again. Identifying that sequence, and the involvement of other family members in it, was central to the treatment. Third, the undesired, "irrational" (e.g., dangerous, harmful, criminal, sick, harmful) behavior that was the basis for the presenting problem was viewed as "a way of adapting to the current social situation" (Haley, 1987, p. 2).

> It appears that the problems brought to therapists commonly arise from difficulties of everyday life that have been mishandled by the parties involved. Although such difficulties at times may involve special or unusual events—accidents, sudden illness, unexpected job loss—most commonly they involve adaptation to an ordinary life change or transition, such as marriage, childbirth, entering school, and so on. The mishandling involved may range from ignoring or denying difficulties on which action should be taken, to attempts to actively resolve difficulties that need not or cannot be resolved, with a wide area between which action is needed but the wrong kind is taken. Bad handling certainly does not correct, and usually increases, the original difficulty, that is then apt to be relabeled as a "problem," which is usually met by more of the same or similar inappropriate mishandling, leading to exacerbation or spreading of the difficulty—and so on and on. (Weakland, 1976, p. 124)

> In people's attempts to deal with life, their solutions most often become the problem. (Guerin, 1976, p. 20)

Thus the problematic behavior was not an expression of an individual disorder or defect. Rather, it was an end product of an ineffective effort to *adapt* to a family situation. The "problem" is often a failed solution attempt.

This casting of human problems and solution attempts in the framework of an adaptation model, of course, was not a new idea. Indeed, we have seen that Dewey's formulation of the nature of problems took this same perspective, as do the evolutionary psychologists. The *presenting problem* can be seen as Dewey's *imbalance* or *disequilibrium* in the *organism–environment* system. In addition, the notion that some solution attempts fail is entirely consistent with the evolutionary thinking (Darwin, 1871) that was the basis for Dewey's adaptation model.

The early family therapists, of course, did not draw specifically from Dewey, whose ideas by then had been widely disseminated into many fields. But in hindsight we can see the distinct imprint of his adaptation model of problems and solutions. Indeed, that model would ultimately come to have an even wider impact.

The adaptation approach of strategic family therapy drew attention away from individual disorder and redirected it to the interaction and organization of the family. The fourth key concept of strategic family therapy was that providing a specific solution to the presenting problem was a primary goal of treatment and a key indicator of the success of therapy. The presenting problem was part of a persistent sequence of behaviors that involved other family members. These problematic sequences expressed and maintained dysfunctional relationships, hierarchies, and structures such as alliances (Haley, 1987; Madanes, 1988). The challenge of the strategic therapist is to adjust these dysfunctional elements of the system by focusing on changes in the behavioral sequencing. A key to this is adjusting the way families perceive the presenting problem: "The first task of the therapist is to define a presenting problem in such a way that it can be solved" (Madanes, 1981, p. 20). "The hope is that intervention will bring about an alteration or redefinition of 'reality' in the form of a more functional solution" (Guerin, 1976, p. 20).

The therapeutic techniques for accomplishing such redefinition will be taken up later. Of interest is the notion that the presenting problem is a primary issue throughout the therapy, and that it is embedded in sequences of family behavior. Discovering the sequence is the key to solving the problem. "The resolution of problems corresponds . . . in primarily requiring a change in the problem-maintaining behavior so as to interrupt the vicious positive feedback cycles. The therapists main task is to promote such changes" (Weakland, 1976, p. 123).

Thus solving the family problem means eliminating the undesirable behavior by adjusting the behavior of more than one family member. This may be relatively easy or difficult, depending on how entrenched the behavior sequences are. It may occur quickly or take a long time. In either case, the ideal outcome is that family members perceive that their original presenting problem has been solved.

In the context of the experimental paradigm that largely ignored the "real" problems of the families they studied, strategic family therapy's riveting focus on the nature of such problems is a revelation. For our purposes, three points are primary. First, family problems are social constructions involving the active participation and perceptions of several family members. Presenting problems such as, "Dad is an alcoholic"; "Jane and her brother fight all the time"; "Johnny gets into fights at school"; "Susan and her brother are having sex" are important. But they are only part of the picture.

Second, efforts to solve perceived problems can lead to changes in the family that are beneficial. In many families, in most situations, such changes are brought about in the normal course of family interaction, based on internal family strengths. That may be based on such factors as cohesion, effective communication, high levels of skills in parents, and so on. But for some families, in some situations, adaptive changes do not emerge naturally. In those cases, the problems often get worse. Help from outside the family may be needed.

Third, adaptation is the key concept in understanding what a family problem is and how it can be solved. Some families have very difficult challenges to face, such as natural disasters, death of a parent, family members with physical disabilities, poverty, and so on. In one sense, these may be viewed as "problems." But if families are successfully adapting to such circumstances, then they are not "family problems" any more. They are only problems if an effective adaptation is not found. Although the viability of this definition can be debated, it nonetheless opened up a new and influential way of thinking about family problems.

As an example of how these concepts are applied in practice, I present segments of a case study of family therapy. I include only some details, and interested readers should refer to the complete text.

> A 13-year-old boy was brought to a department of psychiatry for a consultation. He had been diagnosed as a severe childhood depression at a family service agency. During the psychiatric evaluation at the hospital, it was found that his mother had been severely depressed in the past and that one of the child's cousins had also been severely depressed. . . . The boy had fits of crying, sat around most of the day doing nothing, had refused to go to school for the last two months, and had threatened suicide. He had been in individual treatment with a therapist who felt strongly that the child should not be stressed. (Madanes, 1981, pp. 103–104)

> [It] was decided before the first interview that the therapist would recommend to the parents that the child be forced to go to school as soon as possible, so that he could return to the normal life of a 13 year old. It was assumed that, because the mother had been depressed in the past, the boy's "depression" was a metaphor for the mother's depression and that the child was staying home, keeping his mother company, and helping her by eliciting concerned and protective behavior from her, so that she was focused on her son rather than on her own problems. (p. 104)

> It was planned that at the beginning of the session the therapist would redefine the problem as a refusal to go to school and the depression as a consequence of staying at home doing nothing. The therapist would then appeal to the mother as an expert in overcoming depression, thus defining her as a competent person who, instead of being depressed, had succeeded in overcoming depression. On the basis of this success the mother would be put in charge of making the boy go to school. In this way, if the boy stayed home, his behavior was metaphorical of the mother's depression; but if he went to school, his behavior was the result of the mother's success and competence. (p. 104)

> The therapist started the first interview by saying that he understood that the problem they were consulting about was centered around the boy's

refusal to go to school. The mother immediately corrected him, saying that they were consulting about the child's severe depression, the *consequence* of which was that he could not attend school. The father, however, stated that he had thought that the boy's crying and upset were normal adolescent problems and that the boy should be made to go to school. The therapist took this opportunity to define the problem as one where the boy used to be normally sad but became depressed when he stopped going to school. The depression was presented as the consequence, not the cause, of refusing to go to school. (p. 105)

After some resistance, the boy did attend school regularly and the depression subsided. "At the beginning of therapy, the child's depression had been a metaphor for the mother's depression. At the end of therapy, the boy's success was a metaphor for the mother's success in overcoming her depression" (Madanes, 1981, p. 108). Family therapy involves many more elements than reformulating the problems presented. This case, for example, used metaphors, but also shows the often central importance of working with the family's view of their problem.

Elements of the strategic family therapy approach are the basis for the idea that some serious family problems can be solved quickly, as in brief therapy (Watzlawick, Weakland, Fisch, & Bodin, 1974). Short-term family therapy has major implications for the cost of treatment, mental health care policy, and a broad range of welfare programs. The family preservation movement in social work and other interventions (e.g., Henggeler, 1992; Pecora, Fraser, & Haapala, 1992) are based on the concept of adaptation and on effective short-term solutions. Thus the strategic therapy reformulation of the concept of "family problem" has had a major impact on family practice, even though it did not have a tradition of rigorous quantified research that fit the empirical paradigm of social and behavioral science. This suggests that there is more than one pathway to finding theories and practices that are effective.

The family therapy field continued to develop and expand with problem solving remaining as a key issue addressed in various ways. One influential case study in 1978, *The Family Crucible: One Family's Therapy—An Experience That Illuminates All Our Lives,* brought the details of the therapy in one family to the attention of the public at large (Napier & Whitaker, 1978). Written in lay terms with an engaging style, the book provided an indelible impression of a family system trying to solve its problems and how two family therapists were able to help them. The book remains one of the best introductions to the nature of family problems and family therapy (Napier & Whitaker, 1978; see pp. 273-295 for a brief overview).

Social Learning Theory, Mental Health, and Problem Solving

The idea that problem solving and adaptation were central to mental health was also introduced at the level of the individual person (Jahoda, 1953, 1958). The 1950s and 1960s saw the ascendance of behaviorism and social learning theory as models for explaining human behavior (e.g., Bandura, 1969; Skinner, 1953). Similar to the family therapy models, these theories ultimately sought explanations for mental illness different from the prevailing medical "disease" and psychiatric models. Also, similar to the family therapists, they provided a new definition of what a "problem" is and what it means to "solve" it. This approach has been very influential in current clinical and developmental psychology. Though much of it was not initially applied to the family context, it has come to have a substantial impact on prevention and intervention programs (e.g., Forgatch & Patterson, 1989). In addition, this paradigm has produced the most rigorous empirical tests of treatments based on problem solving techniques.

Perhaps the most seminal early work from this perspective was a review and synthesis paper by D'Zurilla and Goldfried (1971). They embraced the social learning model (Bandura, 1969; Ullmann & Krasner, 1969).

> Rejecting the traditional "medical" view that abnormality is best explained in terms of symptoms of some underlying "disease" process, the social-learning approach places most of its emphasis on the individual's learned response to more or less naturally occurring life circumstances. When the individual's characteristic response is *ineffective* (i.e., results in negative consequences to himself and/or others), it runs the risk of receiving such labels as "abnormal," "disturbed," or "maladjusted," depending on the particular behavioral norms and standards of the person doing the judging. (D'Zurilla & Goldfried, 1971, p. 107)

The concept of "ineffective" behavior and the focus on small units of behavior parallels the strategic family therapy approach. Indeed, both paradigms share the emphasis on adaptation, which can be traced to Dewey. Given the divergent perspectives of Dewey and Freud, it is no coincidence that both strategic family therapy and the social learning models attacked the prevailing psychoanalytic paradigm. What is pertinent is that these attacks were based on new concepts of what problems are, and how to solve them. D'Zurilla and Goldfried were careful in casting their concepts in "behaviorist" terms.

The term *problem* will refer here to a specific *situation* or *set of related situations* to which a person must respond in order to function effectively in his environment. . . . [A] situation is considered problematic if *no effective response alternative is immediately available to the individual confronted with the situation.* (D'Zurilla & Goldfried, 1971, pp. 107–108)

Problem solving may be defined as a behavioral process, whether overt or cognitive in nature, which (a) makes available a variety of potentially effective response alternatives for dealing with the problematic situation and (b) increases the probability of selecting the most effective response from among these various alternatives. (p. 108)

A solution (i.e., an effective response) . . . may be specifically *defined as a response or pattern of responses which alters the situation so that it is no longer problematic to the individual and at the same time maximizes other positive consequences and minimizes other negative ones.* (p. 109)

In these terms, solutions are usually found by learning new, more effective responses. Drawing from the extant research and theory in the rational paradigm, D'Zurilla and Goldfried proposed five stages to the problem solving process that lead to these new responses: (a) general orientation, (b) problem definition, (c) generation of alternatives, (d) decision making, and (e) verification. The imprint of Dewey can hardly be mistaken for anything else. They then gave one case study of how to apply their problem solving behavior modification approach to a client who presented the following situation: "I became upset and depressed last night because my husband was out working late and I was home alone" (p. 122). They provide a detailed description of how a therapist leads or coaches the client through each of the five stages of problem solving. Ultimately, the client generated some new approaches to her problem that were effective (e.g., getting dead bolt locks, asking friends over for card games, enrolling in an adult education class).

This parsimonious formulation boldly reduces mental health and problem solving into stimulus–response terms. As in all behaviorist applications to humans, the catch is in assigning "positive" and "negative" values to relevant behaviors and consequences. A valid and reliable general calculus of reinforcement for humans in everyday life has never been provided. The meaning of D'Zurilla and Goldfried's "effective response" is somewhat vague, open to broad interpretation, and perilously close to being circular. Indeed, it has become increasingly clear that reinforcement is only one of several factors influencing human behavior. But as with family therapy, flawed theoretical models may still produce useful applications. The theoretical model has never really been tested, but the effectiveness of therapy using this theory as a basis has been tested. And there is evidence it works in many cases (e.g., Brasswell & Bloomquist, 1991; Kendall, 1991; Urbain & Kendall, 1980).

There are a number of similarities in the strategic family therapy and social learning models. One of the most significant of these is the idea that the basic nature of problems for "normal" people and families is not more fundamentally different than it is for "abnormal" people and families. These are the routine problems of everyday life, the problems of normal individual and family transitions, and the problems associated with crisis. Thus the analysis of problem solving in families and individuals who have sought help for relatively "serious" problems *is relevant* to families who have not sought help. The search for new solutions to provide a better adaptation to the environment is a process that applies across families with different characteristics. Thus principles from strategic family therapy and the cognitive–behavioral approach should apply to families that are not currently abnormal or dysfunctional. Indeed, such principles should be useful in preventing the escalation of family problems to that level. This thinking has been the basis for applying problem solving components in prevention programs (e.g., Conduct Problems Prevention Research Group, 1992; Spoth & Redmond, 1996; Tolan & McKay, 1996).

The strategic family therapy and social learning models both possess a glorious parsimony that sets them apart from other views of problem solving. This is advantageous conceptually, empirically, and for generating applications. However, the evidence supporting the veracity of these models is not to be found in direct, conclusive tests of the models themselves and their assumptions. Instead, these models have prospered on the basis of some successes in treatment applications based on them. The value of a model that generates useful applications must certainly be acknowledged. However, the success of such applications should not be mistaken for proof that the models provide a true understanding of family problem solving. Indeed, the models may prove to be only useful heuristics.

This may appear to be a fine distinction in the face of much-needed treatment success. However, the treatment success, although encouraging, has not been universal or consistent (Kazdin, Siegel, & Bass, 1992; Reid, 1993). Perhaps the brilliance of both the strategic and social learning approaches is in their selection of key observable components of the adaptation process that are subject to change. In any event, neither model set out to offer a complete model for family problem solving. Research from other perspectives has shown that it is more complex than these reductionist models imply. Models that explicitly capture more of

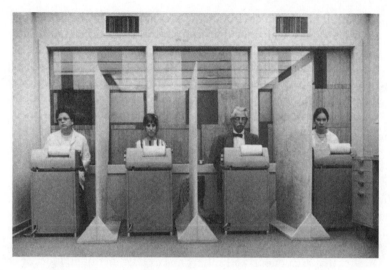

Figure 3.5. Setting for One of Reiss's Family Interaction Tasks (Reiss, 1981)

that complexity may be essential for developing better applications in family problem solving. One line of research stands out as offering a model of family problem solving that faces up to some of that complexity.

Family Paradigms and Problem Solving

David Reiss began studying information processing in families to test whether certain patterns were linked to the emergence of schizophrenia in children. His initial studies led to an entirely new approach to understanding family problem solving and some of the most penetrating empirical analyses of families ever done. As with previous models, his approach was constrained by an ongoing interest in mental illness in family life. But his detailed empirical studies also included families with no mental illness.

Reiss began his research with families doing artificial problem solving tasks (e.g., Reiss, 1967), similar to some studies reviewed previously (Figure 3.5). His tasks involved families in recognizing patterns in sequences of shapes, sorting cards with letters on them, and in completing a puzzle by providing each other with information that had to be shared (Reiss, 1981). To provide some control on the dimensions of interaction under study, some of the tasks placed family members in a setting that did not allow visual communication. Figure 3.6 shows one of the sets of cards used by the families. In one task, individual family

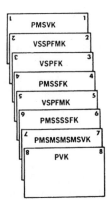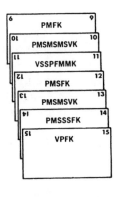

Figure 3.6. Card Sort Deck From One of Reiss's Family Interaction Tasks (Reiss, 1981)

members would sort the cards into the patterns they thought were most appropriate, based on the order of the letters on each card. Then the family as a group would sort the deck. Such card-sorting procedures were common in studies of perception and cognition. Reiss was interested in how family processes might be involved in such basic functions. He was further interested in how the family might be involved in the distortions of perception and cognition that accompany forms of mental illness.

Although the initial experimental results of the studies were fascinating, Reiss and his colleagues began noticing that families seemed to have their own "objectives" in pursuing the experimental procedures.

> For example, in the Friedkin family, father, Frieda, and Betty seemed to work together as if their principal objective was the exclusion of mother. Mother's scattered behavior might reflect a complementary objective—to be excluded by others. This family's objective took precedence over the objective to do the task as well as possible. Our excitement began when we realized our procedure was capturing the consequences of these family-produced objectives with great clarity. The data from the Friedkins . . . clearly revealed the splits and alliances in the family and their devastating effect on family problem solving. We sensed that our families were writing their own script and playing it out with intensity while leaving a vivid, objective record of their deeds in the quantitative data of the laboratory procedure. (Reiss, 1981, p. 57)

Reiss pursued these observations and developed the concept of family paradigm. Family paradigms are "shared, unspoken, and unquestioned assumptions that family members hold about their environment" (Reiss &

Klein, 1989, p. 206). These assumptions shape the way family members interact with each other and with the social environment over long periods of time. They also shape the way families approach, and try to solve, problems. In one respect, the family paradigm can be seen as another family characteristic, such as social class or ethnicity, that influences problem solving. But the family paradigm variable is more complex because it represents a kind of family character, personality, or atmosphere.

Three dimensions of family paradigms have been identified.

> *Configuration* expresses the degree of patterning and lawfulness that the family perceives in its environment. It reflects the degree to which the family believes there are stable, discoverable, noncapricious laws that underlie the critical phenomena of their experienced world. (Reiss & Klein, 1989, p. 207)

> *Coordination* refers to the family's conception of how it is regarded by its social environment. (p. 208)

High coordination means the family believes the environment perceives them as a close-knit group, and they effectively share information consistent with that perception. Low coordination is just the opposite.

> "*Closure* refers to the balance between openness to new experience (delayed closure) and being dominated by tradition (early closure)." (p. 208)

A card-sort procedure efficiently identifies the family profile on these three dimensions. Good problem solving is associated with high levels of configuration, coordination, and delayed closure.

These dimensions are similar to some of those in the experimental problem solving literature. But in Reiss's model, they are not isolated features of a family member's, or the family's, skill. Instead, they are part of a coherent, actively maintained family definition of itself. A family seeks quick solutions, or shares information, because that is part of the way the family does things. That is the way they have done things in the past and that is the right way for them to do things. This has important implications for changing, especially improving, a family's problem solving. More than isolated skills are at stake: The identity of the family is at stake.

Thus simply explaining to a family that there is a more efficient way of solving problems may have little impact. From this perspective simply learning new responses to problem situations may not be sufficient to produce a solution. Coming to grips with the family paradigm would be required.

Reiss has applied his paradigm theory to family crisis, family stress, and a range of issues beyond the scope of our concerns (Reiss, 1981; Reiss & Klein, 1989). Although he has studied "normal" families, this has always been done in comparison to troubled families. Thus the implications of his work for a general theory of family problem solving have a comparative slant. But it is clear that his model is complex enough to capture much more of the detail involved in family problem solving than was previously possible. However, this strength is also a weakness because it renders the model more difficult to test and more difficult to use as a basis for applications. Reiss has pointed out some terrain that research on family problem solving will probably have to examine.

As we have seen, Dewey's link between problem solving and adaptation has been a fundamental principle in most of the research on family problem solving. Reiss extends this tradition by placing the family paradigm concept precisely at the interface of the family and the social environment. Even more strongly than the strategic family therapists, Reiss claims that distinctive characteristics of the family must be taken into account in order to understand adaptation. The notions that each family has a distinct "paradigm," and that the paradigm governs much of their problem solving efforts, add complex new concepts to the science of family problem solving.

It has often been claimed that each family is unique. Reiss's assertion that each family has a unique paradigm seems to take this seriously. Identifying three specific dimensions of family paradigms (i.e., configuration, coordination, and closure) provides some focus to the concept. But classifying families in terms of these three dimensions still results in a complex categorization scheme (e.g., high configuration, low coordination, low closure). It is, of course, difficult to do quantified research with such a complex system of assessing families. Indeed, relatively few researchers have quantitatively pursued Reiss's approach (Reiss & Klein, 1989). But if Reiss is right, understanding family problem solving will require assessment of features of a family's unique "personality" or paradigm. That idea is a valuable contribution to the science of family problem solving in itself.

Cognitive Problem Solving Skills: Thinking and Solving

Dewey was among the first to attempt a complete explanation for *How We Think* (1910/1982). Internal thought processes have appropriately been in the mainstream of psychology ever since. Thus far, my review has focused on group and family processes of problem solving. But because families and groups are made up of individuals, it is pertinent to consider how research on internal cognitive processes informs us about family problem solving. In recent years, significant advances in cognitive psychology and neuroscience have added to the current understanding of how the human brain functions (e.g., Pinker, 1994, 1997; Sternberg, 1994). Most of that work has focused on basic reasoning, language processing, logic, and mathematical thinking. Although these basic processes provide a foundation for "higher-order" thought, they are too fundamental to be directly relevant to the cognitive and affective complexities of group problem solving. Because of this, a special subfield in cognitive psychology has emerged to study social or interpersonal problem solving. Work in that subfield has direct bearing on family problem solving.

The idea that thought processes have social aspects has been acknowledged for some time (e.g., Thorndike, 1920). But much of the research on that topic has focused on group processes in social psychology, not specific cognitive processes in individuals. Models that integrate the specifically social elements in discrete cognitive terms have proven to be somewhat more challenging (e.g., Zajonc, 1969). The stream of research most relevant to family problem solving began with efforts to understand the development of social capabilities in children. Piaget's theory of moral development in children proposed that morality was one way other people entered into the thought processes of children (Piaget, 1932). Kohlberg expanded Piaget's theory to encompass a broad range of social abilities that have come to be known as *social competence* (Kohlberg, 1969). By the 1970s, some researchers were examining cognitive interpersonal problem solving skills (Spivack, Platt, & Shure, 1976) as one aspect of social competence. These skills were specific ways of thinking that promoted resolution of problems, typically conflicts between people. This research focused on a few key elements of the way children dealt with interpersonal problems, such as the ability to generate alternative solutions and the ability to recognize consequences of the alternative solutions (Shure & Spivack, 1978). Again the imprint of Dewey can be recognized. From the beginning, this research was oriented toward applications. Spivack and Shure sought to reduce or prevent aggressive behavior by teaching children cognitive problem solving skills. This applied line of research has continued and become the basis for widely disseminated school-, home-, and clinic-based prevention and intervention programs (Shure & Spivack, 1991; Urbain & Kendall, 1980).

The idea that aggressive behavior in children can be prevented or reduced by training children how to think about problem solving has several advantages. Serious aggression in children is notoriously difficult to treat using any standard treatment paradigm. This has been apparent since alternatives to psychoanalysis were sought in the 1950s. The cognitive model avoids delving into the complexities of personality or past history of the child. The child simply needs to learn more effective ways of thinking about problematic situations.

Another major advantage of this cognitive approach is that a therapist is not needed to teach these thinking skills. They can be taught by schoolteachers or parents. This model was ideal for applications in community psychology (Shure & Spivack, 1982) and is now widely used in school systems in several forms, including violence prevention and peer mediation programs. Applications for parents have also been developed (Shure & Spivack, 1978).

Spivack and Shure's work contributed to an extensive series of detailed studies of social information processing, interpersonal problem solving, and aggressive behavior in children (e.g., Crick & Dodge, 1996; Dodge, 1980, 1993; Rubin, Bream, & Rose-Krasnor, 1991; Rubin & Krasnor, 1986). These studies initially had children describe their perceptions of, and preferred responses to, a series of social situations described by an experimenter. Later on, the situations were presented as videotapes of children involved in routine school or home situations. These studies clearly showed how aggressive and withdrawn children perceive and define social situations differently from other children and use different strategies for solving problems these situations present. For example, aggressive children are more likely to attribute negative intentions to others in social situations, and tend to generate different, and more aggressive, response options. Rubin et al. (1991) proposed an information processing model of social problem solving.

This approach uses the well-known phase model of problem solving, but moves beyond it to specify how children move from one phase to another and sometimes have to return to earlier stages. Such detailed models promote the formulations of specific, testable research hypotheses. They provide one avenue for examining such complex concepts as phased rationality (Klein & Hill, 1979).

The focus of this line of work on social problem solving in aggressive children limited the contribution it can make to general models of family problem solving or a more comprehensive understanding of interpersonal problem solving in children. Nevertheless, the empirical rigor of the experimental designs, the clear conceptualization of the theory, and the programmatic evolution of the studies has produced some findings central to our concerns. First, the way children define situations and the kinds of alternative solutions that they can generate *does* determine how well they can solve interpersonal problems. None of the other paradigms has demonstrated this so definitively or shown that it is already operative so early in life. Second, problem definition and solution generation are part of a broader sequence of events that contribute to a child's social development. For example, how a child learns about social cognition in general will influence these specific aspects of problem solving. Throughout the 1980s, with rare exceptions (Pettit, Dodge, & Brown, 1988), this research did not focus on the antecedents of these social cognitive biases. But since then, the obvious role of parenting and other family factors in the etiology of such patterns has received some attention (e.g., Weiss, Dodge, Bates, & Pettit, 1992). For example, experiencing harsh discipline practices as a child has been shown to distort social cognitions (Weiss et al., 1992), which in turn leads to behavior problems.

From the standpoint of mainstream cognitive psychology, this research program could be seen as taking a few rather simple cognitive processes and working out some of the social and developmental implications. After all, cognitive psychology is close to being able to accurately simulate the thought processes involved in such complex activities as interpreting language (e.g., Graesser, Singer, & Trabasso, 1994) or playing chess. This is convincing evidence that most of the key elements of those processes have been taken into account. Comparable evidence for models of social problem solving has not been forthcoming. Indeed, for the most part, the early social–cognitive program did not actively seek more comprehensive models that would encompass all aspects of social problem solving. There was some movement in that direction, however.

Evidence for this trend is found in a series of studies by Robert Selman and his colleagues (e.g., Selman, Beardslee, Schultz, Krupa, & Podorefsky, 1986; Yeates, Schultz, & Selman, 1991). They were interested in the nature of social competence and how it developed. Impressed with the findings of such researchers as Spivack, Shure, Dodge, and Rubin, they proposed that a functional component of social competence was based on the now familiar phases of interpersonal problem solving: identification of the problem, generation of alternative solutions, evaluation of consequences, and use of different strategies (Selman et al., 1986). But they took a major step forward by stating that this was only half of the picture. They proposed that the functional component must be understood in terms of a structural component that represented the developmental stages of moral and social development as described by Piaget (1932) and Kohlberg (1969).

They (Selman et al., 1986; Yeates et al., 1991) described four levels of Interpersonal Negotiation Strategies (INS). These are strategies that combine behaviors and cognitions that guide the individual's interaction with others. The strategies are most apparent in conflict situations or social dilemmas. Level 0 is the *impulsive* level and is limited to impulsive, egocentric negotiations that do not take the other person's needs, views, or feelings into account. This is typical of young children, but may persist into adolescence and beyond in some individuals. Level 1 is the *unilateral* level that acknowledges the other's position but responds to it by unilaterally attempting to either dominate the other person or else submit to their position. No true negotiation occurs. Level 2 is the *reciprocal* level, in which the individual is able to take the other person's perspective. The individual uses those perceptions to try to influence the other person's position or bargain for solutions that further his or her own interests. Negotiation occurs but it is only seen in zero-sum terms. Level 3 is the *collaborative* level, in which the individual is able to take a third-person perspective and seek solutions that will benefit both parties. Compromise is often used and there is a concern for solutions that promote the ongoing relationship between self and other.

The INS level is assessed with an interview, in which participants indicate how they would handle a series of hypothetical situations (e.g., Selman et al., 1986). Structured probe questions elicit details about how the participants understand the situation and justify their choices. Participants are given the following instructions.

> People are always running into problems with others at school, at work, and at home. Everyone has to work out ways to solve these problems. I am going to read you some examples, and I would like you to tell me some ways that the situations could be dealt with. There are no right or wrong answers to these questions, so I want you to tell me what you think would be the best way to handle the situation. (Selman et al., 1986, p. 458)

Subjects respond to eight different situations. The following is one example given to adolescent participants. Sex of the protagonist in each example is adjusted to match the sex of the participant. "Joe's mother always has him go to a picnic with her friend and her friend's daughter. Joe really doesn't like this girl at all, and he doesn't want to go." The interviewer then asks the participant to answer each of the following questions with regard to that situation. The interview is audiotaped.

1. What is the problem here? Why is it a problem?
2. What is a good way for Joe to deal with his mother?
3. Why is that a good way for Joe to deal with his mother? What do you think will happen if Joe does that?
4. How do you think everyone will feel if Joe does that?

The audiotape of the interview is transcribed and then coded in terms of the four INS levels. Scores were averaged across the eight situations so that each participant had a composite INS score between 0 and 4. The responses were also examined to test whether the INS level used by participants varied by such factors as whether the situations involved peers or adults, and whether the relationships were personal or work-related. Good interrater reliability was demonstrated on these measures. This innovative measurement procedure was a relatively efficient way of assessing complex features of how children and adolescents understand interpersonal problem solving.

Selman and his colleagues maintain that the individual progresses through these levels sequentially in a way that corresponds to the normal development of cognitive and moral abilities. This requires a combination of innate characteristics and environmental stimulation. The research has found evidence for the predicted sequential development across the INS levels from Age 9 through Age 18 (Selman et al., 1986; Yeates et al., 1991). There is also evidence that delays in development in INS levels are associated with behavior problems (Leadbeater, Hellner, Allen, & Aber, 1989; Selman & Demorest, 1984). The INS research is very ambitious in seeking to integrate elements of the cognitive, social, affective, and moral domains in human development. The scope of their model is somewhat daunting. However, it can hardly be denied that all of those domains do play a fundamental role in interpersonal problem solving, especially within the family. Their pioneering efforts at tracing the developmental course of interpersonal problem solving skills has added to, and helped stimulate, other work on this issue in developmental psychology. Problem solving between parent and child has been examined with children as young as 2 years old (e.g., Frankel & Bates, 1990). An important feature of much of this research is that it was done within family groups. Explicitly or implicitly, this research provided the beginnings of an understanding of how interpersonal problem solving developed within the family context.

Although most of the developmental work emphasized the problem solving of children, a few studies focused on parenting as a problem solving activity. Tallman (1961), in a paper 25 years ahead of its time, provided one of the clearest formulations of the linkage between adaptation and problem solving in parent–child relations. Clearly citing Dewey as the first to recognize this linkage, he showed that children whose parents used better problem solving with them had higher levels of adjustment. Developmentalists at that time were unable to absorb this work, in part because Tallman's paradigm was foreign to the field. Years later, the field has come to view parent problem solving with children as an important developmental issue.

The fact that some of the major contributions of the behaviorist and cognitive perspectives to understanding the development of interpersonal problem solving did not address the family context should not be surprising. Indeed, interpersonal problem solving is an exceedingly complex phenomenon. The research record from these perspectives, however, does show an inevitable movement toward considering family interaction as a primary arena in which interpersonal problem solving develops.

Cognitive–Behavioral Family Therapy and Counseling

At the same time the research on "normal" developmental processes was evolving, work on family problem solving as a technique for treating troubled families expanded. Fueled by advances in social learning and cognitive research, therapists developed new approaches to family therapy. Among the first to train families in aspects of family problem solving was Alexander and his colleagues (e.g., Alexander & Parsons, 1973; Klein, Alexander, & Parsons, 1976). Their program integrated several perspectives in a treatment for families with a delinquent adolescent, and included problem solving components. They reported impressive success in reducing aggressive behavior, which stimulated further refinements in training for family problem solving (e.g., Robin & Foster, 1989). The theory behind this was similar to D'Zurilla's social learning approach to treating individuals. Teaching people the mechanics of good problem solving would help them better adapt to their environment and each other.

Patterson and his colleagues introduced a social learning approach to treating families with aggressive children (Patterson, 1974; Patterson, Reid, Jones, & Conger, 1975). Their focus was the pattern of contingencies in parent–child interaction that promoted aggressive and other antisocial behavior in children. Their early programs emphasized changing the parenting behavior of the parents, and included one of the first instruction books for parents trying to cope with antisocial boys prior to adolescence (Patterson, 1971). The early work did not address problem solving specifically. It was designed for families with younger children before much complex cognitive problem solving between parent and child takes place. But extensions of this approach to parents with adolescents included a major component of family problem solving (Forgatch & Patterson, 1989), again expanding the D'Zurilla social learning formulation.

Patterson brilliantly applied the theory and behavior modification techniques of social learning theory to parent–child interaction in families with aggressive boys. He proposed that antisocial child behavior developed as a response to reinforcement contingencies in the family. Parents inadvertently "trained" their children to be antisocial. His documentation of this coercive family process through observational studies in the home marked an unprecedented integration of theory, external validity, data analysis, and implications for treatment. In the context of this coercive family process, it is easy to see that little in the way of productive problem solving could take place. The key to Patterson's approach to treatment was showing parents how to break the coercive cycle between parent and child. After some progress was made on this, and especially as children got older, family problem solving was brought into the treatment program.

Forgatch and Patterson (1989) combined their clinical experience with their research to produce the most comprehensive book available on family problem solving for parents with teenagers. As with Patterson's earlier parenting books (e.g., Patterson, 1971), the problem solving book could be used by parents on their own or in the context of a parent education group or family counseling and therapy. It included detailed descriptions of the phases of problem solving and an entire chapter on family meetings.

Although most of the previous clinical work had emphasized cognitive or behavioral components of problem solving, Forgatch began finding that emotional expression during family problem solving was an important predictor of outcomes (Forgatch, 1989). High levels of expression of emotions such as anger and sadness seemed to inhibit progress toward solutions. The expression of these emotions elicited emotions from other family members. The presence of negative emotions in families with difficulties was no surprise to anyone. But the advent of good measures of emotion, and the isolation of the role of emotion in those difficulties, was new and important. The importance of affective exchanges as causal factors in marital interaction had been clearly established (e.g., Levenson & Gottman, 1985). Forgatch showed that some similar patterns were important in family problem solving.

Studying affective expression in family problem solving raised some formidable measurement challenges. Emotions are inherently internal experiences, not directly accessible to measurement. They are expressed in forms that are difficult to measure, including facial gestures, intonation contours in the voice, as well as in linguistic forms. Gottman adapted Ekman's facial coding system for use in marital interaction and created the Specific Affective Coding System (SPAFF; Capaldi, Forgatch, & Crosby, 1994; Gottman & Krokoff, 1989). Forgatch applied SPAFF to family problem solving. This work provided a quantitative handle on the affective domain, which had long been considered too difficult to study scientifically. Because negative emotions (anger, sadness, frustration) are so prominent in family problems, this research has potential to add important insights to the models based on the cognitive and behavioral domains.

Much of the early excitement about the family communication double-bind approach to schizophrenia subsided when the treatments proved to be no better than other approaches. But a steady stream of successful research results has maintained an ongoing interest in potential for future applications (e.g., Mueser, Bellack, Wade, & Sayers, 1993). Family interaction patterns do seem to be a part of the schizophrenia puzzle. But it is not yet clear how the pieces fit together.

One series of studies reignited interest in this topic. These studies focused on what happens to schizophrenics when they return home from a stay in a mental hospital or other residential psychiatric facility. Falloon developed a psychoeducation training program for the families of the schizophrenic relative (1988). The program included training on the nature of schizophrenia, medications, caregiving, and communication with the schizophrenic. An important part of the training focused on family problem solving. Certain family interaction patterns, such as expressed emotion (Mueser et al., 1993), have been associated with psychotic episodes. This pattern has been linked to ineffective family problem solving, conflict, and complaining. Falloon's family problem solving component sought to reduce those patterns. Falloon showed that his program substantially reduced the time schizophrenics spent in residential care and reduced the number of psychotic episodes that required such hospitalization (Falloon, 1988). The savings in hospitalization costs, as well as personal turmoil, were very large. This family-based approach to treatment has potential for several other disorders (see chapter 6) as well.

Family Conflict and Family Problem Solving

As demonstrated previously, most research and theory on family problem solving conceptualizes it as a prosocial process that begins with defining a problem and then moves forward toward seeking solutions to this problem. The occurrence of conflict before or during this process has typically either been ignored or relegated to the status of a secondary issue. When acknowledged, conflict is usually considered as an undesirable symptom of a "problem" that needs to be solved (e.g., Jacobson,

1977). Thus, in large part, research on family conflict has been separate from the work on family problem solving. At face value, this separation seems appropriate because conflict and problem solving are different processes. But in families, these processes are often intertwined. In the next two chapters, I will show how a better understanding of this overlap expands the utility of research on family problem solving. But first, the contribution of family conflict research must be considered. The most relevant part of that work is research that examined how family conflicts are resolved.

As noted already, some of the earliest research of relevance for family problem solving considered marital conflicts, which contribute to divorce (Burgess & Cottrell, 1939; Terman, 1938). Frequent intense conflict continues to be recognized as a sign of trouble in a marital relationship or in a family. However, it has also been acknowledged that some conflict is healthy for marriages and families (e.g., Gottman, 1993; Vuchinich, 1987). Conflicts are inevitable when there is open communication. Such conflicts provide a mechanism for locating adaptation problems in relationships and families. When managed effectively, conflicts can create the basis for adjustments that improve adaptation. Thus couples or families that never fight may be closed to necessary adaptations. These ideas came to be advanced largely through marriage counseling techniques to teach troubled couples how to manage their conflicts (e.g., Jacobson, 1977). For the most part, these programs advocated "controlled" conflicts with an orientation toward clear statements of the issues involved and specific proposals for resolving the conflict, often with compromise as a theme. Clearly these studies drew heavily from the earlier research and theory on the phases in rational problem solving that was reviewed earlier.

This work proved useful for applications in marriage counseling by prescribing training in problem solving to address the unresolved issues that were causing the excessive conflict. Although beneficial, these studies did not break new ground regarding how conflict was linked with family problem solving. However, one branch of that research began focusing on how marital conflicts ended and the way they were "resolved" (Bell, Chafetz, & Horn, 1980; Billings, 1979). This opened the door to a new approach to understanding what it means to "solve" family problems.

Survey and experimental studies began assessments of how couples "resolved" their conflicts. The results showed that couples in happy marriages had more resolutions, and were able to resolve conflicts with strategies, such as compromising, that reflected more concern for the other person. This is similar to Selman's Level 4 collaboration (Selman et al., 1986), when self and other work together for solutions that benefit both. These studies used somewhat different conceptualizations of conflict and categories to describe the ways conflicts were resolved. But they all clearly demonstrated that the way conflicts were resolved was associated with important features of marital relations.

Integrating such results into the social problem solving literature requires an understanding of how spontaneous conflict episodes in marriages and families are related to the problem solving process. Because the problem solving literature is based largely on experimental situations or the therapy context, such an integration was only rarely considered (Gottman, 1979; Patterson, 1982). In retrospect, this was unfortunate because the gaps between the experimental tasks, the therapy session, and the everyday life of most families are quite large. Yet it is well known that most families have conflicts. And it is generally accepted that certain conflict patterns are indicative of family problems. The question of how family conflicts are related to family problem solving thus takes on significant proportions. The connections between family conflicts and family problem solving will be taken up in chapter 7.

Research on how marital conflict affects children provides further motivation to pursue these connections. For decades, excessive marital conflict has been recognized as having negative consequences for the individuals involved and their marriage. By the early 1980s (e.g., Emery, 1982), it was clear that there were serious risks for children whose parents exposed them to high levels of marital conflict. Cummings began verifying the mechanisms that produce these risks by studying how children reacted to overhearing adults arguing (live or on videotape) in laboratory experiments (e.g., Cummings, Iannotti, & Zahn-Waxler, 1985). In a compelling series of studies, he and his colleagues clearly documented the immediate negative emotional reactions of children in terms of anger, fear, and sadness (see review in Cummings & Davies, 1994).

Pursuing the exact cause of these reactions, they began considering how the conflicts ended. Drawing from the previous research, they tested whether the child reactions differed when the conflicts terminated with resolution, standoff, escalation, or expressions of sadness. To isolate the potential effect of the way conflicts end on child reactions, they used videotapes of actors engaging in conflict and had them tape four different endings to the same conflict episode. Each tape had the same conflict episode except for the way the conflict ended. Children were randomly assigned to see only one of the tapes. Any differences in reactions to the conflicts could then be attributed to the way the conflict ended.

The results were striking. The negative emotional reactions of the children to the conflicts were substantially reduced, and in some cases eliminated, when the conflict ended in resolution. Controls for other variables were included, and the finding was easily replicated. Although there are some limitations to this experimental design, the results invite interpretation. In general terms, the amount of marital conflict to which a child is exposed may be less important for negative outcomes than the way the conflicts are managed. If true, this suggests that if parents are going to argue in front of their children, they should find ways to resolve those conflicts. The measurement of children's emotional reactions to family conflicts provided graphic detail to the hazardous consequences of cycles of unresolved conflicts that had been recognized by the strategic family therapists (Haley, 1987) and clinical researchers (Patterson, 1982; Reid, 1986).

Toward a Theory of Family Problem Solving

Good theories provide systematic explanations for why things happen the way they do. They offer an organizing framework for understanding how a variety of diverse empirical findings fit together. Furthermore, they point the direction for research that can improve this understanding and promote better applications. For the most part, the research on family problem solving has been done in the service of theories about something else. It has been used to explore theories about family therapy, group productivity, divorce, child psychopathology, social cognition, child development, and so on. Only scant attention has ever been given directly to a theory of family problem solving (e.g., Klein & Hill, 1979; Tallman, 1988, 1993). This is simply a historical fact that might be interpreted in a number of ways. In any event, the acknowledgment of this fact is important for interpreting the rather rambling course that the research on this topic has taken. Although some solid theoretical work has been done (e.g., Klein & Hill, 1979; Tallman, 1988, 1993), with few exceptions (e.g., Kieren et al., 1996), efforts to verify the theories have not been actively pursued in the empirical domain. Two barriers may have been responsible for this state of affairs.

First is the conceptual complexity of the causes of family problem solving. The extent of this complexity was made clear in perhaps the most comprehensive paper on the topic to date. Klein and Hill (1979) systematically reviewed the diverse conceptual components that contribute to family problem solving. This effort is distinguished from the previous work that typically focused on only one cause of family problem solving. In a systematic way, Klein and Hill organized the factors that had been shown to contribute to a family's problem solving effectiveness (see Figure 3.7). It was a daunting list indeed, including the individual characteristics of family members, family structural properties, cultural

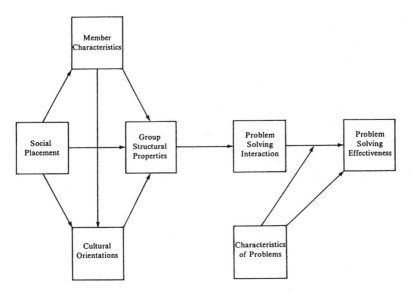

Figure 3.7. Diagram of Factors Affecting Family Problem Solving Effectiveness (Klein & Hill, 1979)

background, social structural placement (e.g., social class), the characteristics of the problem, as well as the family's interaction patterns. Their case for the contributions of these factors was quite convincing. But the prospects of doing research that took all, or even most, of these factors into account was sobering. Previous research had never attempted studies with such a broad scope. The empirical challenges associated with including these factors in a research design have proven to be insurmountable thus far. Behavioral research in other areas has borne out the importance of including these diverse multiple causes. In this light, their theory seems more viable than ever. Klein and Hill (1979) suggested a set of testable hypotheses they derived from the model. These offer specific paths for empirical investigations. But the number of hypotheses and the sheer complexity of their theory may have made researchers somewhat reluctant to try to test something so ambitious. The model was an order of magnitude more complex than anything that went before it. Although it has shaped much of the recent thinking on family problem solving, researchers did not attempt to test parts of it for several years (e.g., Kieren et al., 1996). Thus the question of whether research has led to an adequate theory of family problem solving is still open.

A second barrier to theory-based empirical work is the general problem of quantifying human behavior and perceived future paths of action. A key phase in Dewey's (1910/1982) early formulation of problem solving was the evaluation of alternative potential solutions to the problem. Inevitably, this requires the person to assign some level of value to each of the projected outcomes for each potential solution. This idea is central to the blocked-goal approach to conceptualizing family problem solving. The blocked goal is perceived as a negative value state—such as frustration. Alternative actions are sought to remove the block, and thus transform the situation so that a positive value state is attained—such as gratification. Theoretically, this formulation has many advantages (e.g., Tallman, 1988, 1993), and I have used it in this book. But it also has some serious limitations. One is the fact that individuals and families have many goals operating at any given time. So many, in fact, that it is often difficult to determine which blocked goals for which family members are the sources of the negative emotional state. In addition, family members may not agree on what goals are being blocked, let alone what changes might ultimately remove the blocks. For the blocked-goal theory to be complete, one would need a universal calculus for quantifying the negative states for family members, and the potential value of the positive states that could be attained through specific changes. As we have seen, some research has sought to simulate these processes with games that assign discrete values to specific actions (e.g., Blechman & McEnroe, 1985; Straus, 1968). Although useful, such studies are not informative about the value calculus that families might use in everyday life. Indeed, some research that began with a gaming approach discovered that other family processes were more important (e.g., Reiss, 1981). Overall, there is a substantial gap between the conceptually rigorous rational theoretical models of family problem solving (e.g., Tallman, 1988, 1993), and empirical research to support it. At the core of the gap is one inescapable fact. The theory requires a calculus that quantifies human perceptions and behaviors about family problems, but no one has yet found that calculus. Chapter 4 addresses this issue by showing how family problems are social constructions that create a consensus about what problems are and what can be done to solve them.

Summary

Sciences are judged by how well they can describe, explain, and predict phenomena of interest. In the twentieth century, we have come to expect mature sciences to use their accomplishments to create applications that are useful for society. In these terms, the accumulated research on family problem solving by 1990 could be judged as having attained a moderate level of success on all accounts. There was evidence that family problem solving could be reliably and validly measured. Predicted relationships with other constructs have been found, which allowed some modest accuracy in predictions. Certainly the concept had been applied and been shown to provide some practical benefits in treatment and prevention. By 1990, interest in family problem solving was expanding in developmental psychology, clinical psychology, and family studies. The topic continued to be a focus in family therapy.

This progress was noteworthy, but the accumulated research also made clear that a mature science of family problem solving had a long way to go. Although treatments for serious disorders using family problem solving routinely achieved improvements, they were often not large or sustained for very long (Hazelrigg, Cooper, & Borduin, 1987; Kazdin et al., 1992). Beneficial effects of prevention and parent education programs were not well documented. The research, although voluminous taken as a whole, was largely a patchwork of relatively brief programs of work from divergent theoretical paradigms. Thus there was little long-term systematic accumulation of findings that could be used to verify theories of family problem solving. More often family problem solving was used as a concept in service of seeking to verify more general theories (social learning theory, cognitive theory, small group theory, etc.). Little was yet known about how much problem solving families actually did in real life. Little was yet known about whether family problem solving varied across ethnic group and social class.

By 1990 these circumstances had left the science of family problem solving still in somewhat of a state of disarray. In fact, with rare exception (Klein & Hill, 1979), little interest had been shown in integrating work on the topic from different disciplines. Researchers from diverse fields usually came away from their studies of family problem solving with interesting results that contributed something to their particular field. Pleased with such results, there was little motivation for, and many barriers to, pursuing theoretical integration. One of the goals of this book is to take some steps toward integration. Though diverse and complex, the accumulated research has produced an acceleration of interest in family problem solving in important scientific disciplines.

Through the 1990s, researchers from diverse persuasions continued to be drawn to family problem solving as a topic of study. This period saw important advances in methodology and increased interest in integration of perspectives. The major trends in the recent work will be briefly reviewed next, with more details given in succeeding chapters. During the 1990s, family problem solving became a popular topic of research in developmental psychology, clinical psychology, and family studies. This ascendance grew naturally out of the fascinating results of the previous research, an increasing realization that family interaction patterns have a major impact on the development of children, and that family problem solving is a valuable tool in treating a variety of psychological disorders.

The primary subject matter of the science of psychology is the individual person. In keeping with this, developmental psychology has naturally focused on the development of the individual. The importance of parent–child relationships has been increasingly acknowledged over the past 50 years, with attention for most of that time given to mother–child relations. Characteristics of the family in which the child develops, especially family interaction patterns, were largely relegated to a minor, passing interest in the early history of developmental psychology. This may have been entirely appropriate, as unraveling the complex details of all the essential domains of individual development is a monumental challenge. But as more was learned about the factors that affect developmental trajectories, it became increasingly apparent that features of the family context were key contributing factors. Bronfenbrenner (1979) captured this significance in his influential developmental–ecological model that highlighted family and community contexts as determinants of developmental outcomes. Partially in response to these trends, research on the causes and impacts of parenting increased. But the dominant paradigms in developmental psychology were not easily adapted to bring the family into the picture. Thus, as we have seen, most of the work on social problem solving dealt with the individual child's characteristics without much concern for the family context (e.g., Dodge, 1980; Rubin & Krasnor, 1986; Selman et al., 1986). A few studies did acknowledge family linkages (Pettit et al., 1988; Shure & Spivack, 1978) but sustained treatments would not appear until later (Weiss et al., 1992).

From the psychological perspective, parenting was usually considered in a manner similar to a personality characteristic. Specific types of parenting were defined—permissive, authoritarian, authoritative (Baumrind, 1991). These types were linked with different child outcomes—with authoritative parenting yielding the best child outcomes. Authoritative parenting is characterized by a balance of parental warmth and moderate discipline practices. Authoritative parents set limits but always explain the reasons for the limits. When rules are broken, negative consequences follow. But they are not extreme, and avoid excessive power assertion by parents. In most respects, these parenting types describe some limited patterns of parent–child problem solving in families with children up to about age 12. The child breaking rules is the typical problem and the parenting style prescribes how the parent goes about solving it. This model of parenting still dominates research on parenting in developmental psychology.

Although useful for younger children, this model proved to be too narrow for parenting adolescents. The most critical developmental issues in adolescence focus on autonomy from parents and identity formation. In addition, adolescents have developed social skills and cognitive abilities that can challenge those of the parents. Therefore, effective parenting of adolescents requires more than the traditional authoritative parenting. Researchers had begun the necessary expansions to existing models (e.g., Grotevant & Cooper, 1984; Hauser, Powers, Noam, Jacobson, Weiss, & Follansbee, 1984; Steinberg & Silverberg, 1986). The adaptations that emerged included a new focus on what was often labeled family decision making (Dornbusch, Ritter, Liederman, Roberts, & Fraleigh, 1987). This concept was typically assessed by measuring the extent to which the adolescent perceived that he or she contributed to family decisions. More open decision making was correlated with better adolescent outcomes. The literature on adolescent delinquency and psychopathology had already shown similar correlations (Henggeler & Borduin, 1990). Although the family decision-making variable improved the conceptualization of parenting for adolescents, it was becoming clear that it captured only a small part of a family process that could improve predictions of adolescent outcomes.

This led to an increased interest in studies of family problem solving from a developmental perspective. By 1990, there was a record of previous research that provided a sound theoretical and methodological basis for further work. Prominent in this regard was a set of procedures for assessing family problem solving. Over the years, the structured family problem solving task had been proven and refined. The technique of observing a small group trying to solve a problem dated back to the Bales era. External validity was enhanced by having the family discuss a problem that had been of concern to them *at home*. Quantitative techniques for assessing family characteristics from observations had been honed to a fine edge through 20 years of work (Brody, Stoneman, McCoy, & Forehand, 1992; Forgatch, 1989; Rueter & Conger, 1995; Vuchinich et al., 1996). Details on the developmental approach to family problem solving are addressed in chapter 7.

Since 1990 there has been a steady increase in the use of problem solving components for the clinical treatment of several child and adolescent disorders (Hibbs & Jensen, 1996). This includes treatment for depression (Stark, Swearer, Kurowski, Sommer, & Bowen, 1996), anxiety disorders (Kendall, 1991), conduct disorder (Kazdin, 1996; Kazdin et al., 1992; Vuchinich, Wood, & Angelelli, 1996), attention deficit hyperactive disorder (Anastopoulos, Barkley, & Sheldon, 1996; Brasswell & Bloomquist, 1991), anorexia nervosa (Robin, Bedway, Siegel, &

Gilroy, 1996), and other problems (Robin & Foster, 1989). Details on these treatments are given in chapter 6. In general terms, these treatments include a component that focuses on teaching the child and family members better interpersonal problem solving skills. Typically, this is some form of the cognitive–behavioral stage models reviewed previously—for example, clearly define the problem, consider possible solutions and their consequences, select a solution to try, reevaluate its success. Other components of the programs are tailored to address the specific disorder.

The expanded use of family problem solving in these treatments is a result of several factors. First, there was early evidence that such training improved the success of treatment of difficult clinical cases (e.g., Alexander & Parsons, 1973). More recent studies continue to show positive effects—even in the most recalcitrant disorders (Kazdin et al., 1992). Second, family problem solving training easily fits into a psychoeducational strategy of treatment (Hibbs & Jensen, 1996) in which clients receive training in how to do specific things. Framing the treatment as merely a matter of learning to do some things a little differently provides clients with hope and steady indications of progress. It tends to defuse traumatic confrontations, blaming, labeling, resistance, and other processes that disrupt progress in therapy. Problem solving skills seem to provide a generic benefit for a broad range of specific disorders. The basis for this generic benefit has not yet been isolated. I will consider this issue further in chapter 6.

Third, another contributing factor to expanded clinical applications has been an increased realization that involving family members in treatment of children and adolescents can improve treatment success. Although this has always been a basic principle in family therapy, it is a relatively new concept in much of clinical psychology, which traditionally emphasized individual treatment. For many years, Patterson, Alexander, and their colleagues were among the few groups of clinicians to apply social learning treatment principles in the family context. The success of their work on conduct disorders, long known as one of the most difficult to treat, drew much attention to family-based treatments.

Fourth, an additional factor is that a wide variety of delivery methods can be used in family problem solving training. This includes films, videos, manuals, pamphlets, group sessions, and Internet services. In addition, they can be delivered by specialists who do not have advanced clinical training (e.g., persons without PhDs or MDs). These delivery options can provide cost effective components for treatment. Problem solving training thus fits into a health care environment in which shorter, less expensive treatments are sought.

In the flurry of this expansion, only a few studies have sought to isolate the distinct effect of problem solving training in multicomponent treatments (e.g., Kazdin et al., 1992). These studies show that the problem solving *combined with* the other components yield the best success rates. Thus even though the "family problem solving effect" is not fully understood in clinical terms, evidence for its effectiveness in treatment is continuing to accumulate. In terms of the ideal of how empirical science should lead to applications, it is fair to conclude that the applications of family problem solving are running well ahead of its science. Medical science has several examples of remedies that are quite effective even though no one knows why they work. In the case of family problem solving, we have some general ideas of why it works, but not a clear, specific understanding.

Much of the main work on family problem solving predated the full emergence of the field of family studies as an academic discipline. However, in recent years, the field has maintained an increasing interest in the concept and how it is measured (see Appendixes F and G; e.g., Coughlin & Vuchinich, 1996; Forgatch, 1989; Kieren et al., 1996; Rueter & Conger, 1995). Of particular interest is a new concept of "conflict resolution styles" in marriage (Heavey, Larson, Zumtobel, & Christensen, 1996; Kurdek, 1995). Based on accumulated work in psychology (Gottman, 1994; Heavey, Layne, & Christensen, 1993) researchers have concluded that individual partners in an ongoing dyadic relationship develop one of only a few characteristic styles for trying to resolve conflicts.

Kurdek, for example, identified four styles: positive problem solving (e.g., focusing on the problem at hand), conflict engagement (exploding and getting out of control), withdrawal (reaching a limit, refusing to talk any more), compliance (e.g., giving in with little attempt to present my side of the issue). The overlap with previous studies of family conflict management is clear (e.g., Vuchinich, 1987, 1990). In a longitudinal study, Kurdek found that the style of conflict resolution was associated with marital satisfaction (Kurdek, 1995). The patterns of association were complex. But the lowest marital satisfaction was found when the wife used conflict engagement and the husband used the withdraw style. This replicated earlier studies (Heavey et al., 1993), which drew out the implications of these findings for marriage counseling. The clinical challenge is to stop the demand–withdraw pattern and replace it with something more effective. Again, training in interpersonal problem solving is recommended.

These studies demonstrate a steadily increasing interest and sophistication in problem solving within the family. Here, conflict resolution style is posited to be a key indicator of marital satisfaction, one of the best predictors of divorce. Thus, as in the developmental work, family studies has found family problem solving to be predictive of important outcomes. It is feasible that the concept of conflict resolution style will be applied to the family as a whole. However, some efforts to characterize the way a family resolves conflicts suggest that the concept of a single "family style" of conflict resolution greatly oversimplifies what families actually do (Reiss, 1981; Vuchinich & DeBaryshe, 1997).

There have been many twists and turns in the historical record of research on family problem solving. The past 50 years have seen a patchwork of studies that have borne more applied fruit than their level of scientific rigor would seem to merit. Despite the complex and elusive nature of family problem solving, researchers have doggedly persisted in attempting to capture, measure, and understand it. In strict scientific terms, it would still have to be concluded that we know relatively little about if, when, or how family problem solving takes place in the real world. This is not a new conclusion (De Waal, 1989, 1996). Based on the available research, as Weick (1971) implied, family problem solving as it is usually understood could be largely an image in the eye of the research community. Qualitative field studies of problem solving in the context of routine home life would be very instructive in this regard.

Perhaps a little knowledge about family problem solving goes a long way. Its success in clinical applications would certainly suggest that this is the case. Problem solving may be such a central feature of family life that even modest improvements can yield significant beneficial results. Some branches of family therapy have maintained, from a theoretical viewpoint, that this, indeed, should be the case (Haley, 1987). This idea is also consistent with family applications of chaos theory (Gottman, 1991). This is a rather sweeping conclusion to ponder. But reviewing the research history, one cannot find evidence that refutes it.

One of the most perplexing features of the research record is the phenomenal resilience of Dewey's ancient formulation of the phases of problem solving. With relatively little evidence of its validity (Bales & Strodtbeck, 1951; Gottman, 1979; Kieren et al., 1996), it has been the single most widely used model for how family problem solving happens or should happen. Although cognitive psychology abandoned it long ago in favor of more cybernetic models, it has lived on and on in models of interpersonal and family problem solving. This widespread use far exceeds empirical scientific evidence in favor of it.

One way to account for this popularity is the notion that Dewey's model has great heuristic value. It has conceptual flaws and has not been adequately verified with rigorous empirical research. Nonetheless, it does seem to provide a way of making sense out of some very complex processes. In addition, applying it has produced successes, as predicted. But even as this success is acknowledged, it must be noted that we do not know exactly how it seems to work. Because of that, the rational model cannot be considered a good theory, even if it is the best one currently available. It still is not clear how often families actually engage in focused problem solving. And when they do, it is not clear how often they follow the rational stages, unless they have been trained or instructed to do so. Some research is addressing these issues (e.g., Kieren et al., 1996). The question of whether the rational model of family problem solving will ultimately be verified is taken up in chapter 4.

It is possible that Dewey was simply correct by virtue of a colossal effort of philosophical insight. If Dewey was right, the phases could follow directly from the adaptation concept in the theory of evolution. Indeed, those phases could be a genetically transmitted product of the evolution of cognitive and social structures in humans and other organisms (e.g., De Waal, 1989, 1996; Wilson, 1975). That would certainly be the position of the evolutionary psychologists (Barkow et al., 1992; Pinker, 1994, 1997; Tooby & Cosmides, 1997). Viewed in these terms, the resilience of the unproven phases is simply evidence of the central function adaptation plays in human family life. Perhaps we keep coming back to it because it is a primal human process. But our research methods may not have been sophisticated enough to fully conceptualize and demonstrate this. Proof of the evolutionary argument would require the isolation of a gene that transmits problem solving behaviors. Such a discovery is not likely in the near future, but it is not outside the realm of possibility. Although the reasoning is speculative, it nonetheless offers an explanation for the dogged persistence of Dewey's phase concept. In the next two chapters, I synthesize elements of the current paradigms and present some new approaches to family problem solving. These provide a distinctive approach to interpreting the limitations of the previous research on this topic and suggest directions for future research.

4

Families, Problems,
and Solutions

As soon as a problem is clearly defined, its solution is often simple.
                                    Bishop, Fienberg, and Holland (1975)

After decades of research on family problem solving, one might well expect that there would be little to gain by further probes into self-important what family problems are. However, as was apparent in chapter 3, most work in the area has focused on what happens *after* the family problem has been defined. The overwhelming emphasis has been on the nature of the "solving" process—not on the nature of family problems and how they come to receive attention. The small group experiments, for example, typically began with a problem already defined. The beginning point for most of strategic family therapy is the "presenting" problem.

This emphasis on solving is a natural by-product of the paradigms that guided research and theory in psychology and family therapy. Although paradigms illuminate certain aspects of the phenomena under study, they necessarily ignore other aspects that may be of fundamental importance (Kuhn, 1970). In the case of family problem solving, the nature of problems in nonclinical families, and how they come to be discussed are issues that have been largely ignored. With a few notable exceptions (e.g., Aldous & Ganey, 1989; Weick, 1971), the nature of family problems has been taken for granted.

The emphasis on "solving" processes has certainly proven to be fruitful. However, it is unlikely that it will ever provide an adequate understanding of family problem solving. The reason is that the nature of problem solving depends in part on the nature of the problem that is to be solved. The idea that there exists some universal solving process independent of the kind of problem at hand has been appealing since the time of Dewey. This kind of abstract concept has an esteemed history that can be traced to Plato's notion of "forms," or the ideal tradition of nineteenth-century German philosophy (Klein & White, 1996). This one-strategy-fits-all logic is parsimonious to a fault (Tallman et al., 1993). Indeed, there are some recurrent strategies that families use in trying to solve their problems. But these strategies are not uniformly distributed across families. Different families emphasize different strategies (Klein & Hill, 1979). Furthermore, the strategies applied vary according to the type of family problem and other family factors (e.g., the mood, recent events). Rationally weighing the benefits and costs of each possible solution will only be effective if all family members agree on what each of the costs and benefits are. In most families, what is a benefit to one person is often a cost to someone else.

In this chapter, I propose that it is necessary to have a more comprehensive grasp of the nature of family problems before one can fully understand how they are solved. I present a new approach to conceptualizing what family problems are and the nature of solutions to them. This analysis is developed with concepts outside of the paradigms that have dominated previous research and theory in the area. In that respect, a paradigm shift is encouraged (Kuhn, 1970). Readers should prepare themselves for an entirely different strategy for understanding family problem solving. In this chapter, I will neither try to test a theory about it, nor try to improve the way troubled families do it. These are *deductive* strategies that begin with a theoretical model and then interpret the observed data in those terms. Instead of that, an *inductive* strategy will be pursued. This strategy begins by observing the raw data of family life to see if there are patterns or structures. Such patterns are then studied to determine if they display systematic organization. If they do, the inductive researcher seeks to build concepts and principles that seem to be guiding the family behavior. Families may be observed and interviewed in this research process. Many families must be studied to be sure the patterns are not unique to one family. Ultimately, these inductively generated concepts and principles may fit together in a way that allows most of the behavior to be explained in a coherent, parsimonious manner. If that explanation provides a useful way of describing, understanding, and predicting important aspects of family problem solving, it gains the status of a theory.

Inductive research strategies are well-known in the social sciences and have always been used in combination with deductive strategies, whether it was acknowledged or not. In recent years, this approach has been called qualitative research and has frequently been applied to family life (e.g., Ambert, Adler, Adler, & Detzner, 1995; Gilgun, Daly, & Handel, 1992; Gubrium & Holstein, 1990). It is used in other disciplines such as conversation analysis, anthropological field work, and sociolinguistics, and a classic statement of the method was written by sociologists (Glaser & Strauss, 1967). But it has rarely been used to study elements of family problem solving (e.g., Vuchinich, 1990; Vuchinich, Vuchinich, & Coughlin, 1991). My purpose in this chapter is to begin an inductive analysis of family problem solving. I will not go so far as to propose an inductive theory but instead I will focus on some patterns and structures I have observed in families.

This chapter is organized in terms of three principles. First, *family problems are social constructions*. They do not suddenly take shape in the course of family life as objects that are well-defined, clearly formulated, and understood by all family members. Instead, they are social constructions that family members must actively create, sustain, and promote to others. The importance of social construction in families has been demonstrated in work that is based on such fields as ethnomethodology, phenomenology, and sociology of knowledge (e.g., Berger & Luckmann, 1966; Gergen, 1985, 1994; Gilgun et al., 1992; Gubrium & Holstein, 1990, 1993). This perspective will be applied to clarify the nature of family problems. Although this approach shares some views with postmodern theory (Cheal, 1991; Klein & White, 1996), it does not reject the rationalism of "modernity" out of hand. The purpose is to complement rational models, not eliminate them.

Second, *solutions to family problems must fit and adjust the family system*. Much of the work on problem solving has focused on intelligence, power, and creativity as factors that produce effective problem solving. Such factors clearly make a contribution in some domains. But the family context includes constraints that render intelligence and creativity less important, and other characteristics such as features of the family system, cohesion, and social skills more important. These factors require a new focus on what good solutions are, and how they can be attained.

Third, *family rituals structure the emergence and solution of family problems*. Family problems are rarely easy or enjoyable to deal with. They usually involve the expression of some form of negative emotion and often bring into question the actions, attitudes, or feelings of other family members. Elements of ritual behavior patterns are used in several aspects of family life to effectively manage a wide range of emotional issues (Bossard & Boll, 1950; Fiese, 1992; Imber-Black, Roberts, & Whiting, 1988; Vuchinich, 1986; Wolin, Bennett, & Noonan, 1979). Families often develop ritual patterns for formulating family problems and trying to solve them. These ritual patterns have been largely overlooked, but their form can shape important elements of family problem solving (Reiss, 1981). Indeed, many applications of family problem solving include ritual elements such as family meetings (Dinkmeyer & McKay, 1989; Forgatch & Patterson, 1989).

Each of these principles will be presented in turn. They are motivated in part by the successes and failures in the history of work reviewed in chapters 2 and 3. But more directly, these principles emerged from the analysis of hundreds of videotapes of families in their homes. The videotapes were products of several research projects spanning more than 10 years (e.g., Vuchinich, 1984; Vuchinich et al., 1996). A primary goal of those studies was to capture family interaction patterns as they "normally" occur at home. Details of the studies will be described as needed. Though initially unanticipated, it soon became apparent that these videotapes provided an unprecedented window on how problems naturally emerged in the flow of family life and how families tried, successfully or unsuccessfully, to come to grips with them.

This chapter is a result of an effort to reconcile the published research on family problem solving with what the videotapes showed the families doing at home. Some transcripts will be used as examples. But the chapter focuses on clear description and explanation of concepts, rather than formal quantitative or qualitative analysis. It should be understood as field notes toward a grounded theory of family problem solving.

The Social Construction
of Family Problems

Problems of one sort or another are prevalent in virtually all families. Any family member can readily give examples of problems, difficulties, or "issues" that have come up in the past month. But something interesting happens if you ask two members of the same family if their family has ever had any "problems." They do not always agree on what was a problem. Typically there will be some circumstances in which those polled agree there was a family problem. But for others, one person will say it was a problem and the other will say it was not. Often such interviews lead to the family members asking what *you* mean by a "family problem."

This exercise is instructive because it suggests that there is no a priori objective consensus on what a specific family problem is. On a day-to-day basis, the definition of family problems is up for grabs. The following transcript from a family dinner shows an example of a disagreement about whether or not something is a problem. The rural southern family has decided to move out of their present dwelling. The father wants to move to an existing house. The mother wants to build a new house. For reference, statements are numbered by turn.

1. Father: Why should we move out there and pay $80 a square foot to build one when I can buy one for less than $70 already built and not have that trouble?

2. Mother: Cause it ain't big enough is what. We—What am I supposed to do, give away my furniture?

3. Father: Dat house is almost as big as this house right here.

4. Mother: JOHN IT DON'T GOT NO DEN IN IT and a dinin' room neither.

5. Father: Now that ain't no—no problem to put up a . . . *(Mother interrupts)*

6. Mother: That's a big problem for me. I ain't arguin'.

7. Father: NO IT AIN'T. It ain't no damn problem for you 'cause you ain't gonna drive a single nail in it. Now, how can it be a problem for you. It'll be there when you move in it. *(Six second silence)*

8. Daughter: It looks like it's gonna rain.

In number 5, the father begins suggesting that the mother's concerns about space could be met by adding a room, which is not a "problem" to do. The mother refutes this in number 6, stating that it is a problem for her. In number 7, the father rejects this, stating that it cannot be a problem for the mother because she will not be doing any of the construction work. The mother does not respond and the daughter, in number 8, seeks to change the topic by talking about the weather. As is often the case, no agreement on whether adding the room was a "problem" was achieved in this interchange. Indeed, this couple could not agree on what problem they should argue about. It was Simmel who first pointed out that some agreement on points at issue is necessary for conflict to proceed (Simmel, 1950). This is even more true in the case of problem solving.

In many respects, family problems are not different from many other features of social life. Roles, relationships, identities, and other social forms may be viewed as social constructions (e.g., Berger & Luckmann, 1966; Gergen, 1985, 1994; Gubrium & Holstein, 1990; Mead, 1934; Reiss, 1981). The processes involved in such constructions are often subtle and complex. Fields such as ethnomethodology, constructionist theory, symbolic interactionism, and conversation analysis (Goodwin, 1982; Gubrium & Holstein, 1993; Maynard, 1985; Sacks, Schegloff, & Jefferson, 1974) have revealed key elements of how they occur by focusing on the details of exactly what family members say to each other. These theories provide some unique insights that are essential in understanding the nature of family problems, although a detailed application of these theories is beyond the scope of this book. They provide a new approach to what is generally acknowledged as the first step in family problem solving: defining the problem.

The constructionist approach to family problems is based on a different paradigm than the psychological or family therapy paradigms that have dominated work on family problem solving. With roots in 19th-century German phenomenology, and little interest in positivistic science or clinical treatment, the various strands of constructionism have focused on the order in and experience of everyday life. Before applying elements of this approach, it is useful to point out that fundamental difficulties in the way these paradigms have conceptualized family problems have been acknowledged for some time. These difficulties begin with Dewey's claim that problems essentially *present themselves* to the individual.

We saw in chapter 2 how Dewey's theory maintained that problems were "imbalances" in the adaptation of the individual to the environment. When they became serious enough, an organismic tension naturally drew the individual's attention to the "problem" and provided the motivation to solve it. Dewey's primary example of a problem was hunger for food. Although brilliant in many respects, flaws in this organismic model of problems are apparent. Many problems that individuals deal with do not have a built-in physical problem alarm system analogous to hunger (e.g., Lewis & Smith, 1980). In such cases, some additional cognitive activity by the individual is needed to identify the problem (Lewis & Smith, 1980). Dewey did not consider that.

Of course, being more concerned with internal thought than social units, Dewey did not consider the possibility of a dyad, or a family having a problem. This limits the applicability of his theory to defining family problems. However, his idea that the essence of a problem is an unmet need is entirely consistent with the popular view that problems are based on blocked goals (e.g., Tallman, 1988). Because blocked individual or group goals can produce physical or psychological tension, Dewey's model can be extended to the dyadic or family context. The key is that tensions based on ineffective adaptation create the motivational energy for seeking a source of the tension and eliminating it.

How that energy is used in the family context is an important question for any theory of family problems. In some families, the tension is expressed as conflict; in other families it is suppressed and turned inward. In still other families, a family meeting is called. Of course, Dewey was never concerned with any of this. Though he established a solid foundation for understanding the nature of problems, he did not pursue the implications beyond the simplest possible problems (hunger for food). Some have suggested that the choice not to pursue this matter was tantamount to begging the question of what a problem is, and that this shortcoming compromises his entire theory (Lewis & Smith, 1980). Such retrospective judgments are perhaps harsh given that Dewey was a psychologist concerned only with the nature of thought.

However it may have been more than coincidence that much of the existing history of work on problem solving has tended to beg that same question.

The Social Nature of Problems

The first description of the social nature of problems in groups came about through efforts to adapt a rational model of decision making to actual situations in the business world. In his early work, Simon had recognized the folly of any model of decision making that assumed that a systematic weighing of benefits and disadvantages could actually be carried out in real-life situations (Simon, 1945). One never has full information about what results any decision will have. In pursuing this important deduction with further observations, he and his colleagues brilliantly described how people in groups systematically merged efforts to weigh benefits and costs with more practical methods for making choices (e.g., Newell & Simon, 1972; Simon, 1956).

For example, they pointed out that rationality calls for systematically evaluating alternatives to determine the *best* solution to the problem that maximizes benefits and minimizes costs. Simon and his colleagues claimed that in real life people instead must seek solutions that "satisfice." That is, they seek solutions that are sufficient to satisfy the immediate needs in the situation. Here pure rationality is tempered by the existential conditions of reality. Both Aldous (1971) and Weick (1971) applied this key point to family life.

They further claimed that the environments of most social groups are far too complex and fluid to allow accurate, detailed assessment of the benefits and costs of decisions. In light of this fact, groups develop simplified images of their environments that only take into account certain features that are believed to be most important. Decisions can thus be made in a timely manner by focusing on only the key indicators of the environment and filtering out the rest of the complexity. Because that complexity produces uncertainty about what decision to make, this process was called *uncertainty absorption* (March & Simon, 1958).

For our concerns these uncertainty-absorbing images of the environment are important because they are social constructions. March and Simon suggested that it was the function of effective management to know what should be filtered out and what should be filtered in to the decision process. A good understanding of the group environment would produce good decisions. In the family context, these ideas are closely linked to Reiss's concept of a family paradigm (e.g., Reiss, 1981). Family paradigms are social constructions that simplify the family's understanding of its environment and thus constrain many decisions. This includes understanding the nature of family problems.

Pursuing this line of reasoning, along with informal observational research, led to the "garbage can" model of organizational choice (Cyert & March, 1963), which provided an entirely new way of conceptualizing group problems and solutions. Consistent with Dewey's theory, traditional decision-making models saw problems as occasional situations (imbalances) that signaled the need for some change in the way the group is adapting to the environment. However, following up on Simon's view of uncertainty absorption, it was found that problems were often stable, social constructions of groups that were acknowledged as ongoing issues to be dealt with again and again. In the organizational context, such problems would be low morale, foreign competition, unfair government regulations, inadequate computer support, and so on. Once a set of these problems became established in a group, they were part of the image the group had of itself and its environment. They became an ongoing set of "garbage cans" for the group—part of the organizational structure.

Solutions had a dual purpose in this model. First, individuals proposed solutions that would further their interests or position in the organization. Second, the solution might help eliminate the problem. But as often as not, the problem was simply used to justify the changes implicit in the solution. In this regard, solutions were changes that were simply tossed into the problem "garbage cans" with little expectation that the problem would really be eliminated.

It is perhaps easier to apply this "garbage can" model to families than to organizations. Consistent with Reiss's paradigm theory, most people can verbalize specific ongoing problems that their families have had. Whether an objective outsider would agree with their assessment is beside the point. Families do seem to create images of their problems that are social constructions. They may include a vast variety of issues, such as Mother's failing health, Billy's trouble with the police, Dad's drinking, Jane's arguments with Mom, and so on. Problems may involve long-standing skeletons in the closet or new issues with little long-term baggage. Many problems are not the occasional occurrences that just come up as imbalances in the group–environment interface. They are stable fixtures of the family. Efforts to propose solutions to such problems are the occasional occurrences that come up. And a true solution may require changing the way a family understands itself, not just relieving a transient imbalance.

The following transcript shows an example of how long-standing family issues shape the formulation of problems. All family problems have a history of events and relationships. That history is often complex, and this transcript is a typical example. Specific details of this history, some of which may seem inane, are absolutely essential to gain any understanding of what transpires. I depart from the research tradition of ignoring such contexts. The reader should be prepared to find out more about this family than he or she may want to know.

This interaction centers on two adult sisters at a holiday party in a low-income, urban setting. Two of them are sitting around the kitchen table with their male partners drinking and talking. Trish has allowed her unemployed sister Jane and her two children to live in her subsidized apartment for more than a year for free. Jane's male partner is in jail. Trish also has the sisters' parents living in her apartment. In the transcript, the third sister, Marge, is talking with Trish. Trish is complaining about Jane not paying for rent, utilities, food, or for damage her children have done in the apartment. She implies that this is unfair to her. Marge validates Trish's complaint.

> Marge: Trish, I'll tell 'ya. Here's my hand to God. If Jane says, "Marge, me 'an the kids are comin' here overnight"—overnight or day 'an a half. That's ONE thing. But a whole year. That's ANOTHER thing. . . . If I come to stay with y'all a year or more, I would try to pay for more food. . . . I think Jane's wrong. . . . Jane should help Trish.

Marge provides some emotional support to Trish and offers a solution to Trish's long-standing problem—that is, Jane should help Trish with living expenses. Having Marge agree that there is a problem also raises the possibility of Marge helping to put some social pressure on Jane to help Trish with expenses. Trish takes this validation as an occasion to give several specific detailed examples of how Jane not only offers no help with expenses, but also has an arrogant, resentful attitude when Trish suggests that she should help out more. As the conversation continues, Trish becomes more emotional and negative in her complaints about Jane. She is formulating a long-term family problem.

After several minutes of this, Marge apparently begins to feel that Trish's verbal attack is going too far and begins to subtly try to stop Trish by interrupting her. Trish responds to this by giving an example of how Marge was involved in an incident that resulted in one of Trish's windows being broken. The previous Easter, Marge had taken their grandmother out for dinner. When she took her back to Trish's apartment, the door was locked. It was very cold, so Marge tried to get Gram into the apartment through the window. In the process, the window was broken, and Trish had to pay for the repairs. After listing several examples of

Jane's irresponsibility, Trish adds the incident involving Marge and Gram. Marge, who is seated directly across the table from Trish, takes umbrage to this implied claim that she, as well as Jane, is irresponsible toward family members, and the discussion escalates from there.

1. Trish: It's the same as when—when, uh. What hurt me was when we went out for Easter. An Marge gonna try to get Gram in the damn window and then break out my windows an all that shit.

2. Marge: Trish, if you knew how much Gram [was] worryin' me and botherin' me.

3. Trish: No. Wait a minute. I'm just talkin' about if she worry you for that one day, what the hell you think she's doin' for me five and seven days a week.

4. Marge: Did I tell you you had to take her?

5. Trish: Who?

6. Marge: Didn't I tell you you didn't have to take her and Grandaddy? If I had enough room I woulda' taken them.

7. Trish: But you didn't *have* enough room though. You didn't have the room.

8. Marge: How I'm [gonna] take them?

9. Trish: Well, as far as that, as far as that goes—

10. Marge: You—if you put—As you put it, if you w'd get technical, then I gotta—you gotta pay rent where the hell you at. Right?

11. Trish: That's right. That's right. That's right.

12. Marge: An' if Gram and Grandaddy stayin' with you all you need is [to] put out for food, damn it cuz, they done raised you, wiped your ass, cooked your food, and everything. I'm sick—I'm fed up with the whole— it's just a whole bunch of damn shit that's goin' around.

13. Trish: NOW LOOK. LOOK. Now wait a minute. Now I'm not sayin' that.

14. Marge: LOOK. ALRIGHT. LOOK, I'M A TELL YOU. ALRIGHT.

15. Trish: THEY CLEANED YOUR ASS AS MUCH AS THEY CLEAN MINE NOW. *(The argument continues for several minutes with Marge becoming increasingly irate)*

In number 1, Trish puts Marge in the same irresponsible sister role as Jane when she states that the window-breaking incident is "the same thing" as the other things Jane had done—or failed to do. Marge seeks to deflect this in number 2 by stating how much concern she has for her elderly mother (Gram). In number 3, Trish belittles this concern by reminding Marge that the parents are living in *her* apartment. In this interchange the problem at issue shifts away from sibling responsibilities for each other to the long-standing problem of which of the siblings are taking responsibility for caring for their aging parents. In numbers 4 through 11, Trish implies that Marge has not been making a fair contribution to the burden of caring for their parents. In number 6, Marge indicates that she would have taken them in if she had the room. By number 12, Marge has become very upset about Trish's implication that she is not doing her fair share in caring for their parents. In number 13, Trish realizes how upset Marge has become and tries to clarify her point. Her phrase, "NOW I'M NOT SAYIN' THAT," suggests that she might not have intended to imply that Marge was irresponsible. In any event, Marge and Trish both became more angry and a loud argument continued for several minutes before Marge's partner convinced her to leave the room, and in fact pulled her by the arm out of the room. She returned some time later and a calmer discussion of sibling responsibilities continued.

No problems were solved that day. But some progress may have been made in formulating the "problem." It was clearly established that Marge agrees with Trish about Jane's irresponsibility in the living arrangements. But Trish may have lost some active support from Marge in dealing with that by what was probably an inadvertent implication—that Marge was also irresponsible in her family responsibilities. In any event, the immediate impact of Trish bringing the elderly parents into the discussion is of special interest. Caring for their parents has obviously been an ongoing problem for these adult siblings. No solutions to it were offered. But we can see that it lurks in the background and can quickly generate emotional outbursts when it is mentioned. All families have such long-standing problems that may or may not be overtly addressed.

Another important way of conceptualizing family problems and solutions was derived from a general theory of how people make sense of everyday life. Garfinkel (1967) pointed out that people often make sense out of situations after the fact. Similar to March and Simon, he emphasized the enormous complexity of real-life situations. Making sense of what is going on often cannot be done at the time. Often it is only after events have occurred that we look back and develop an understanding of what happened. Weick (1971) was the first to apply these ideas to family problem solving. He suggested that family events often occur quickly, are complex and emotionally intense. Consider an intense, potentially injurious physical fight between preadolescent siblings. In such a situation, actions and "solutions" may have to be implemented *before* the problem is clearly defined or understood. Indeed, families typically have a set of standard solutions that are implemented to deal with problems. For example, parents, on discovering a family rule violation, may immediately "ground" children, send them to their rooms, demand an apology, require a handshake, revoke privileges, and so on as typical solutions to the problematic situation. The full story of what the problem was, and why a certain solution was applied, may be constructed only in retrospect.

Crime and Punishment at the Dinner Table

In the following example (set in the rural deep South, circa 1975), two parents and their four daughters (ages 9, 12, 14, and 16) are having dinner. One daughter's transgression is revealed (by another daughter) and the father immediately issues a punishment. However, the full nature of the problem is discussed only after the punishment was given. Daughters' statements are referenced by their age—for example, the 14-year-old is labeled D14. D14 has a small summer job working at the school with some of her friends. On Thursdays, they go out for lunch.

1. D14: I had steak today.
2. Mother: Where?
3. D14: At the Hungry Bull. [a restaurant]
4. D12: She went to the Hungry Bull for lunch.
5. D16: THE HUNGRY BULL?
6. D12: Isn't that sick.
7. D14: That's where we decided to go because we didn't want to have hamburg—
8. D16: OH MY GOSH. I DON'T BELIEVE HER.
9. D14: You can get a meal at the Hungry Bull for as cheap as you can get a buffet at—
10. D12: She spent $2.95 today or $2.50—
11. Father: Where did you get the money for this meal?
12. D12: Mother's purse.
13. D16: She goes to work and then she comes home for money to have lunch.
14. D14: On Thursdays, on Thursdays. . .
15. Father: THAT'S THE LAST TIME. You've already spent your quota for the whole summer.
16. D12: That's all she gets, about 30 cents an hour.
17. Father: YOU CAN EITHER COME UP WITH YOUR OWN MONEY TO FLY OR YOU TAKE A BROWN BAG. You're not makin' anything. It's costing you as much—
18. D14: I AM TOO. I'm makin' $40. That's something. Are they makin' anything all summer long?
19. D12: Don't compare yourself to us.

20. Father: FORTY DOLLARS. You've already—by the time the summer's over you will have spent more 'an 'at fer yer meals that you go out on the town.
21. D14: I—We—Dad, we only go out on Thursdays.
22. Father: Well how many Thursdays are there?
23. D14: And we go to places like McDonald's and today is the first time—
24. Father: AND THE HUNGRY BULL.
25. D14: Today is the first time.
26. D16: The HUNGRY BULL. I don't BELIEVE that.

D14's sisters ferret out the facts of the case and express their outrage in numbers 4 through 16. The mother was not aware of this lunch, as indicated by her question ("Where?") in number 2. The father clinches the inquisition by asking where the money came from (number 10). Thus it was clear that D14 took the money from the mother's purse without asking permission. This apparently was a violation of family rules. Initially, the sisters seemed to be formulating the lunch as an excessive act, about which they may simply have been jealous. But taking money out of the mother's purse was a different kind of problem altogether. Within seconds of this revelation the father (number 15) was moved to loudly forbid D14 from using any family money for her lunches with coworkers. Only in the aftermath of this punishment (numbers 17–24) does the father present his formulation of the problem—that is, the costs of her special lunches will use up all the money she is making in her job. Dad considers this unacceptable. In retrospect, this formulation merges the sisters' complaints about excessiveness with his own point about violating a family rule. The father's solution to the problem occurred *before* it was clearly defined. This punishment was hardly severe, but the daughter did try to escape it in numbers 21 and 23. The videotape shows her cringing and hanging her head afterward. Such a public display of her crimes, as well as the punishment, may have had a shaming effect that was more punishing than the limits placed on her lunches.

Aldous and Ganey (1989) found evidence that solutions may often *precede* defining the problem. In a laboratory living room setting, families were given a list of family vignettes (e.g., the teenager is not happy with the amount he is receiving for his allowance; see Appendix E). They asked families "to consider the items one at a time and to express thoughts or feelings that they had." They assessed several aspects of the family members' comments. Of particular interest was a code for comments that *defined the problem* more clearly, and a code for *providing solutions*. They further coded the sequence in which the defining and solution comments occurred. Contrary to the rational model of problem solving, the solutions tended to occur *before* the defining comments. They suggested that this was evidence for Weick's notion that family problem solving often does not follow the rational model. Instead, problems are defined retrospectively, after solutions have already been implemented.

These theories suggest that there is much more to defining problems in family groups than the basic rational model would imply. However, the additional layers of social constructions do not alter two fundamental features of problems that were part of Dewey's original formulation. First, problems are based on tensions that can be traced to unmet needs. Second, these problems signal a faulty adaptation of the family (or one of its subsytems) to the environment. The key constructionist insight is simply that families create their own images of these unmet needs and adaptations. They then use them in practical ways that allow action in the face of a complex and uncertain social environment.

Although this constructionist insight is straightforward, it has two major implications for understanding family problems. First, because they are social constructions of a family group that creates its own internal standards, objective criteria are not used for a family's definition of their problems. Second, an interactive group process must be involved in creating and sustaining the definitions.

What Makes Something a
Family Problem?

Strictly speaking, family problems can be anything the family creates. In most families, problems are defined in a way that allows for beneficial adaptations to the environment that promote the well-being of family members. But in some families, problems are defined in such a way that healthy adaptations do not occur and the well-being of family members is sacrificed. For example, a family may define one of their children as the main "problem" the family has. The solution might be to abuse or kill that child. This scapegoating pattern is well-known in research on dysfunctional family systems (e.g., Minuchin et al., 1978; Vuchinich, Wood, & Vuchinich, 1994). Enmeshed family systems with permissive parents might define problems in such a way that there are no perceived internal family problems because "anything goes."

There are numerous dysfunctional variations in the way family problems are defined. But the key point is that families create their own image of what their problems are. A paraphrase of W. I. Thomas's famous quote on defining the situation (Thomas & Thomas, 1928) is pertinent: "Family problems defined as real are real in their consequences." Although

families are free to define their problems in any way, there are consequences that follow from the definitions. In the long term, following the
logic of Dewey and Darwin, one would predict that families that view
problems in a way that promotes effective adaptations survive, and the
other families do not. Defining family problems is only one part of
adaptation, but it is an important one.

The criteria a family uses to define their problems may be quite
different from those used by social systems outside the family, such as
schools, therapists, police, counselors, religions, child protective service
agencies, extended kin, or neighbors. The right to determine whether a
specific family circumstance is a "problem" requiring action is distributed
among these systems. This distribution varies across different types of
society. In a well-functioning society, the socialization practices produce
parents who organize their family life, including their view of what family
problems are, in a manner consistent with the standards applied by those
institutions that interface with the family. Ideally, those standards should
promote the well-being of family members in the society. Of course,
societies approach the ideals of socialization and beneficial standards
with varying degrees of success that may change over time. As a result,
some families may believe that they have no serious problems but must
deal with institutions that believe that they do have a problem requiring
attention.

In American society, specific professions have the responsibility to
establish and apply standards for behavior in families that are the basis
for determining whether a serious family problem exists. These include
the professions of social work, family therapy, medicine, nursing, law,
clinical psychology, developmental psychology, and family studies. The
basic criteria usually applied is whether the family situation produces a
risk to the physical or psychological well-being of family members. For
most of American history, the threshold of perceived risk has had to be
very high before intervention in the family was allowed. For example,
evidence of child abuse had to be very strong before any intervention in
the family could take place.

Thus societies do establish "objective" criteria for determining that a
family problem exists. But because much of family life typically takes
place outside of the surveillance of other institutions, families have
considerable leeway in establishing their own definitions. Within families, a health or adaptive criteria may not be at all prominent. The social
constructionist perspective shows how family systems impose restrictive
constraints on how problems are defined. These constraints are of
fundamental importance to the problem solving process. Solving problems of no consequence to the family's well-being or adaptation cannot
be considered effective. Getting the appropriate problems on the table is

a prerequisite for adequate family problem solving. How that happens depends on the family's social construction of the problem.

Constructing a Family Problem

A second implication of the social constructionist view is that definitions of family problems are actively created through family interaction. Over long spans of a family's life cycle, the residue of face-to-face interactions results in some stable beliefs about a family's problems. These are consistent with the family paradigm, and they become fixtures to be used by family members. Such images of problems typically are not those defined in a 20-minute family problem solving session to deal with an immediate situation. However, those images serve as an important context for defining and managing problems on a day-to-day basis. The ultimate definition of a problem combines these images with a set of procedures and patterns in family interaction.

This composite defining process is crucial to problem solving because an adaptive solution is only possible (a) if an appropriate problem is formulated; (b) if it is accepted by at least two family members (preferably by all); and (c) if it is then implemented, which usually requires cooperation from most of the family. In what follows, I provide an outline to that composite process.

When all family members feel that their needs are met, as far as they are concerned, there are no family problems. The amount of time families spend in this state of "no family problems" varies greatly across the family life cycle and across families. Some families have problems every day. Other families deny that any problems exist and thus, from their perspective, never have any family problems. Of course, most families fall somewhere between these extremes, with some periods that are relatively problem free and others that are problem laden.

The beginning of a family problem is a physical or psychological tension resulting from the perception of an unmet need by at least one family member. This tension could be focused on a specific individual need (e.g., sex, control, a kind word of support, encouragement, a hug, a compliment), or it could be a diffuse sense of dissatisfaction. The tension could be based on one person's perception of a family need (e.g., the family needs money for housing, the family needs a cemetery plot). A tension deriving from a legitimate unmet need (e.g., for emotional support after a trauma) could be suppressed and lead to no overt action at all. In this case, the definition process does not proceed. Or an individual's tension could be based on irrational or unrealistic perceptions about what one's needs are. For example, an older sibling may feel the need to physically punish a younger sibling to show dominance. The tension experienced by the older sibling is real and may well move toward being defined as a family problem. The point is that the defining process itself does not distinguish between legitimate or illegitimate, healthy or unhealthy perceptions of need in family members. The same basic defining process operates in functional and dysfunctional families.

The definition process proceeds *only* if the person expresses the tension to another family member. One person's experience of an unmet need is simply his or her experience. But once it is communicated to another family member it may become a social object. Typically, this takes the form of a complaint or a request. The process moves ahead another step if that family member acknowledges the validity of the complaint or request. A preadolescent might complain to the father that his eight o'clock bedtime is too early for someone his age. If the father accepts that complaint as reasonable, then a preliminary basis for defining the problem is established. But if the validity of the complaint is denied, then you have a complaining preadolescent and no progress toward defining a family problem.

This communication can work in the opposite direction. A mother may see her child moping around and ask, "What's bothering you?" The child can then state a complaint or request, or just admit to negative feelings. If so, this kind of interaction can lead to a formulation of a problem on which both mother and child agree. If the child says in effect, "Nothing is bothering me, I'm just tired," the issue may be dropped, at least for the time being.

After two family members acknowledge the validity of an unmet need, they may move to the next step of proposing a definition for a problem. In the bedtime example, the problem may be defined by the father to be a rule for bedtime that was once appropriate but has become inappropriate because the child has gotten older. At this point, the unmet need and complaint (or request) are transformed into a new social construction—a problem. Of course many, if not most, unmet needs, complaints, requests, and so on are never transformed in this manner. Complaints often lead to countercomplaints, threats, conflict, or they may simply be ignored or discounted.

Complaints and requests can also be delivered with prepackaged definitions of a problem as well as a proposed solution. The preadolescent could have presented his complaint along with the definition of the problem (i.e., inappropriate rule), and a solution (i.e., change his bedtime to nine o'clock). This may tend to stimulate the defining process. But until a definition is validated by another family member, a "family problem" has not been defined. One family member cannot, by fiat, define a family problem without getting at least one other family member to accept it. Many influence tactics may be used to get others to accept one's definition, ranging from brutal physical coercion, through rational discourse, to subtle seduction.

Once two family members construct an initial definition of a family problem, the pursuant course of events varies according to family structure. If the father and preadolescent are in a single-parent family with no siblings, then the bedtime rule may be changed once these two agree. That may be a solution to the problem, at least for the time being. However, if there is also a mother and other siblings in the family, the problem defined by the father and preadolescent would probably have to go through further validation.

At this point, the definition becomes a matter of family politics. The way the matter gets handled depends on how power is distributed in the family and whether acceptance can be gained from key family members. If the father has controlling power over that domain of the family, he might simply accept this definition and change the bedtime rule. If the mother has controlling power, the definition of the problem would have to be accepted by her. As other family members become involved, the initially proposed definition may have to be changed in order to arrive at a definition that can be accepted by the family power structure.

Under ideal circumstances, all relevant family members come to accept a single definition of the problem (e.g., the preadolescent's bedtime is too early). When such a consensus is achieved, the ideal type of family problem has been constructed. But if complete consensus was a prerequisite for a true definition of a family problem, it would be a rare occurrence indeed. That is why I propose the more practical, and more frequently attained, criterion that at least two family members validate a definition. Once that occurs, a problem has a "social life," as opposed to being just tension within one individual. That is a minimal basis for family-based social movement toward solution.

This constructionist view of family problems means that at any given time there can be two or more partially formulated, competing definitions for problems based on tensions and unmet needs of family members. The defining process may take place in a matter of minutes or it could drag out for weeks or even years. Definitions of family problems may be shared by only part of the family. Indeed, part of the family may move toward solutions to the problem, leaving other family members out of the process. In addition, complex characteristics of the family such as the power structure, cohesiveness, influence patterns, and coalitions can shape important parts of the definition process—well before any problem solving actually takes place.

In the following example from a dinner, the father presents a complaint against his teenage son. He claims the son has excessive expectations about how much time parents should spend in transporting him to his hockey practice. The mother then forms a coalition with the father by agreeing with and pursuing the same problem. The son does not drive and needs transportation to his hockey practice tomorrow. He has asked his parents to take him there, but the final arrangements have not been made. Again, I will not spare the reader the details necessary to understand what happens.

1. Father *(to son):* When are you gonna find out what, like how long you're gonna be tomorrow and . . .

2. Son: I won't, I won't know 'til tomorrow when we get there. Why?

3. Father: What are we supposed to do, sit by the phone and wait for your call to get picked up and then take you to the other place?

4. Son: Wull have mom call Schmidts. [his friend's residence near the practice rink where he will be dropped off and picked up]

5. Father: Why? It's not her practice. It's *your* practice.

6. Mother *(to son):* Yeah. Its *your* arrangements.

7. Father *(to son):* We're providing the rides. YOU COULD AT LEAST find out what time and how long.

8. Son *(to mother):* Oh. Okay, then you are gonna drive me there?

9. Mother: It depends on what time it is. If it's dark at 5:30, I could get you there at 5:00.

10. Son: Why would I want to be there at 5:00 if it starts at 5:30?

11. Mother: 'Cause I gotta come home from work, GIVE YOU SOMETHING TO EAT!

12. Son: DON'T WORRY ABOUT GETTIN' ME SOMETHING TO EAT THEN!

13. Father: It's still a trip back from the office—to here, to there . . .

14. Son: That's why I suggest, I thought that's why I suggested Schmidts's. [as the drop-off location]

15. Mother: WULL WHY DON'T YOU CALL AND ASK IF THEY'LL PICK YOU UP. Tell 'em that your mother has an appointment at 5:30.

16. Son: Because I do it all—every time.

17. Mother: WULL IT'S FOR YOU. WHY SHOULDN'T—YOU SHOULD DO IT? WHO SHOULD DO IT, THE GUY DOWN THE STREET? Who else is gonna do it? It's for your benefit.

18. Daughter: Mom, you don't have to yell.

19. Mother: I'm not yelling.

In number 3, the father points out a problem with the son's plan to wait until tomorrow to finalize the transportation schedule. He implies that the loose plan is not fair to the parents and would leave them "waiting by the phone" until his practice was over. The son's response in number 4 is rejected with the implication again that the son's plan is unacceptable, and that it is *his* responsibility to make the plan more specific. In number 6, the mother forms the coalition by agreeing with the father that the plan is problematic and changes will be necessary. The mother had not yet agreed that she would provide transportation, though she had apparently told the father that she would. The son notices this and in number 8 seeks confirmation that mother will provide transportation for him. Mother indicates (number 9) that the time may create another problem. The son seeks to eliminate this difficulty by absolving the mother of responsibility to provide him with food. But father reaffirms the coalition with mother by agreeing with the time difficulty (number 13). As the son tries to deflect this, the mother, in a loud voice, suggests that *he* ask the Schmidts to pick him up, in number 15. The son tries to get the mother to take care of this (number 16), but the mother, again using the father's initial responsibility logic, insists that the son should be responsible for making the arrangements. The daughter suggests that the mother's tone is excessive (number 18), which mother denies (number 19). After some silence, the topic was changed and the arrangements were not mentioned again at the dinner. The main point of interest is how the mother and father work in tandem to create and sustain a definition of a problem: the son's inappropriate expectations and lack of responsibility for his hockey transportation arrangements.

As we have seen, most prior work on problem solving begins with a problem already defined, or forces the family to choose a prepackaged one. Although such procedures help to meet the research demands of certain scientific paradigms, they ignore some of the most important processes in family problem solving. The way a family problem gets defined places constraints on the ways it *can* be solved. How shared definitions of family problems are constructed is of primary importance because a shared definition is a prerequisite for group action toward a solution. The goal is to describe some parts of the definition process and point out its importance. Many families cannot get past square one in family problem solving because they cannot construct a meaningful family problem. Better understanding of how that happens can be beneficial to such families.

The problem-defining process can be a multilayered, hopelessly muddled affair in some families. But for most families, the process is streamlined in a way that allows serious unmet needs to be formulated into defined problems that can be addressed by family action. Tensions and unmet needs get interpreted in terms of a limited number of structured elements of the family system such as family rules, roles, and identities. Families typically settle on a subset of these elements, which provides a simplified but practical way of transforming tensions, complaints, requests, and conflicts into defined problems. Consider some examples of what I will call *problem structures.*

One of the most frequently used is the *rule violation* structure in which tension is based on someone violating a family rule. Because such rules often organize the way needs get met, their violation creates tension for some family members. A three-generation household may include some adult smokers and nonsmokers, which precipitates some smoking rules. Smoking or leaving ashes or tobacco debris in certain areas of the living quarters would violate a family rule. This would produce tension in the nonsmokers, which could easily lead to defining a problem in terms of the smoking rules being violated. If this definition—a smoker broke a smoking rule—is accepted by key family members, movement toward a solution could begin.

In the following example, two parents and their 12-year-old son are doing a problem solving task in a community mental health center. The parents chose to talk about homework as a problem they have had with their son.

1. Father *(to son):* Did you bring spelling home today?
2. Son: Yeah.
3. Father: How come you didn't bring none of it home last night?
4. Son: I did.
5. Mother: Did you study it last night?
6. Son *(to father):* You—you said, "Go outside."
7. Father: I told you to go outside when you got done with your homework.
8. Mother: And that's part of your homework.
9. Son: But—
10. Father: You don't go outside until after you've done with your homework. And you, you were in your pajamas, right? 'Cause you were on restriction.
11. Son: And then you said, "Get on your clothes and go outside."
12. Father: After you got done with your homework. You picked up your things and put 'em back in your room. Didn't ya'?
13. Son: Yeah.
14. Father: And I said "Are you done with homework?" And you said, "Yes." And I said "Okay then, you can put on your clothes and go outside." Didn't I? Didn't I?

15. Son: I was just about to study spelling and you said, "Get your clothes on and—"
16. Father: You didn't say, you didn't say you had any spelling. Why didn't you say you had spelling? You know you're supposed to study.
17. Son: You asked me if I had spelling and I said, "Yes."
18. Father: Now when I ask if you were done with your homework what are you supposed to say? You're supposed to say, "No, I've got spelling." Then you would have had to study your spelling. But you didn't say that. I asked if you were done with your homework, didn't I?
19. Son: *(sulking)* Yes.
20. Father: And what'd you say?
21. Son: Yes.
22. Father: Then I said "Okay, go ahead and put on your—take off your pajamas and go outside and play." Didn't I?
23. Son: Yes.
24. Mother: So what are you going to have to do tonight?
25. Son: Study spelling.
26. Mother: Twice as hard, right?
27. Son: Right.
28. Mother: To make up for last night, right?
29. Son: Right.

Persistent questioning was needed to get the son to admit that he had broken a family rule—that homework should be done before playing. This example also shows how minute details are often important in dealing with rule violations. In this case, the father *had* said that the son could play—after the son had indicated that his homework was done. The 12-year-old implicitly sought to get off the hook because the father had not asked specifically if his spelling was done. But the mother pointed out (number 8) that spelling is part of homework. In number 14, the father makes it clear that spelling is part of homework and what the appropriate response should have been. Here, the parents go to great lengths to identify what the child did in terms of the rule-violation structure.

A second problem structure that is especially common when children are in the family is the *unfair rule* structure. In this structure, a family member experiences frustration because of the constraints imposed by some family rule, and seeks to challenge it. Most parents sooner or later have heard their child whine, or yell, "But that's unfair." The previous example of the preadolescent wanting a later bedtime is an example of this problem structure. Because children develop so quickly, rule changes are inevitable. In addition, family transitions such as divorce, remarriage, death of spouse, and so on require changes in family rules. As a result, the adjustment of family rules can be quite frequent in some families. Child and adolescent tensions are often funneled into the unfair rule structure. Although this structure can be troubling to parents, it has distinct advantages. Animosity is directed toward a rule, not toward other family members. In addition, this structure invites specifications in family rules, and perhaps important changes to them. Such changes may provide a better adaptation for all family members.

A third problem structure is a *breach of responsibility*. Family members depend on each other for getting several physical, psychological, and social needs met. Family roles specify responsibilities in this domain. Husbands and wives should meet each other's sexual needs. Parents should meet their children's psychological needs. Tensions arise when one person perceives that a need is not being met by the family member who has responsibility to provide for that need. A husband might complain that his wife is not meeting his sexual needs. A teenager might complain that her parents do not care about her the way they should. A parent might complain that a child is not fulfilling the family's need to have the garbage taken out. This problem structure is related to the rule violation structure, but focuses on role responsibilities and individual personalities rather than specific family rules. The breach of responsibility structure thus involves a personal accusation that calls into question not only his or her action, but his or her character. This problem structure was evident in the previous transcript of adult sisters arguing about family responsibilities.

In the following example, a mother complains that her 12-year-old son talks back to her and argues with her. They obviously do not have a specific family rule about this issue. But she believes it is the child's responsibility to show respect for her and accept her viewpoint on some issues.

1. Mother: I don't appreciate you talking back to me. And I don't appreciate you *arguing* with me, 'cause I'm always having, to defend something that um I feel is right. . . . I want you to stop talking back to me and I want you to stop arguing with me. *(5 second pause)*

2. Son: I want you to stop screaming at me. *(3 second pause)*

3. Mother: A lot of times that you start arguing with me are the times that I don't scream at you. The times I scream at you, you only scream back— there's no arguing or talking back. It's like scream for scream.

4. Son: Of course, what am I supposed . . . you're AH-H-H-H *(mimics mother's scream)*

5. Mother: Well, I'm not talkin' about . . .

6. Son: To get over your voice I have to scream.

7. Mother: No, we're talking about talking back.

The mother's effort to apply a breach of responsibility structure in number 1 is deftly thwarted by the son in number 2. Here, he turns the tables on her by demanding that she "stop screaming" at him. Because screaming at a child is generally acknowledged as undesirable parental behavior, he is essentially claiming that *she* is the one who is guilty of breaching her role responsibility as a parent. In number 3, the mother admits to screaming at him, which the son uses to justify his screaming back. The mother ineffectively tries to separate the screaming issue from the talking-back issue (number 7). This example demonstrates the breach of responsibility problem structure, and also shows that application of a problem structure is not necessarily a straightforward matter. These structures can be manipulated as family members pursue their own ends. As shown, other family members must accept a given problem structure in order for it to be effective in framing a problem definition.

Other common problem structures include the *scapegoat* problem structure and the *external threat* problem structure. In the scapegoat structure, one person is labeled as the cause of tensions because of flawed personal characteristics. For example, a child may be defined by the family as aggressive, cruel, or mentally ill. Most unmet family needs are then blamed on the scapegoat. The same structure can also be applied to physically or psychologically disabled children or adults. Similarly this structure appears in families with impaired elderly members. This problem structure is quite simple in form and can be devastating to the scapegoated individual and to family functioning, as has been well documented (e.g., Minuchin et al., 1978).

Physically or mentally impaired family members can create special challenges in the way the needs of family members are met. Other family members may have to make sacrifices for the benefit of the impaired person. In some families, these individuals are often targeted as scapegoats when difficulties arise. The impaired person may be perceived as the primary source of family problems. The scapegoat problem structure can occur in tandem with the breach of responsibility problem structure. Family members typically feel responsible for the care of the impaired person, but the scapegoat structure can erode and eliminate that sense of responsibility. The scapegoat problem structure leaves open few alternatives for adaptive solutions.

A less prevalent, but important, problem structure is the *external threat* problem structure. Here, the unmet needs are formulated in terms of circumstances outside of the control of the family. Natural disasters routinely create situations where this problem structure is applied. Family members are hungry because the flood cut off food supplies. This structure can provide a definition that tends to unify family members and mobilize good problem solving. As Simmel (1908/1950) was first to point out, external threats strengthen group bonds. However, this structure can also be used to isolate dysfunctional families from external social systems that could provide much-needed help. For example, an incestuous family may define their problems in terms of harassment from police and child protective service agencies. To the family, the incest is not their problem, the outside interference is.

Families create and use problem structures as practical devices for interpreting and understanding their problems. They are applied within the context of the general features of the family paradigm. In the next two sections, I consider how this constructionist nature of problem definition influences the development of solutions, and how family rituals are used in applying problem structures.

Solutions as Social Constructions

Our review of the literature found that much of the work on problem solving has focused on intelligence and creativity as factors that promote effective solutions. Other things being equal, more intelligence and creativity do probably lead to better solutions. But in the realm of family problem solving, "other things" are hardly ever equal. The social constructionist view of family problems suggests that those other things may be as important as IQ or creativity for solving family problems. This section considers some implications of our constructionist view for understanding solutions to family problems.

The constructionist perspective does not change the nature of solutions—which are, as described previously, changes in the family system that remove blocked goals or needs. The perspective, however, does provide some important detail on how those solutions come about. In the most popular rational model of family problem solving, a specific definition of a family problem and some brainstorming "naturally" generates at least one good approach to solving the problem. Effective implementation, or follow-through with that solution, perhaps with some minor adjustments, should solve the problem. The emphasis is on getting families to go through these stages. But there is no empirical basis for explaining why or how this phase model produces good solutions in family groups. Presumably, it is in the nature of human families to come up with good, adaptive solutions. That would be consistent with the adaptational theories of Darwin, Dewey, and the evolutionary psychologists. Although this is theoretically plausible, it does little to provide an understanding of *how* this takes place in the context of family problem solving. The details of that *how* are essential in verifying the theory, and for finding applications that can benefit families. Let us turn to some more of these details.

Two implications of the constructionist perspective will be presented. First, *solutions to family problems must fit the family system*. Second, *solutions to family problems depend on individual and family characteristics that promote negotiated consent*. These implications place constraints on the kinds of solutions that are proposed and the kind that will be effective. Most solutions to family problems are not brilliantly conceived deductions that come from a family member's penetrating insight. Nor are they immediately hailed as "the solution" by the entire family. Instead, they more typically are products of hashing over ongoing complaints through stonewalling, foot-dragging, and begrudging willingness to try doing something a little different. Creativity and insight are essential elements in getting the process going and for keeping it going through the inevitable quagmires and pitfalls. But their role in the process must be understood in the broader context of family systems.

Earlier, I demonstrated how family problems come to be defined in terms of key features of the family system. These include family rules, roles, power structure, and identities. The family paradigm and a set of problem structures further constrain how family problems are formulated. Consider the following example of the Smith family. The problem begins with an adult son-in-law's persistent complaint that his 80-year-old live-in mother-in-law is disrupting his marriage by taking too much of his wife's time. As a result of a combination of features of the family system, the problem comes to be formulated by the husband, wife, and their two teenage children. It is defined as the wife's 80-year-old mother having a demanding personality, and thus unrealistic expectations about her claims to her daughter's time and energy. Several elements of the family system constrained the ultimate form of this definition. (a) The Smith family paradigm holds that the Smiths are strong and independent individuals. Excessive dependency is disapproved. (b) The husband has the most power in the family because of his economic position and his social skills. (c) The family tends to use the scapegoat problem structure to define problems. (d) The mother role in the family focuses on care of children, not care of other kin. Other elements could be involved but these will suffice for the example.

Once a problem is defined within such a context, the options for solutions are quite limited. Many purely logical solutions are ruled out because they would create other problems for family members. For example, the husband could simply get a divorce and move out. But the family members want to keep the bonds linked to the marriage. Another potential solution could be to send the 80-year-old to a nursing home. But if the family cannot afford that, it is not really a possible solution.

These "impossible solutions" are often offered in jest during brainstorming, however.

More realistic solutions are evaluated within more detailed constraints. The wife might suggest that the husband spend more time with the teenage children, thus freeing her to care for her mother. The father may use his power to reject this option and his social skills to convince other family members that his mother-in-law's dependency is exaggerated and out of line. Other family characteristics would rule out other solutions.

After taking into account constraints of the family system, there are always some alternatives available. For example, the teenagers might be assigned to spend more time with their grandmother, thus allowing the wife to spend more time with the husband. Or the wife might simply place stricter limits on what she will do for her mother. Or respite care services might be used to provide temporary care for the mother. Creativity and social skills can be beneficial in coming up with a solution within the constraints that will actually work. If the relationship between the teenagers and the grandmother is already strained, the first solution might be difficult to implement.

Thus an important part of solving a problem is in understanding the constraints that were used in defining it. That makes it possible to propose solutions that will fit within the family system. All solutions require some, perhaps minor, change in the family system. An effective solution is one that makes the necessary change without disrupting other effective elements of the family system. A proposed solution that requires too much change will ultimately not be effective in providing a solution. This applies to any well-functioning family system.

In some cases, family systems are unhealthy and the family members would be better off if the family system changed radically, perhaps even breaking up altogether. In dealing with troubled families, family therapists may propose solutions that are intended to make major changes in the family system (e.g., Haley, 1987; Madanes, 1981). Such therapy techniques highlight the importance of solutions to family problems and their intimate link to basic family characteristics.

Cohesion and Social Skills
in Family Problem Solving

Understanding which possible solutions fit the constraints of the family system is one key to effective solutions. Getting family members to accept and apply solutions requires consideration of separate characteristics of the family and its individual members. In general terms, these characteristics could be referred to as *cohesion* and *social skills* (Aldous, 1971). They are features of the family that "grease the wheels" of social construction for both definitions and solutions to problems. Families with low levels of cohesion or social skills typically have difficulty formulating effective problem definitions and solutions.

Cohesion is the family-level characteristic (Olson, 1986) that represents the level of positive emotional bonding in the family. Families with healthy levels of cohesion have empathy for each other and have some understanding of why other family members have the viewpoints and feelings that they do. In addition, cohesion means that family members care about each other so that the tensions, frustrations, unmet needs, and well-being of other family members are taken into account in one's own actions. Cohesive families propose definitions and solutions for problems that consider the feelings and viewpoints of other family members. Thus initial definitions of problems by the person seeking change are tempered by concern for the others' reaction. Inflammatory personal attacks are avoided. Similarly, responses to initial complaints and problem definitions are tempered by the ability to perceive how that person might well feel that a problem exists (Forgatch & Patterson, 1989).

Cohesion fosters a more cooperative approach to defining and solving family problems. When it is lacking, these processes can become adversarial. In that case, definitions and solutions can be forced on family members through various types of coercion. Cohesion also increases the likelihood that there will be follow-through with solutions that emerge. Family members who believe that the solutions took their best interests, and the interests of the family, into account are more likely to help implement those solutions. When solutions are forced through coercion, follow-through is likely only to the extent that the powerful family members have surveillance over those less powerful.

It is well-known that cohesion can be excessive and lead to enmeshed family relationships (e.g., Olson, 1986). In such cases, there is too much empathy and family members are unable to recognize and act on their own unmet needs. They are too concerned with the needs of other family members. Codependent family relationships have this characteristic. Problem solving in enmeshed families may appear to be positive and productive, because enthusiastic support and agreement will lead to consensus on definitions and solutions. However, the problem solving mechanism is undermined from the beginning because the tensions, unmet needs, and blocked goals were not authentic. Some research has suggested that enmeshment sugarcoats family problem solving, and can have negative developmental consequences for children (Coughlin & Vuchinich, 1996).

Although cohesion provides an important foundation for effective problem solving, the communication and negotiation that must occur during the construction of definitions and solutions requires that some family members have a minimal level of social skills. At the most basic level, this refers to the ability to actively listen to what people say and interpret the meaning (Galvin & Brommel, 1996). It also includes the ability to clearly express one's own ideas and feelings. Such skills are usually taken for granted as rudimentary features of social competence that all people naturally acquire by middle childhood. However, family therapy, social work, and research on diverse populations have found that many families do not have a critical mass of socially competent members. Indeed, social competence requires a complex set of cognitive, affective, and behavioral orientations that must be developed (e.g., Selman et al., 1986). Without basic communication skills in place, the definition and solution of family problems is inhibited.

In the following example, two parents and their children (son aged 10, daughter aged 12) discuss the mother's complaint that the children leave their clothes on the floor. It shows several types of social competence in action during family problem solving.

1. Father *(to mother):* The problem is they put too much on the shelf. They need to take it [the clothes] up as it's done. And they need to take it up every day.
2. Mother: I've always said daily. That's kind of like, you know, after dinner take your clothes up. So it's just kind of like a routine . . .
3. Daughter: I pick mine up once a week.
4. Father: Well, every day.
5. Daughter: Heh heh heh. *(giggles, indicating she was making a joke previously)*
6. Father: There's no reason it can't be taken up every day.
7. Daughter: Uh huh.
8. Father *(to daughter):* Okay? Do you agree?
9. Daughter: Yeah.
10. Father *(turning to son):* Do you agree?
11. Son: Yep.
12. Father *(to son):* What's the consequences if it's not taken up every day?
13. Mother: That's what I'd like to know.
14. Father: You lose it.
15. Son: You lose what?
16. Father: The clothes.
17. Son: *(laughing)* No-o-o-o-o.

18. Mother *(to father touching his chin)*: No sir. You know what the consequences are? You're responsible for all the ironing in the basket.

19. Son: NO. No. No.

20. Daughter: Yeah. Yeah. *(laughing)*

21. Father *(to son)*: All you gotta do is take it up. It's not that hard. You go upstairs twenty times a day.

22. Mother *(to father)*: They think that the problem is ironing because they don't like to iron. SO that would be a great consequence. In fact, I'm (thinking about) using ironing as a consequence all summer because . . .

23. Father: Every day.

24. Son: I love ironing.

25. Father *(to son, laughing)*: Shoot. You're gonna love it a lot more cause you're gonna end up—Every day. SO the bottom line is that every day the clothes get picked up. *(to daughter)* Okay?

26. Daughter: Okay.

27. Father *(to son)*: Okay?

28. Son: Yeah.

This rather positive interaction includes several elements of social skills, humor, and family cohesion. For simplicity, I focus on some skills demonstrated by the father. For example, he solicits the approval of the new proposed family rule about picking up clothes from both children (numbers 8, 10, 25, and 27). Even though these are simple acts, they are important because he shows that he respects the children's viewpoint, and explicitly offers them the opportunity to disagree with the new rule or amend it. Although he is somewhat directive (number 1) and persistent, he also uses encouragement and reasoning to convince the children of the benefits of the rule. For example, in number 21 he points out to the son that picking up clothes is "not that hard," in part because the son goes upstairs "twenty times a day" anyway. In addition, he uses humor in responding to the children. In number 24 ("I love ironing"), the son jokingly disagrees with the mother's statement (number 22) that the children do not like ironing. The father responds to the son by laughingly agreeing with his statement and adding to his joke with "You're gonna love it more, cause you're gonna end up . . . [doing more]." The father was suggesting that the son would end up doing more ironing as a result of not picking up his clothes. Although this is not much of a joke, his response in kind to the son's joke is a supportive action that short-circuits any authoritarian implications that might be taken from the parents establishing a new family rule. Finally, the father persists in making clear statements on what the new rule is, and what the consequences of violating it are. The give and take of such family discussions often creates a challenge for maintaining a focus on the basic issues at hand and creating specific outcomes. Providing summary statements and soliciting the approval of these statements from others requires considerable skill.

Beyond the basic skill level, there are more advanced social skills that promote effective definitions and solutions. Most pertinent is the ability to negotiate opposing viewpoints to generate agreement and compromise (e.g., Selman et al., 1986). The early experimental research on small groups often referred to the natural emergence of a social–emotional leader who managed the emotional well-being of the group to promote agreement and compromise (e.g., Bales & Slater, 1955). Although that model is perhaps too simplistic to apply to families (e.g., Steinhauer, 1989), it was nonetheless the first research to show what is now an undisputed finding: that group members do take on distinct roles during problem solving.

The intricate nature of family relationships and personalities that emerge during problem solving are beyond any simple classification. However, it is clear from my observations that some family members have exceptional skills in encouraging and orchestrating the social construction of problem definitions and solutions. Klein and Hill (1979) have addressed some elements of these skills in their discussion of how the characteristics of one family member can greatly expand the family's problem solving effectiveness. Elaborating the nature of these complex skills is beyond the scope of this presentation. But some family members are able to draw out the cohesive and cooperative elements of family members and negotiate solutions that tend to be applied. Most families, of course, do not have negotiation "superstars" in them. But the extent that even one member has such skills can greatly increase the effectiveness of family problem solving.

Ritual in Family Problem Solving

Proposing solutions that fit the family system, and having the skills to get consensus on applying them, are two features of problem solving brought into focus through the constructionist perspective. These features show how solutions to family problems are constrained. Although these constraints are important, this perspective says little about *when,* in the social ecology of family life, these constructions, constraints, and skills go into operation. Weick's (1971) landmark paper made fun of the image of the family gathering around the fireplace to engage in "problem solving." He wondered when, and even if, that ever really happened. Unfortunately, there is little more data on that question today than there was then. I will not attempt to redress that gap here. But our observations of family dinners and problem solving situations have led to one conclusion. Key elements of family problem solving are organized in terms of rituals. These rituals provide locations in the family ecosystem for problem solving to take place, and provide some structure for the family interactions that occur during that time.

Rituals are often thought of in terms of relatively infrequent religious or cult-like ceremonies that evoke images of rigid behavior patterns with some special symbolic significance. Although these are pertinent exemplars, elements of ritual organization are involved in a much broader range of human, and especially, family behavior. Erving Goffman (1967, 1971, 1981) showed how ritual was a central organizing principle in several fundamental components of face-to-face interaction. Bossard and Boll (1950) were the first to show how important rituals were for family life. More recent work in family studies (Fiese, 1992; Imber-Black et al., 1988; Wolin et al., 1979) and family therapy (Madanes, 1981) have clarified the important implications of ritual organization in the family context. With this work as background, our interest is in pointing out some ways that ritual organization functions in family problem solving.

Why should rituals have anything to do with family problem solving? The main reason is that symbolic constructions such as social groups (e.g., families) must be actively maintained in order to survive. Human existence is filled with opportunities for distraction and random behavior. Once social order is created through groups and other mechanisms, it is necessary to continue to maintain the symbolic structures and the dutiful participation of members. In a nutshell, that is what rituals do. They organize the behavior of members and provide regular, structured emotional experiences that reaffirm the value of the group for the members. Thus when a church member participates in a communion ritual, its purpose is to reaffirm the value of the church and the member's commitment to it (Durkheim, 1926). There are ritual features of family problem solving that similarly affirm the value of the family.

Not all families use rituals in solving problems. Indeed, some families never solve problems at all. But I have found that many families do use ritual elements in problem solving. Because of limited sampling, these observations should be taken as initial steps toward a grounded theory of family problem solving. I want ultimately to suggest that the popular rational phase model for family problem solving can be most effective when some of the phases are ritualized. Indeed, this may be seen as one implicit goal of having regular family meetings (Dreikurs, 1948; Forgatch & Patterson, 1989).

Rituals have numerous interesting characteristics and come in many shapes and sizes. For our concerns, I focus on three primary properties. First, there is a structured sequence of actions that occurs in the same order each time the ritual is performed. Second, the sequence of actions has a specific meaning that is basically the same at each performance.

Third, the meaning includes the expression of respect or affective attachment to a valued symbol. These properties are easily seen in the communion ritual. They can also be seen in the way some families organize their dinners. Consider a family that holds hands and has a moment of silence before dinner as a gesture of togetherness. It is a sequence that is repeated. It has the same meaning each time. And it expresses attachment to the family: a valued ongoing symbolic structure. Many more aspects of family dinners can be ritualized. In fact, the entire preparation and aftermath of dinner can have ritual elements. However, the most extensive ritualizations are usually saved for the special occasions such as Thanksgiving or Christmas in American society.

Rituals provide family members with regular opportunities to make connections with each other. These include the husband–wife obligatory hug and kiss greeting, the parent–child "How was school today?" questioning sequence, the sibling dispute over who gets the last chicken leg, and so on. Ritual organization extends to more serious matters. A parent and child, as mentioned earlier, may have a "What's bothering you?" ritual in which the child signals that he or she is experiencing some difficulty and the parent proceeds to draw out the description in an extended sequence that ultimately ends in the parent comforting the stressed child. Marital sexual behavior may also have ritual components. And there are many other examples.

This classification of more serious family rituals includes three that are especially relevant for problem solving. These rituals can play an essential part in the successful functioning of the phases of problem solving that have been studied for many years. Two of them are linked to problem structures described previously. The first is a *complaint ritual* in which one family member makes a complaint against another family member or some part of the family system. In this ritual, the complaint is followed by denial or a countercomplaint, and that sequence is then extended again and again. Gottman (1979) has labeled this pattern *cross-complaining* in the marital context.

This ritual is frequently seen in conflict-ridden families. The meaning repeated is that "we don't get along." The symbol given homage is the barrier between the participants. Goffman (1971) distinguished positive rituals that affirm bonds that connect members from negative rituals that reaffirm important boundaries between members. The *complaint ritual* is a negative ritual that affirms the self and the boundary between self and other. This ritual can stop problem solving before it begins because it precludes any validation of the other's feelings or agreement on a definition of the problem. Viewing these sequences as rituals provides an explanation for why family members go on and on in meaningless, irrational attacks on each other. They must tirelessly defend the symbolic self against perceived challenges from other family members.

A second, more positive family ritual is a *validation ritual* in which a complaint or proposal by one family member is followed by an acceptance by another. As described earlier, this validation is an essential step in defining something as a family problem. The acceptance means that the complaint or proposal is acknowledged as having value and is worthy of consideration. This sequence has ritual elements because, when it operates, the validation response is made regardless of how ridiculous, unpleasant, or illogical the complaint or proposal is perceived to be. The meaning conveyed is that the individual making the complaint or proposal is a worthy person. He or she has a right to have viewpoints, feelings, and so on acknowledged. The acceptance displays respect for that person and respect for a family unit that at least acknowledges its members' viewpoints and feelings. This ritual is important as a basis for both presenting problems for consideration and for brainstorming (e.g., Forgatch and Patterson, 1989). Both of those processes require family members to accept, without criticism, whatever is presented regardless of the implications for oneself, which may be negative. Ritualization transforms the meaning of the actions from the level of individual defensiveness to the level of family maintenance. The practical importance of validation is well-known in the family communication literature (e.g., Galvin & Brommel, 1996). Ritualization provides an explanation of how some families develop validation sequences naturally. Validation does not mean that everyone agrees that what was said is accurate or appropriate. It means that the person is a family member who has a right to have his or her viewpoint heard.

The *selection ritual* is a third mechanism families use in solving problems. It begins with the presentation of two or more options for the solution to a problem that has been defined. This is followed by proposals either to delete, accept, or amend a specific option. The selection ritual cycles through evaluations of these proposals. After several cycles, a proposal to accept one of the solutions is approved.

The following example is from a family doing a problem solving session at home. Two parents and two daughters, 10 (D10) and 12 (D12) years old, discuss the children's bedtime. The daughters want to stay up later than their current bedtime.

1. D10: I think I should stay up later. I think I should be able to stay up later. At least I'm in bed. If I'm in bed, I can stay up a little later . . . as long as I'm still in bed.

2. Mother: What do you mean? I'm not sure I understand.

3. D12: You can do anything, er stay up as late as you can, as long as you are in bed.

4. Mother: Oh.

5. D10: No, not as late . . . about a half an hour later . . . than I usually go to bed. Like 8:00 . . . usually in the summer it's more than 8:00.

6. Mother: So yer sayin' that if if . . . if I said it was time to go to bed at 9:00 that as long as you were IN BED you should be able to keep the light on and read or play Legos or something 'til 9:30?

7. D12: You cannot get out of bed. Like you were goin' to sleep.

8. Mother *(to D12):* And you agree with that?

9. D12: Yes.

10. Mother: Well, why can't I just have you go to bed a half-hour earlier. Have you go to bed at 8:30 and then you can do that . . .

11. D12: I don't like that.

12. Mother: Hah, hah.

13. Father: Hah, hah.

14. Mother: But the fact is that I'm responsible for making sure you get a certain amount of sleep at night.

15. D12: But what if "Star Trek" is like an extra special er something and it goes on 'til our bedtime. Wull, we don't want to miss a half an hour of it.

16. Mother: Uh huh.

17. D12: And we don't feel like taping it because I like seeing it all at one time.

18. Mother: Um huhm.

19. D12: Unless you feel like taping the whole thing which you don't have to do—you don't have to.

20. Mother: Hummm. I'm all . . . I will be honest, I am all for you having some time to read in bed.

21. D10: It doesn't matter what time I start. At least it's not like kindergartners, 7:00.

22. Mother: Right.

23. D10: 7:30. Like 8:00. Like maybe 8:00, 8:30, 9:00 er somethin'.

24. Mother: Yes.

25. D10: As long as I'm in bed. Not as long as I want. Maybe for a half an hour.

26. Mother and Father *(simultaneously):* HUHMMMMMMM.

27. Mother: Well, Susan.

28. Father: Well, if you really just want to lay there and read er something, why can't you just go in there at 2:00 in the afternoon or sometime during the day.

29. D12: We're in school.

30. Father: No. We're talkin' about summer time right now. Not school time, right?

31. D12: It is school time.

32. Father: Well, it's summer now so let's talk about it right now. Why can't you do that, Susan?

33. D10: Do what?

34. Father: Take a . . . if you want to read for a half hour in bed, then go at 2:00 in the afternoon.

35. D10: We've got better things to do.

36. D12: That's our free time.

37. Father *(several turns later):* . . . There's a TIME for everything. Okay. Like when it's TIME for bed. Whenever that time is, then it's time for bed. Time to turn the light off and go to sleep. That's bedtime. Otherwise, it could just stretch out for ever and ever and there's no real . . . you end up doing whatever you feel like doing 'til however long you feel like doing it. And we simply can't allow that. We're responsible for providing some structure . . . some guidelines and some set things for you. NOW, if you would like to stay up a little bit later than you're doin' in the summer time, then maybe we can do that. Maybe you can stay up later. But what I'm sayin' is that at some point, and I'm not sure what time that is, that's when it's bedtime—it's time to turn off the light and go to sleep. [After further discussion, the daughters were given a later bedtime during the summer]

In this example, the family considers several options for a new bedtime for the daughters. This was perceived as a problem by both daughters, and they quickly proposed, and amended, a new family rule (numbers 1 through 5) that would have solved the problem, in their view. In number 6, the mother clearly states her understanding of their proposal, which the girls validate. The parents are reluctant to accept the new rule and suggest that it is not necessary because the girls can read in bed at any time. However, the daughters counter that position because school and their other activities prevent them from reading in the afternoon.

The mother seems to be on the verge of accepting the new rule when the father takes sides with the mother and pursues her position even further. He evokes a parental right to set rules (number 37), but provides an explanation based on the responsibility of parents to provide for the well-being of the children. Ultimately, the parents did not allow the daughters to read after their bedtime, but they did make the summer bedtime a half hour later than it was when the discussion started. This may be seen as a compromise in which both the parents and the daughters get something they wanted. The parents got their bedtime rule clarified and avoided the difficulties inherent in a rule that allowed the children to read after they went to bed. The daughters got their bedtime moved back a half hour.

The selection ritual is in evidence as more than one option is considered, and several proposals are made to amend, justify, reject, and accept them. The ritual element operating in the example is the sustained willingness of the family members to continue to entertain proposals, amendments, and justifications. Reasoning, logic, and rational rhetoric are woven into this sequence of events. But it is the sequential structure of proposing alternatives and then selecting one that organizes this interchange. This structure is followed in the face of often poorly formulated options, discussing them through some unconvincing justifications, and then selecting one with little apparent logic that, in fact, makes a trivial change in family rules. Fragments of rationality do appear in this interchange. But rationality does not govern the process or outcome. This family has obviously used such a ritual before, and will probably use it again. In some respects, their entire discussion might be considered as being quite trivial, with little at stake, and with little meaningful outcome. After all, how important is a half-hour change in the bedtime of two preadolescents? But the selection ritual affirms that this family can, as a group, work through the problems of its members. And beyond that, their coordinated actions and affective expressions create a symbolic representation of the family unit itself.

This ritual is often the key to what is usually referred to as the evaluation phase in family problem solving. The term *evaluation* implies that rational calculation is at the basis of this phase and that family members rationally weigh pros and cons of each option. I suggest that rational evaluation is only a rhetorical metaphor in most families. Following the observations of Simon, March, and others on the limits of rationality (March & Simon, 1958; Simon, 1956), I propose that true rational evaluation is impossible because precise, objective values for pros and cons of the options do not exist. Instead, family members are seeking to construct sufficient consent that one option should be tried. The ritual requires that several be discussed and that one solution be selected. The repeated sequence carries the meaning that all family members contribute to the selection. The ultimate selection displays attachment to the symbolic unified family. In that respect, the ritual is similar to holding hands before dinner.

Can a ritualized process arrive at good family decisions? It can if the ritual is conducted within the constraints described and the family members have the appropriate characteristics. A primary advantage of the selection ritual is that family members will tend to accept and apply the solution because it has been ritually approved. So, following through on the solution displays one's connection to the family. Of course, the selection ritual must also be bounded by the rational limits of common sense. But efforts at more strict adherence to rigorous rational criteria for evaluation are probably pointless. Family problems and solutions cannot be reduced to a precise calculus of costs and benefits.

These ritual components can be extended to create larger ritual occasions. Of most interest is the family meeting, which, as discussed earlier, has been part of the parent education literature for 50 years (Dreikurs, 1948). Although the family meeting has the appearance of and some formal elements of a business meeting (Dinkmeyer & McKay,

1989; Forgatch & Patterson, 1989), the key to its functioning are the rituals described previously. This is an important fact because efforts at using strictly rational methods will fail without the rituals in place to make the meetings work. In most applications, only the rational shell of these meetings are addressed. This will be considered in more detail in chapter 6.

Summary

In this chapter, I have offered some new ways of thinking about family problems and solutions. Three principles were proposed. First, *family problems are social constructions.* Second, *solutions to problems must fit, and adjust to, the family system.* And third, *family rituals structure the emergence of, and the solution to, family problems.* The purpose has been to describe patterns and suggest a direction of inquiry, rather than report on conclusive findings. Our interpretation of prior work pointed out some fundamental flaws in the available theories. These flaws are too basic to be repaired within the currently prevalent theoretical context. Our approach to a remedy is to go back to the raw data of normal family life and pursue an inductive, qualitative analysis strategy. The three principles can be used to begin building theory (Glaser & Straus, 1967) or to generate hypotheses that are subject to empirical test. Ultimately, these principles might be reconciled with elements of the rational model. But at the heart of the effort is the consideration of family problem solving *without presupposing the rational model.* Observations should allow families to demonstrate that they are behaving rationally. The ultimate scientific status of these observations will depend on replications, whether these structures can be organized into useful concepts and principles, and whether they promote a better understanding of family problem solving for researchers, practitioners, and families.

At one level, an inductive analysis of family problem solving may be viewed as yet another approach to a topic that has already seen many interesting approaches. But from another perspective, it has a greater significance. It offers a new way of testing and perhaps amending a paradigm that may be seriously flawed. As was shown in chapter 3, the rational paradigm has come to dominate most research and practice in family problem solving. Although this has served to organize and simplify thinking about a complex process, it also may conceptualize essential elements of that process out of existence. For example, if problem solving is fundamentally rational, then it really does not matter from where the problems come. In the next chapter, key features of the rational model are examined in detail.

5

The Rational Model and Beyond

The concept of family problem solving is laden with positive value. It is a concept that most people would probably say is a good thing. Although it does not hold the revered status of "God, Mother, and Apple Pie," it might well hold a solid position in the second echelon of indisputably virtuous things. This status is derived from the value usually attached to "the family" in American culture. If families have problems, then they should be solved to protect the valued object. Family problem solving also carries with it the problem solving component that is closely associated with rationality. Of course, rationality is also a highly valued concept in American culture. Thus the topic of this book has a double dose of cultural value.

An interesting feature of culturally valued concepts is that their truth and desirability are accepted without the need for proof. A functionalist (Parsons, 1951) would maintain that such valued concepts are essential to preserve the social order. Regardless of their basis, valued concepts enjoy a favored status compared to concepts without such associations. Because of this status, people are more likely to accept the viability of a concept such as family problem solving than they are to accept a concept such as the role of conflict, bounded rationality, or triangulation. Valued concepts get passed from generation to generation without proof of their accuracy. Even though positivistic science is supposed to be objective and value free, researchers and theorists are humans and have always been influenced by their cultural values.

I raise these points to entertain the possibility that the concept of rational family problem solving has been so widely disseminated and accepted, in part, because it embodies two American values: family and rationality. This means that the model of rational family problem solving may well be fundamentally flawed, even though it is widely accepted. Of course, a concept can be valued and true at the same time. Ideally, value-free scientific methods can test for truth, independent of the cultural value attached to the concept. But in the real world, values often surreptitiously creep into scientific tests. Scientific work on family problem solving is a prime candidate for such bias.

In light of these concerns, this chapter reassesses the rational model of family problem solving. I consider the strength of the empirical evidence that supports it, the methods used to test it, and propose some new approaches to understanding it. But the reader should be forewarned about the reasoning that will be applied. When a single paradigm becomes as dominant as the rational model has been, research from alternative perspectives is scant. There are few studies that even consider alternative models. It could be argued that the reason for this is that no other models are as correct as the rational model. Although plausible, there are equally plausible alternative explanations. The one advanced in this chapter is that the rational model has generated supportive scientific findings in a very narrow domain: mostly structured tasks in laboratory or clinical settings. Part of that success has been a result of the narrow domain that has been examined empirically. Success within that domain has stimulated further work along that line, to the exclusion of alternative models. The logic seems to have been, "why try other models when the rational one seems to do fairly well?" This reasoning is convincing. But the history of science shows that it can lead research down the garden path (Kuhn, 1970).

Evolution is an adaptive process of change in response to features of the environment. This process has been observed in plants, animals, humans, and human groups (e.g., Wilson, 1975). The opposite process is *involution* in which the organism or group does not make adaptive changes but instead continues to create increasingly complex ways of doing exactly what it has been doing all along (e.g., Geertz, 1970). This preoccupation makes any adaptation to changes in the environment impossible. The organism becomes a closed system. The organism may survive, as long as there are no substantial changes in the environment. However, when such changes occur, as they inevitably do, the organism cannot make the necessary adjustments and perishes. The rational model may be an organism that has lapsed into an involutionary process. Its paradigm accepts only information from structured tasks with presupposed concrete problems to be solved. Studies of such tasks continue to be propagated in endless variations. But the model is relatively closed to information about other elements of problem solving. It survives in part because its environment has maintained a steady state and it has enjoyed a dominant position in that environment. It will continue to thrive unless its environment changes. Such changes could potentially come about through findings from evolutionary psychology or social constructionism. Though such speculations could be pursued, the purpose of raising the involution analogy is to invite some new ways of thinking about the rational model.

The value of the research in favor of the rational model should certainly not be discounted. Aspects of it are bound to be correct for certain family contexts, and it has earned its dominant status through diligent application of the scientific method. But open scientific inquiry requires that alternative models be considered even as a dominant model is actively pursued. In the case of family problem solving, I propose that the rational model provides only a partial explanation of family problem solving.

The tactics applied in this chapter are conceptual rather than empirical in nature. Conclusive empirical proof for an alternative model is not provided. Instead, a critical evaluation of the research designs and ecological validity of most studies of family problem solving will be the focus of attention. Design and validity issues in this research tradition that have rarely been addressed, and that have been largely taken for granted, are highlighted. These issues have been raised in previous work (Aldous, 1971; Aldous & Ganey, 1989; Vuchinich et al., 1991; Weick, 1971). They will be pursued further in this chapter because they have great significance for how family problem solving is conceptualized and how it should be studied in the future. Consideration of these issues may serve to expand the viability of the rational model, as well as suggest complementary alternate approaches.

The review in chapters 2 and 3 traced the historical development of the rational model of family problem solving dating back to Dewey's early formulations (1910/1982). It has been described in several sources (e.g., Kieren et al., 1996; Klein & Hill, 1979). Although there are variations, the focus of the model is on the phases families and other small groups sometimes go through in the process of solving problems. The following is a typical list of the phases:

1. Define the problem.
2. Generate alternative possible solutions.
3. Evaluate the alternative solutions.
4. Select one solution to implement.
5. Follow through with the solution and adjust it if necessary.

These are the basic *elements* of family problem solving according to the rational model. They specify the fundamental components and the order in which they occur. The ordering of the *phases* provides an organizing format for the problem solving process.

Human Groups, Families, and the Rational Model

Dewey (1910/1982) developed the rational model to describe a thought process in individuals. There is little doubt that such a process is used by human individuals, at least part of the time. Reflection on personal experience and observations of others can readily produce some evidence for this. But whether such a process governs small group problem solving is not at all apparent. The group problem solving studies cited in chapters 2 and 3 demonstrated that the group context sets in motion some entirely different processes (e.g., power, conflict, conformity, leadership, affiliation, influence, coalitions) that may explain more of how problems are solved than Dewey's rational process. Efforts to take such processes into account have taken a variety of forms. The concept of the social–emotional leader (Bales & Slater, 1955) was one approach. Other efforts have described specific group factors that promote poor decisions. For example, the concept of "groupthink" was used to capture a process that includes perceived unanimity, pressure to stifle dissent, high confidence level, and belief in the morality of the group (Janis, 1967). Janis claimed that groupthink was the basis for the decision to escalate the war in Vietnam and other American foreign policy blunders. Some of that work indicated that small groups, especially those in formal organizations, try to be rational (Simon, 1956). But such trying explains only one part, perhaps a minor part, of how groups go about solving problems.

It is certainly noteworthy that humans often *try* to use Dewey's rational process. But even a brief consideration of the small group research reveals the inadequacy of the rational model for small group problem solving. It is probably even less likely to be an adequate model for problem solving in family groups. Chapter 1 described the affective and structural features of families that distinguish them from other small groups. Family problem solving involves more intense emotional expressions, greater power differentials (e.g., parent vs. child), and more persistent change and long-term patterns than other small groups. These factors can wreak havoc in any of the phases of rational problem solving.

Consider the simplest phase: Define the problem. This is an essential step because it allows the family members to focus on one topic as the focus of problem solving efforts. But assume a father and adolescent son have been feuding for weeks about the son not doing his assigned chores around the house. We are all familiar with such ongoing family conflicts that may simmer for months. Let us assume that the mother sits down with father and son to try to iron out the problem.

Mother: Okay, what's the problem?

Father: He never does his chores anymore. He just lays around and watches TV. He's not pulling his weight around here.

Son: I do as much as you do. I'm not a slave. It's like . . . Ahh! Whatever. *(The discussion deteriorates into further father–son conflict, and the son finally storms out of the room in a huff)*

The father–son conflict prevents any single problem from being defined, and thus derails the entire problem solving process. Such events can happen in any kind of small group, but the close interdependent nature of family life make them a fundamental feature of family problem solving. This nature affects all the problem solving phases. For example, even if a problem is defined and alternatives are generated, picking the "best" is often another locus of conflict, emotional outbursts, power relations, coalitions, and so on. Even if a "solution" is agreed on, follow-through may be totally ignored.

Certain family constructs may be primary features of family problem solving. For example, a cohesive family has emotional bonds that motivate resolution of difficulties for the benefits of other family members and the group as a whole. Problem definitions, alternative solutions, evaluation, and follow-through may all occur naturally in a cohesive family. But they may be impossible in a family without cohesion. If such family features as cohesion, trust, and open communication are absolutely essential for problem solving, then the following question must be raised: Are some of these features part of the problem solving itself? As was noted in chapter 1, such features (e.g., cohesion) have usually been considered separate from the problem solving process. However, some researchers have found it necessary to include family features beyond Dewey's phases within a conceptualization of family problem solving phenomena. Olson's circumplex model (1986), for example, acknowledged cohesion and adaptability as two primary dimensions of family functioning. Adaptability was a family characteristic that encompassed problem solving and other family features such as flexibility.

One might maintain that these various family processes and structures are conceptually separate from the problem solving process. Such processes and structures should be taken into account, but only as adjunct elements that impinge on problem solving itself. That is a viable theoretical position and reflects the way the rational model is typically used. It is conceptually convenient and consistent with prevailing paradigms. But the accumulating mixed research support for the model, and the persistent challenges from researchers who look outside of the laboratory context, simply cannot be ignored. It is possible that the strict separation of rational and other family processes is a fatally flawed concept. To pursue that possibility requires considering ways that purely rational and other family processes work together.

Thus far, this has been done in a piecemeal fashion. In one realm, effective clinical training materials in family problem solving typically spend as much time on the nonrational processes as they do on the rational processes (e.g., Dinkmeyer & McKay, 1989; Forgatch & Patterson, 1989; Kendall, 1991; Robin & Foster, 1989). For example, Forgatch and Patterson (1989) provided elaborate detail on how to "present" and "receive" complaints, issues, and so on, while defining a problem. Their instructions seek to avoid the kind of conflicts that are typical when families try to define problems. The need to adjust the rational model has become even more theoretically apparent in integrative analyses such as Robin and Foster's (1989) behavioral–family systems approach to parent–adolescent conflict. Such work adds further credence to previous studies that have called for a reconceptualization of family problem solving (e.g., Aldous, 1971; Aldous & Ganey, 1989; Klein & Hill, 1979; Reiss, 1981; Weick, 1971).

The impetus for chapter 4 was that problem solving, cohesion, trust, and so on are all reified abstractions that give only a partial picture of family problem solving. These concepts have a long history and make good conceptual sense within the prevailing paradigms. They have provided researchers and practitioners a way of making sense of what families do. They have offered a way of seeing order in a swirling arena of family life. They have afforded some much-needed concreteness in the shifting sands of family problem solving. But the emerging awareness of flaws in the rational model suggests that there is more to this phenomenon than these constructs can capture. One strategy for finding out what concepts might be needed is to use inductive tactics on a raw form of data. Some steps along that line were taken in chapter 4. Such a constructionist approach might ultimately verify the rational model or discover concepts that complement it or seriously challenge it. In chapter 4, some patterns consistent with the rational model were found (e.g., selection ritual). But these were embedded in elements outside the rational model (e.g., ritual). The outcome of such investigations is not known. The key issue is that a constructionist approach may find concepts that integrate the rational model with family constructs.

Thus far, a viable model that integrates the rational and family processes has not yet been established, though some promising proposals have been made (e.g., Klein & Hill, 1979; Olson, 1986). The future will undoubtedly see further efforts to supplement, adjust, reject, revise, and reformulate the rational model of family problem solving. This book is an effort in that direction. But as such work proceeds, it is important to fully understand the methodological foundations of the rational model. Those foundations have been a basis for the growth and acceptance of the model. But those foundations are also at the core of its pervasive limitations. In this chapter these limitations are examined, along with strategies for overcoming them.

The Scope of the Rational Model
of Family Problem Solving

One issue is paramount in any assessment of the rational model. That is the scope of the model. How much of what phenomena is this model supposed to explain? It has been used to represent two different phenomena. First, it has been used to describe the way normal families solve their problems. This use of the model has broad scope because it covers such a wide variety of families and situations. Second, the rational model has been used as a basis for components of treatment for troubled families and children. The thrust of these applications is to train troubled families to use the rational phases so that some of their negative symptoms will be reduced. This application of the model has a much more narrow scope because it includes only troubled families and focuses on whether or not their negative symptoms are reduced.

In assessing the broad-scope application, a key question is: Does the rational model explain how normal families solve the problems that come up in their lives? The fact is that, despite 50 years of research, no study has ever tested the rational model on a representative sample of any large population. Most of the research has been on small, convenience samples of families in laboratory situations. On this basis alone, one might well conclude that the evidence supporting the broad-scope application is marginal at best. Indeed, the view that the rational model does not apply to most families has been voiced for decades (e.g., Aldous, 1971; Weick, 1971).

Rational problem solving may be beneficial for troubled and other families even if it does not describe what most families do. Dewey originally presented his model as a description of how people *should* think, not how most of them actually do. One goal of his work in education was to promote rational thinking. Furthermore, the most influential applications of the rational model to family problem solving (e.g., Alexander & Parsons, 1973; Forgatch & Patterson, 1989; Robin & Foster, 1989; Shure & Spivack, 1978) have developed through a therapeutic paradigm (D'Zurilla & Goldfried, 1971). The criteria for assessing the rational model in this context must focus on whether its application helps families. As was seen in chapter 3, there is ample evidence that such applications do have some beneficial effects. These will be pursued further in chapter 6.

With convincing evidence supporting the limited-scope version of the rational model, let us consider the broader-scope version: Does the rational model describe how families *normally* solve their problems? The research results from the rational model have always been somewhat mixed. For example, studies have found that some families do have phases in their problem solving consistent with the rational model (e.g., Bales & Strodtbeck, 1951; Gottman, 1979; Kieren et al., 1996). But these same studies also show that families often do not follow these phases. The limits of the rational model have led to a persistent series of analyses that directly challenge the rational model (e.g., Aldous, 1971; Aldous & Ganey, 1989; Simon, 1956; Vuchinich, 1990; Weick, 1971). However, a coherent paradigm to replace the rational model did not emerge. These critiques, along with inconclusive empirical results, suggest the extent to which the rational model explains the way most families function is still very much an open question. In the rest of this chapter, this question is examined in terms of some basic research issues.

The Tyranny of 20-Minute Problem Solving

One reason the rational model has dominated empirical research on family problem solving is that it can be conveniently examined within the context of well-established theory and methods in the behavioral sciences. It is assumed, for example, that observing a family trying to "solve a problem" in 10 or 20 minutes is a legitimate way of gathering data about family problem solving. Concerns about the external validity of such data, noted in chapter 3, are sometimes acknowledged, but are relegated to a minor paragraph or footnote. Experiments of this kind, and the way the rational model conceptualizes them, are an efficient way of reducing a very complex set of phenomena down to a manageable set of procedures and analytic techniques. Indeed, these studies may be considered as examples of good science because of their adherence to standards of precision, measurement, and statistical analysis. This has helped the rational model to garner the stamp of approval of prevailing science. But if the rational model is fundamentally flawed, its utility for producing better applications will ultimately be strictly limited and perhaps dangerously misleading.

One of the most important limitations of the rational model is its dependence on the time-limited problem solving task. The well-known advantage is that it is a practical way to get data on problem solving. But the disadvantage is that it may prevent researchers from ever finding out how family problem solving usually occurs. How many studies have rigorously tested the rational model of family problem solving in ordinary family behavior at home? To my knowledge the answer is *zero*. Such an enterprise would have to find families solving problems at home. As Weick (1971) observed, we do not even know if or when it ever really happens. The interesting point is that if one takes away the artificial procedure universally used for testing the rational model, one may not be able to find the phenomenon of interest. This casts some doubt on the model itself. Evidence for an accurate model should be available from more than just one artificial research procedure. This does not disprove the rational model, but does suggest that it may stand on some shaky ground.

Consider further the hazards of dependence on the time-limited problem solving task. I know of no empirical evidence that *any* family has ever gone through all the hypothesized phases of problem solving in the routine home environment. This presents a major challenge to the rational model. The tendency to gingerly acknowledge, but largely ignore, this external validity issue is part of the dominant research paradigm. If the rational model cannot be tested on routine family behavior in the home, then it can never be verified.

What would it take to do such tests? Many of the techniques used in the laboratory procedures can be applied to family behavior in the home. For example, one of the primary techniques in testing the rational model has always been the coding of verbal behavior (e.g., Bales & Strodtbeck, 1951; Kieren et al., 1996). From videotapes, audiotapes, or direct observation, statements by family members are assigned codes by trained objective observers. These codes represent the function or intent of the comment (e.g., makes suggestion, gives support, disagreement, etc.). Predictions about what kinds of statements should occur in what phases can be derived from the rational model (e.g., disagreements should occur in the evaluation phases after the problem has been defined). Statistical comparisons of the predicted and observed pattern of statements allows a test of the rational model (Kieren et al., 1996). Such techniques could be applied to family behavior at home as well as family behavior in the lab. They have been applied in studying other aspects of family interaction (e.g., Vuchinich, 1986, 1987). In terms of the coding itself, assessments of the rational model in the home setting should be straightforward. Once the family behavior is recorded on audio- or videotape, the measurement procedure can be the same for the home or the lab.

In Search of Family Problem Solving
in the Home

However, getting appropriate home observations raises a different, and quite thorny, research issue. When can a family be observed or taped "in the act" of problem solving at home? There is virtually no systematic empirical work on this question, in part because it lies outside of the prevailing paradigm. Simple logic dictates that family members would have to be able to communicate in order to do problem solving. Thus those times and places in the family's home ecology when communication can occur would be occasions when home problem solving might be expected to take place. The expanding research on family time together (e.g., Daly, 1996) can be useful in finding home family problem solving to study. But pursuing this ecological line of inquiry leads to additional complexity. Does family problem solving take place when only two family members are involved? Does family problem solving take place in telephone calls between family members or through notes stuck to the refrigerator? Pondering how to systematically include such variations empirically is enough to make most researchers long for the comfort and security of the 20-minute problem solving session in the lab. Though the challenge is substantial, progress on such issues has considerable potential for expanding the current understanding of family problem solving.

Much of the research on family interaction in the home has taken advantage of one ecological niche: the family dinner (e.g., Vuchinich, 1986, 1987, 1990). This setting brings several family members together at one time around a table that facilitates audio or video recordings with good sound quality. The dinner, furthermore, is also a regular part of most families' lives, though not always on a daily basis. Thus the situation has some ecological validity (Bronfenbrenner, 1979; Vuchinich et al., 1991). It is known that conflicts do spontaneously occur during dinners (e.g., Gottman, 1979; Vuchinich, 1987, 1990). But the question of whether rational problem solving occurs during dinner has only been considered tangentially (Vuchinich, 1987).

The research on family dinners in the home at least demonstrates that systematic analysis can be done in ecologically valid home settings. But it is unlikely that most family problem solving occurs during dinner. Whether problem solving during dinner is representative of problem solving in other home settings is an open question. Thus observations in other home settings would be needed. From a technical standpoint, this presents no insurmountable problems. With appropriate informed consent, it is entirely feasible to audio- and videotape every room in a home 24 hours a day. This is a hypothetical extreme and there is little point in having hours of tapes of empty rooms. Appropriate times and places for taping could easily be sampled. For some, any kind of home taping conjures up negative images of Big Brother and unethical invasion of privacy.

But many families feel they have nothing to hide and have few reservations about being taped. Researchers have created apartments wired for videotaping and had couples or family groups live in them for extended periods (e.g., Gottman, 1994). Other researchers have left recording equipment in homes over long periods of time (Christensen & Hazzard, 1983; Vuchinich et al., 1996). Such studies have shown that families are not harmed by these procedures. This was a concern because being observed could theoretically induce stress or other negative reactions.

Another concern was subject reactivity, which refers to the possibility that the taping procedures create behavior patterns in the research participants that are different from their "normal" behaviors. Of course, such reactivity biases are also possible, and perhaps more serious, in the laboratory observations of family problem solving. In any event, research on the home setting found that, after an adjustment period, there is negligible reactivity to the taping (e.g., Christensen & Hazzard, 1983). Family members apparently tend to get used to taping equipment when it is in the home over time. The home is their environment, and interaction patterns in it have developed over many years. The addition of some taping equipment in the background (especially if it is small and blends into the physical setting) is not a sufficiently powerful force to significantly change the family (Vuchinich et al., 1991).

This issue got attention in the 1970s when professionally made films of the Loud family home life were shown on a national television series ("An American Family," Public Broadcasting System) in 12 hour-long segments. Two filmmakers were present during all of the filming, which took place over a year. During that period Mr. and Mrs. Loud got a divorce, and some suggested that the taping contributed to the divorce. A Hollywood movie ("Real Life"), an effective comedy, was made loosely based on the Loud family experience. This was one of the more flamboyant episodes in the history of taping family life at home. Though it had little systematic research value, it raised a specter of doubt about the advisability of taping families at home. As a historical note, it should be pointed out that one of the programs did have Mrs. Loud, then a single mother, with her four children engaging in a spontaneous extended family meeting in which efforts at problem solving did occur. Strictly speaking, one would have to count that as at least one small piece of evidence that family problem solving *does* occur in the home setting.

The Loud family has been largely forgotten, but the broadcast media and those who view their products seem to have ongoing fascination with videotapes of home life. Network programs such as "America's Funniest

Home Videos" were built entirely around videotapes of funny things that families have captured in and around their homes. MTV's "Real World" series "bugs" an apartment for video then has a group of young people live there for several months. Events taped in this "home" are edited into programs that are broadcast several times a week. Videotapes of families at home often find their way onto various forms of "reality TV" programming. None of this seeks to contribute to research on family problem solving. But by "legitimating" the idea of videotaping in the home for a large segment of the American population, such programs may facilitate home taping research. Families may be more willing to participate in such studies and may be less susceptible to any reactivity biases. Of course, exposure to the media may lead some family members to try to mimic what they have seen families do on television (e.g., a preadolescent may try to feed the toddler dog food). But such antics should subside if taping continues over time.

Overall, despite some challenges, home audio- or videotaping has considerable untapped potential for evaluating the external validity of models of problem solving, or for more inductive approaches aimed at generating alternative concepts or theories (Glaser & Strauss, 1967). But there are also other useful research techniques that do not involve taping. For example, family members can be interviewed about problems they have had recently. Retrospective reports on these experiences can provide information on the ecology of problem solving (e.g., when, where, how long), but also data on how family members perceived and understood what took place (Zvonkovic, Schmiege, & Hall, 1994). Independent reports from different family members can be used as a check against biased reporting and as a way of comparing perceptions (Smetana, 1989).

Another relevant technique is the use of "beepers," telephone reports, or diary reports to sample routine family behavior (e.g., Larson & Richards, 1995). Beeper sampling prompts a family member to briefly write down a summary of current activity, typically on a forced-choice form. This avoids various forms of memory bias, because the participant simply reports on who they are with and what they are doing at the time. Over a long study period, problem solving activities could be mapped. Regular telephone or written diary reports (daily or less frequently) could provide similar information with perhaps relatively little memory bias. Relying on participants' reports of their behavior related to problem solving would, without doubt, provide some rich data. However, reconciling divergent reports or divergent perspectives from different family members might be quite difficult. An advantage of taping techniques is that objective observers can be used in assessing behaviors so that such inconsistencies are minimized. Ideally, studies that combined participant perceptions with objective coding of taped interaction would provide the most complete information.

Other techniques have also been developed to capture ecologically valid problem solving. Burman, Margolin, and John (1993), for example, recruited married couples for a study in which they were asked to call the researchers immediately *whenever* they were having a conflict. The researchers immediately sent someone to their residence to videotape the couple recreating the conflict they had just engaged in. The researchers sought to capture the emotion and much of the detail of the conflict that had occurred spontaneously.

These considerations make it clear that there are several viable options for studying family problem solving outside of the artificial lab sessions so prominent in research on the rational model. These techniques create research challenges of their own. There are no perfect research techniques. Some of them are costly and have a certain painstaking character. But they may make possible a more comprehensive understanding of family problem solving than is likely to be achieved by any further laboratory studies. It is possible that studies of problem solving at home will ultimately confirm the rational model. If they did, it would still be a substantial advance over the current state of affairs because the lingering cloud of doubt over the lab studies of the rational model would be eliminated. In light of a growing body of work questioning that model (e.g., Aldous, 1971; Aldous & Ganey, 1989; Vuchinich, 1990; Weick, 1971), it is more likely that only parts of the rational model would survive the test of external validity.

The Existential Status of Family Problems

This book began with the claim that families have had their problems since the beginning. Few readers probably disputed that statement. Nor were there probably too many complaints with the claim that most Americans have a general idea of what "family problems" are. Family problems exist as a cultural concept. In chapter 4, it was proposed that a substantive analysis of this concept requires that family problems be considered as social constructions, not as mere terms in the vernacular language. It was further maintained that the rational model largely presupposes that discretely defined "family problems" exist, and focuses on how to deal with them. This is a deceptively important issue that has implications for moving beyond the rational model. The rational model assumes focused, discretely defined family problems exist for all families. This may or may not be true. It is certainly more likely in families that seek family therapy, as some kind of problem is the reason for seeking treatment. But for most families, the existence of discrete problems may be objects imposed on families by researchers or others. Such impositions may be beneficial or scientifically useful. But it is important to separate what families actually do from how analysts interpret it.

A fundamental error may be made by setting out to study "family problem solving." One may distort reality by forcing a given concept on the phenomena of interest. For example, if most families do not view themselves as ever having to deal with what they consider to be family problems, then it may be a distortion to interpret their behavior in terms of family problems. Inductive qualitative research perhaps should be used to discover how families conceptualize their concerns, tensions, or conflicts. Of course, one has to start with some concepts to focus the analysis. Otherwise, a muddle of stream-of-consciousness reports may result. But the degree of specificity of those beginning concepts can vary greatly.

In the case of the experimental studies of the rational model, the degree of specificity is quite high. Family members typically are given a defined hypothetical situation to role-play, or are asked to select a relevant problem from a list, or are asked to discuss a problem they have had recently. Families are able to do such tasks with apparently sincere behavior. There are some very limited informal reports that family members say that their behavior in such tasks is similar to their behavior in such situations at home (Kieren et al., 1996). In such tasks, the concept of a family problem being presented for solving is reified, perhaps prematurely. Families do seem to be able to do credible 20-minute problem solving performances, and some family members say this is similar to what they do at home (Keiren et al., 1996). That is a form of evidence that the family problem concept is valid. But it is also possible that families, much like individuals, tend to behave in experiments the way they think the experimenters want them to behave. Rosenthal's famous discovery of the "experimenter effect" revolutionized the use of human participants in experiments (Rosenthal, 1966). Family behavior in experimental conditions is also likely to be influenced by social desirability biases. A parent who routinely slaps a child in discussions at home is less likely to do that in a lab because it is not socially accepted.

The difficulty is that such research can never discover if most families use entirely different ways of conceptualizing and dealing with their tensions and unmet needs. The rational paradigm thus may promote a closed system with self-fulfilling prophecies. Constraining families to try to solve a problem in a brief time period may artificially create "phases" of family problem solving. Once the time period is started, family members are implicitly confronted with the task of defining the situation

(McHugh, 1968; Rosenthal, 1966; Thomas & Thomas, 1928). This may be a challenge in itself if the family does not usually do this sort of thing at home. Indeed, the videotapes of such situations suggest that some families are quite unsure of how to proceed in this task. If the situation is ambiguous for them, then defining a specific meaningful problem may be difficult.

But if a given problem is identified and there is 20 minutes to be filled, it might well be assumed by family members that more than one possible solution is expected to be discussed. If there was only one solution to the problem, 10 minutes would not be needed. Some families may generate alternate solutions because the experimental task seems to demand it. Then, once more than one solution is on the table, some kind of evaluating or controlling behavior would be necessary in order to come up with the "solution," which is presumably expected by the end of the time period. Such expectations are elicited by tasks that typically ask families to "try to solve the problem" during the allotted time period. Thus the generation of alternatives, evaluations of them, and pressure toward a single solution may well be created by the time-limited task and what participants believe is expected of them. If this is true, it means that the empirical evidence of rational phases in family problem solving may be, in part, an artifact of the procedures used to study the phenomenon. It may have little to do with how families usually deal with problems at home.

Paradigm shifts are always controversial affairs (Kuhn, 1970). Years of debate usually occur before it becomes apparent, in retrospect, that a shift has occurred. The rejection of the rational model is not imminent, in part, because there is no model that is an "heir apparent." The aim here is to point out some limitations to the rational paradigm, which make it more vulnerable than is generally acknowledged. This book has used, and will continue to use, the concepts of family problems and solutions because they are such a fundamental part of most previous work. But I am suggesting that further advances may require reconceptualization of these time-honored constructs. In the next section, I take a critical look at two other fundamental features of the rational model: phases of problem solving and the sequential ordering of phases.

Phases and Sequences in Family Problem Solving

The concept of a phase has been at the core of the rational model of problem solving since Dewey (1910/1982). The early definition of Bales and Strodtbeck (1951) is still generally in use (e.g., Kieren et al., 1996).

For them, *phases* are "qualitatively different subperiods within a total continuous period of interaction in which a group proceeds from initiation to completion of a problem involving group decision" (Bales & Strodtbeck, 1951, p. 485). Each subperiod is further hypothesized to focus on one specific function in the problem solving process. For Bales and Strodtbeck, there were three phases: orientation, evaluation, and control. During orientation, the nature of the problem was specified and solutions were proposed. The evaluation phase raised pros and cons to each alternative. Then, in the control phase, group influence processes (e.g., coercion, authority, bargaining) were used to ensure that one solution was accepted by the group. More recent research, however, has come to define the functions of the subperiods in different ways. Gottman (1979) tested for agenda building, arguing, and negotiation phases. Kieren et al. (1996) focused on four phases: identification–clarification, alternatives, consensus building, and decision. Although these various phase models have some similarities, they represent quite different conceptualizations of what the primary phases are. No studies have sought to test which of these variations provides the best fit to data. Thus, even if the validity of the phase concept is assumed, the available research has not established what the phases are.

Klein and Hill (1979) implicitly suggested that the way the phase concept is usually applied may be too rigid. Instead of one set of fixed phases, they suggest that sequencing during problem solving may be more accurately conceptualized in terms of somewhat more flexible patterns. They proposed the concept of *phasing rationality* to refer to "the orderliness with which a family progresses through the problem-solving process" (Klein & Hill, 1979, p. 522). They suggested the following as possible operationalizations: time spent on problem identification relative to time spent seeking and selecting a solution; extent to which potential problems are labeled and allocated to separate treatments; time spent searching for information relative to total time problem solving; time to solution; extent to which earlier phases are reinitiated when a later phase either stagnates or receives insufficient attention. Klein and Hill acknowledged the difficulty of empirical work on phasing rationality, and indeed the concept has not been actively pursued. It does not fit neatly into the paradigm of the rational model. The phasing rationality concept is pertinent because it suggests that a simple phase model is not adequate.

The idea of a phase in group interaction is more complex than is usually acknowledged. For behavioral scientists, the notion of a functional stage in group interaction is so analytically comfortable that it is often accepted on the basis of little proof. We know segments of group interaction focus on identifiable activities. Groups engage in such activities as conflicts, stories, jokes, and the like, which have identifiable beginnings and endings in the informal realm (e.g., Gumperz, 1982; Vuchinich, 1986, 1987, 1990). In the formal realm, business and other meetings have agendas that create functional phases of interaction. Family problem solving might well be expected to have phases along these formal and informal lines. But a closer consideration of what it means to "be in a phase" of family problem solving suggests that some applications of the concept may be premature.

Being in a phase of family problem solving means that all or most of the family members are acting to accomplish the functions of that phase (e.g., define the problems, generate alternative solutions, evaluate them). It is easy enough to imagine this kind of consensus and coherence of family effort. Indeed, it is likely that it does happen sometimes. But one must be skeptical that such a focused consensus of effort is typical of most families when difficulties arise. Such a consensus would be something of a challenge discussing any issue. But when the issue is an actual family problem about which there is likely to be some frustrations, different perceptions, past histories, and possible animosities, the challenge of achieving and maintaining consensus on how to proceed is great. A majority of family members must essentially agree that a given phase is under way and agree to participate in pursuing the function of that phase. Individual family members may instead have their own ideas of what phase is taking place and what needs to happen next.

From the beginning, some phase models have acknowledged that active effort is needed to help align the divergent views or orientations of participants. Bales and Strodtbeck (1951), for example, proposed control as the mechanism. Kieren et al. (1996) proposed consensus building as the mechanism. These were seen as phases that occurred toward the end of problem solving, and the issue of consensus was the solution to the problem. I suggest that such consensus building and control must occur at a much broader level from the very beginning of problem solving. They must be used in the social construction of the phases themselves, and the coordination of transitions between phases. They are used in signaling and negotiating the definition of the situation within each phase.

Phase models have been tested by coding all statements family members make during a problem solving session in terms of their function. Bales and Strodtbeck (1951) used basic codes such as *gives suggestion* or *shows support*. More recent research (e.g., Kieren et al., 1996) has used higher-order codes such as *identifies problem, proposes an alternative,* or *exerts power.* A set of behaviors is identified as being expected in a given phase. Thus, for example, the *identifies problem* category is one code expected to occur in the problem definition phase.

TABLE 5.1. Behavior Types by Phases of Problem Solving (Kieren et al., 1996)

Frequency of Behavior Clusters in Phases

Clusters of Behaviors	Problem Solving Phases 1	2	3	4	Total
	A[a] 1,041	B 91	C 663	—[b]	1,795
Alternatives	—[b]	D[a] 419	E	672	1,091[b]
Consensus building	F 981	—[b]	G[a] 1,611	—[b]	2,592
Decisions	H 462	I 55	—[b]	J[a] 489	1,006
Total	2,484	565	2,946	489	6,484[c]

a. Cells A, D, G, and J are phase-appropriate.
b. By definition, these clusters of behaviors cannot occur in the phases so designated.
c. Data are based on the interaction of 40 families completing three problem vignettes.
From "A Marker Method to Test a Phasing Hypothesis in Family Problem-Solving Interaction," *Journal of Marriage and the Family, 58,* 448. Reprinted by permission of the National Council on Family Relations.

Problem solving sessions are then divided into segments that presumably correspond to the different phases of the problem solving. Bales and Strodtbeck (1951) simply divided the sessions into three equal time periods that they expected to capture orientation, evaluation, and control phases. Gottman (1979) divided his sessions into equal thirds based on the number of statements the participants made. Other research has used a marker method that divides the session by the first occurrence of statements that indicate a new phase is under way (Kieren et al., 1996). The frequency of each behavior type that occurred in each phase is then calculated. Statistics are used to test whether more of the appropriate behaviors (e.g., *identifies problem)* occurred in expected phase (e.g., the identification–clarification phase) than would be expected by chance. Finding more of the expected behaviors in the proper phase is taken as evidence for the phase model.

Table 5.1 gives an example of such data from the Kieren et al. (1996) study of 40 families with a diabetic adolescent. The columns indicate the four phases of problem solving. The rows give the clusters of specific behaviors expected in that phase. Thus the upper-left cell (row 1, column 1) shows that there were 1,041 problem-defining behaviors in the identification– clarification phase. It further shows that there were 663 problem-defining behaviors in the consensus-building phase. If the model were perfect, one would expect no problem-defining behaviors in any phase except the identification–clarification phase. But the fact that there were more in the expected phase is at least some evidence for the model.

The previous studies of phasing have had similar mixed results with many of the "wrong" behaviors occurring in a given phase (Bales & Strodtbeck, 1951; Gottman, 1979). Such findings are consistent with my view that most families do not coordinate their problem solving behavior in terms of the rigid phases of the rational model. Some researchers have suggested variations on the basic phase model by suggesting that the order of phases may be different in different groups or that problem solving may involve more than one "loop" through the phases (Kieren et al., 1996; Klein & Hill, 1979).

Overall, it has become clear that evidence for the basic rational model for family problem solving is empirically mixed. There is some persistent evidence for a distribution of actions loosely consistent with the phase concept. But there is no agreement on what the phases are, and there is ample evidence for considerable out-of-phase behavior. It is likely that families develop a patterned way of dealing with their problems. Addressing problems in a random way is not likely to get needs met and reduce tensions. Thus some temporal patterns are perhaps inevitable. Such patterns may well involve some kinds of phases that include forms of intended rationality.

Klein and Hill's (1979) less rigid concept of "phasing rationality" may ultimately be useful in moving beyond the current rational model. It is conceptually appealing but difficult to specify empirically. Moving beyond the model, or even making major modifications to it, will not be an easy enterprise. Even after acknowledging some of the difficulties with the rational model made clear by Simon (1956), Weick (1971), and Aldous (1971), Kieren et al. (1996) recently concluded that, "No one has proposed an appropriate test for bounded rationality for families" (p. 452). The rational model lends itself to tests using the techniques of the dominant paradigms, and other models do not.

Before suggesting an approach to breaking this impasse, the question of how to test for sequential patterns must be considered. Testing for sequential patterns involves a separate set of issues than determining whether or not phases exist. The tests for phase sequencing used in past research have often been limited to piecemeal pairwise comparisons (Gottman, 1979; Kieren et al., 1996). Although adequate for exploratory work, they do not provide a strong empirical basis for assessing sequential patterns in family problem solving (Vuchinich & Angelelli, 1995).

Assume that the existence of a set of phases was established and that the beginning and end point of each phase could be located. Assume further, following the work of Kieren et al. (1996) as well as Klein and Hill (1979), that families might recycle phases or loop back to phases

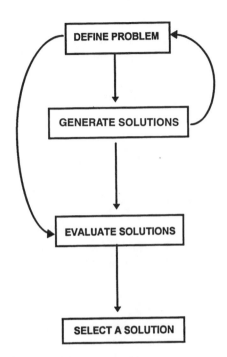

Figure 5.1. Some Possible Transitions in the Phases of Problem Solving

already covered. Assume that the main concern is the ordering of the sequences and that the amount of time spent in each phase is not of interest.

Taking this approach, each problem solving session would be coded as an ordered sequence of phases. In simplest terms, we would expect the following sequence: define problem → generate alternative solutions → evaluate solutions. But if the family looped back through the define phase once, the sequence would be define → generate → define → generate → evaluate. For rigorous tests of sequential patterns each transition is one data point, such as define → generate. To test for such patterns, a sample of problem solving sessions is needed. An important feature of the analysis would be the consideration of transitions observed but *not* predicted by the rational model. For example, a family might move from the define phase directly to the evaluate solutions phase, a transition that is not part of the rational model (see Figure 5.1).

The frequency of transitions can be usefully displayed as a transition matrix (e.g., Gottman & Roy, 1990) in which rows represent the first phase in the sequence and columns represent the second phase. The number of rows, as well as columns, is the number of phases being examined. Thus each cell represents the frequency of transitions from one phase to a different phase. The main diagonal would be zeroes in an analysis of problem solving phases because one phase cannot immediately follow itself. For descriptive purposes, each cell can be expressed as a transition probability, which gives the raw probability of moving from each phase to each other phase. According to the rational model, for example, there should be a high transition probability from the defining phase to the generating phase. But a statistically meaningful test of sequential patterns requires an analysis that takes into account the fact that some phases occur more frequently than others.

In the realm of sequential modeling, Markov models are typically used for such tests. Mathematically, a Markov model is a sequential process in which there is a fixed probability of moving from one type of phase to another possible phase (Gottman & Roy, 1990). In the present application, once a family is in a given phase, say the generating phase, the Markov model holds that there is a given probability of it moving to the evaluation phase next, a different probability of it moving to the define phase next, and so on for each other phase being studied. An important advantage is that it includes consideration of all possible transitions. The analysis is not limited to one rigid sequence of phases.

A Markov analysis can be done with log-linear statistical procedures that use the transition matrix frequencies as the input data (e.g., Gottman & Roy, 1990; Vuchinich, 1984; Vuchinich, Hetherington, Vuchinich, & Clingempeel, 1991). The analysis specifies how likely each type of transition is, and tests can be done for whether one transition is more likely than another. Such an analysis supplies rigorous tests of expected transitions from one phase to another and also provides valuable information about transitions not predicted.

An advantage of the Markov analysis is that it can also test for more complex types of sequencing. For example, the transition matrix tests for two-slot sequences (known as first-order sequences). That analysis assumes that the next phase the family moves to depends only on the current phase. But it is conceivable that the phase the family moves to next depends on the one they are in currently *and* the one they just left. Families may not move to the evaluating phase until they have been in both the defining and generating phases. The Markov approach is so widely applied because it provides both flexibility and rigorous testing. Both of these features are needed in examining sequencing beyond the rational model. Other mathematical approaches to sequencing, in addition to the Markov models, are also available, including those used for genetic sequencing (Abbott, 1995). Perhaps the most important issue is to move beyond piecemeal two-slot tests.

Summary

In chapters 4 and 5, I have suggested some ways to begin developing more accurate models of family problem solving. The first step is to open the analysis to concepts outside of the rational model. Dominant paradigms can be insidious in their ability to constrain the way phenomena are conceptualized. I do not advocate abandoning the rational model but rather opening it up for more rigorous empirical tests and potential integration with other conceptual models (e.g., social constructionism). The second step is to observe what families actually do in the home, and ask them how they think about the problems they have. Although this sounds easy enough, it is not. Family problem solving involves the fundamental inner core of any family. It is a private and personal area. Brief 20-minute (or even 60-minute) observations may indeed accurately reflect how families normally deal with their problems. But the extent to which this is true remains an open question. Learning more about this issue may require some new strategies in this complex area of study. The methodological difficulties will probably challenge the most dedicated researchers. But it is only through such efforts that we will ever find out whether the current theories of family problem solving only apply to what families do in 20-minute laboratory tasks.

One conceptual starting point for moving toward a more comprehensive understanding of family problem solving is to focus on family problems as social constructions. That approach provides a framework for organizing observations about what families do to manage tensions and how they think about them. Family behavior is not random. Families create recurring structures, situations, definitions, rituals, and other patterns that allow them to organize their family life. Linking these observable patterns with what we already know about family problem solving holds great promise for improving the ability to explain this important aspect of family life. In the next chapter, applications of family problem solving in prevention and intervention programs are reviewed. Many benefits from these have already been realized, even though we have a limited understanding of family problem solving. The issues raised in chapters 4 and 5 seek a deeper empirical comprehension that has the potential to extend these benefits even further.

6

Applications in
Family Problem Solving

The existential conditions of human life dictate that we cannot have what we want all the time. Considerable cultural and individual effort must be expended in order to meet even the most basic physical and psychological needs of the humans who are alive at any point in time. The human condition allows for the survival of a large population. But that human condition seems to also carry with it a great deal of whining and grumbling along the way. All humans experience some degree of frustration as a result of unmet wants and needs. It is the nature of the beast. We might imagine a human condition in which all needs are met and everyone is happy. Indeed, such visions have been created in images such as those of heaven or nirvana. But any substantial observations of actual humans will find unmet wants and needs. It is in this realm that we find the basis for many mental health problems that are linked to the family. It is within this realm that we must begin an explanation of how prevention and treatment programs apply training in family problem solving.

Unmet Needs, Negative Emotions,
and Troubled Family Systems

Families are social units that function as a locus for organizing the way many wants and needs of individuals are met. A fundamental feature of a well-functioning family is the ability to manage the tensions and frustrations of unmet wants and needs. Some families do this effectively, and some families do not. The members of families who do not function effectively are vulnerable to a range of negative mental health outcomes. The basic principle underlying most applications of family problem solving is that *improving a family's ability to manage unmet needs can reduce the risk of negative outcomes.* This chapter reviews the logic of applying problem solving techniques in family-based programs to prevent or treat mental health problems. The aim is to explain how family problem solving techniques are used in such programs, to evaluate how successful they have been, and to describe how they produce the beneficial effects. Several diverse applications will be reviewed, along with suggestions for potential improvements.

The individual human is a physical and psychological system. It requires specific types of input from its environment in order to survive in both a physical and psychological sense. When these needs are not fulfilled at a threshold level, the organism experiences physical or psychological stress. The organism may react to this stress in a variety of ways. Because humans usually develop in some form of family context, reactions to stress are shaped by the family system. For many years, the source of the individual's need fulfillment is the family. The individual's innate reaction to stress is the expression of negative emotion. The crying infant is the archetypical beginning point. The comforting of a parental caregiver at that point initiates an attachment bond that is the beginning of connection to a family system.

There is considerable variation in the extent to which family systems actually meet the needs of their children. But regardless of how effective they are in that regard, the basic reaction of the individual to unmet needs is the expression of negative emotion. The family system may suppress those reactions, forcing a child to withdraw, or it may promote unbridled expressions and encourage tantrum-like behavior. Ideally, the family shapes the behavior in a more positive way that allows the child's needs to be met. This may not be easy for some families to do. As a result, given human proclivity toward reciprocity in interaction (e.g., Patterson, 1982), the expression of negative emotion naturally tends to elicit negative reactions from other family members. This ultimately produces the well-known patterns of conflict that are often observed in troubled families.

This may take the form of frequent complaining, whining, sniping, and grumbling, which Gottman (1979) has labeled cross-complaining, and Patterson has referred to as "nattering" (1982). This results in a simmering level of negative emotion even without overt conflict. At the next level, low intensity conflict occurs in the form of bickering, where disagreements and corrections drag on but usually do not erupt. These low-level patterns may be accompanied by explicit conflict avoidance. Before nattering or bickering becomes more confrontational, family members may back away from the issue saying, "I don't want to talk about it," "Forget it," "Let's not argue about it," or some similar avoidance mechanism. Such avoidance may or may not be beneficial depending on other aspects of the family system. But what is important is that these patterns are common in troubled families and they often do not provide a way for the unmet needs that are the source of the negative emotion to be addressed. Frequent interactions of this nature undermine family cohesion and adaptability. Indeed, it has been shown that the expression of negative emotion suppresses family problem solving (Forgatch, 1989).

Of course, expressions of negative emotion often lead to overt conflicts that can take many forms (e.g., Vuchinich, 1987, 1990). They may escalate into violent encounters that are either psychological or physical in form. The intensity of the conflict depends on several factors. Ultimately, one of the most fundamental of these is the level of unmet need experienced by one or more family member. The greater the frustrated need, the more intense the conflict.

Some conflict is inevitable. It can be very useful in understanding unmet needs and bringing them to the attention of the family. Sources of conflict can be removed or changed. Thus conflict does not necessarily escalate. It may give way to a process of defining a problem and moving toward a solution. Most families, through what sometimes seems like a mystical combination of cohesion and adaptability, manage to come up with ways of accomplishing this. In doing so they provide for the basic needs of their members.

But in families where this does not happen, unmet needs and negative emotions tend to accumulate. When the family system does not provide for the individual's needs, they are left to their own devices to get them met. Typically, this leads the negative emotions to become more prominent in the individual's life. These become recognized in a variety of forms such as anger, blame, aggression, denial, shame, withdrawal, externalizing behaviors, internalizing behaviors, and so on. The child experiences prolonged, intense negative emotions that can disrupt normal emotional development. Dysfunctional thought and action patterns, such as depression and antisocial behavior, often result. Once such combinations of extreme emotions, cognitions, and behaviors are in place, it becomes increasingly difficult for the individual's needs to be met in the family system. Indeed, family systems that have allowed such difficulties to reach this level are least likely to be able to effectively cope with the additional challenges to normal development that they create.

Troubled family members may seek to get their needs met outside of the family system. This may or may not produce good results. Individuals may find peers, relatives, teachers, counselors, social workers, or others who are able to provide for needs that are not met within the immediate family system (Henggeler & Borduin, 1990). However, they may also find deviant peer groups, promiscuous sexual affairs, drugs, or other negative influences that either allow them to give vent to their intense negative emotions or else provide risky ways of numbing them.

Which of these extra-family options occurs depends, in part, on the community environment in which the family exists (Sim & Vuchinich, 1996). It is in this environment that most applications of family problem solving are found. They are provided through schools, churches, community organizations, social service agencies, or government programs interested in preventing, or intervening in the development of, negative child and adolescent outcomes. They are oriented toward making it possible for families to more effectively meet the needs of their members. Many of them are designed to help families with children or adolescents who are at risk for some negative outcome (e.g., delinquency, suicide, teenage pregnancy, drug abuse), or who have been diagnosed with a mental health disorder. They are based on the assumption that the family has greatest and most cost-effective potential for meeting the needs of its members (Henggeler, 1992).

The Logic of Family Problem Solving Applications

The concept of mental health has a long and interesting history. Well before the advent of science, certain individuals were recognized as being "different" and perhaps abnormal. Various cultures have had distinctive ways of understanding such individuals. The scientific analysis of abnormal behavior has been increasingly active during the twentieth century. Debates have raged over what the causes of such behavior are and what can be done to treat or prevent it. Family problem solving came into the picture in the early 1970s. In chapter 3, I described how the family became implicated as a contributing cause, and locus for treatment, for some serious mental health problems including schizophrenia, depression, and child conduct disorder.

Chapter 3 described how the family came to be a focus for treatment for mental health and other disorders. Abnormal, maladaptive behavior came to be seen as a product of behavior sequences that included family members. The social behaviorists became interested in reinforcement contingencies and coercive family cycles. The family therapists focused on tactics for changing dysfunctional patterns. The cognitive approach was primarily interested in sequences in thinking about problems but ultimately expanded the approach to include the family context (Shure & Spivack, 1978).

The extent to which behavior sequences and abnormal behaviors are causes or effects of each other has been a matter of ongoing debate. Family therapists and clinical researchers have actively pursued the idea that changes in dysfunctional family behavior sequences could reduce abnormal behavior. This approach has proven to have beneficial results, even though there is still no consensus on exactly why such results are obtained. Years of trial and error have been invested in trying various ways of replacing negative family behavior sequences with more functional interaction patterns. Training families to address their interpersonal problems through rational problem solving has emerged as a straightforward and practical way of promoting such changes.

From the behavioral standpoint, the basic program concept is simple. The goal is to teach families to try to solve their perceived problems by using the well-known phases of rational problem solving. Families are instructed in defining problems, generating alternative solutions, evaluating the alternatives to select the best one, and implementing the solution. Problem solving components are typically based on a psychoeducational model. That means that clients are simply taught some new skills and ways of thinking about their problems. No in-depth psychodynamic changes are attempted in the problem solving components of programs. At first glance, it may appear that such relatively low-key training would have little chance of having a substantial impact on any serious family problems, let alone a serious mental health problem such as schizophrenia or child conduct disorder. As we have seen in the past two chapters, there is little evidence that "normal" families even use rational problem solving. That fact turns out to be of little consequence in helping families with troubled members. The key to the benefits of training in family problem solving is the primary significance of family interaction patterns in promoting and maintaining individual well-being. The effectiveness of such training depends on how the program fits into the context of the family system. Three factors are prominent: (a) the use of such training in conjunction with other intervention components; (b) the low level of interpersonal skills in many dysfunctional families; and (c) getting the family actively involved in the treatment of the most troubled family members.

The Context of Training in
Family Problem Solving

Training in family problem solving is usually applied in conjunction with other program components. These may include drug therapy, individual therapy, group counseling, or other modalities. Mental health professionals have a variety of techniques to draw on in developing a treatment plan for any individual case. Family problem solving is often used as a secondary or cotreatment component. In most applications, it is not the only component used in treating the major symptoms of a disorder, though it is sometimes the primary modality. More frequently, it is a treatment component that increases the effectiveness of other components. For example, treatments for depression or attention deficit disorder often include drug therapy components to address chemical imbalances in the brain that are viewed as primary causes of the disorder. Training in family problem solving is used in conjunction with drug therapy to help adjust family relationships that may contribute to the difficulties. Such training is uniquely suited to facilitate the adaptations a family needs to make as treatment and recovery progress. The training is also used in prevention programs in tandem with other components found in parent education programs, school-based peer programs, community crisis counseling, and conflict mediation services.

Further, the level of interpersonal skill in many families with serious problems is often very low. Indeed, serious mental health or behavior problems often promote negative interactions or the reduction in the amount of family interaction that occurs. For example, a child with attention deficit disorder may constantly be in conflict with parents and siblings. A depressed grandmother may simply be cut off from most family interaction. Such patterns eliminate the family as source of social and emotional support to the individuals most in need of it. Once such patterns are established, many family members have neither the knowledge to realize what is going on, nor the skills needed to change the patterns.

In this context, basic training in family problem solving can be an important impetus to begin some change and provide guidance on using more effective patterns. Most families have some valuable individual or interpersonal resources that may be more easily accessed once negative patterns are reduced or some small positive changes occur. For example, there may be a history of a strong emotional bond between a father and his depressed son. But the son's depression has caused him to avoid interacting with his parents. Family problem solving training may promote some positive father–son interaction that reactivates the suppressed emotional bond. Similarly such training may allow a family bogged down in seemingly endless conflicts to reduce the negative cycles enough so that more supportive family interactions can take place. If family problem solving can allow suppressed positive interaction patterns to resurface, the benefit of the training can be disproportionate to the effort invested.

Another key to the success of problem solving training is that it gets the family actively involved in treatment. American culture often views mental health problems in terms of an individual disease model. Thus, for example, the family may believe that mother is depressed because she got a disease. The treatment for disease in American culture typically focuses on the individual who has it. Drugs, for example, are often the appropriate treatment for individual disease, and family members are relegated to a minor role of trying to comfort the diseased person. Regardless of the veracity of the disease model, such beliefs leave the family with little active role in the treatment–recovery process. In many cases, some family members would just as soon not deal with their troubled kin until they are cured. The additional difficulty is that these other family members may well be part of the mental health problem. Even if they are not part of it, they could make useful contributions to the recovery process.

Training in family problem solving provides a nonjudgmental way of getting other family members actively involved in recovery. Other family members do not have to accept any responsibility for the mental illness or other problem. They can be asked to help a little with the recovery. Their participation not only shows support for the recovery process but also streamlines the implementation of adjustments that family members have to make during and after treatment. A good example of this is the successful psychoeducational program to reduce rehospitalization of schizophrenic individuals (Falloon, 1988), to be discussed later. The program includes education about the nature of schizophrenia as well as techniques of family problem solving.

Why Training in
Family Problem Solving Works

Before providing more details on specific prevention and intervention programs, it is useful to consider general reasons why training in family problem solving should be effective. Most of the literature on applications of family problem solving focuses on the specific techniques that are used or evaluations of program success. In the realm of applications, what works is the primary concern. Why it works is often a secondary issue. Family problem solving is often used as an all-purpose family tonic that clinicians have found to promote success in treatment. Exactly how this is accomplished is not elaborated. But this question is critical for any efforts to improve on the beneficial effects.

In general terms, family problem solving training is effective because it uniquely serves to improve the family system's adaptation to the environment. Problem solving has been intimately linked to adaptation since Dewey's original formulation. D'Zurilla and Goldfried's (1971) seminal work brilliantly applied this linkage to mental health. Concurrent work with the family's role in mental health naturally moved problem solving into the family context (e.g., Alexander & Parsons, 1973; Reiss, 1981; Weakland, 1976). Most families, through natural processes, are able to adapt to each other internally and to the external environment. But some families are not successful at this, and some of their members have substantial unmet needs that lead to negative outcomes. Training in family problem solving provides a way of making changes in the family system that allow such needs to be more effectively met. The rational problem solving model focuses directly on specific prerequisites for family system change. It does this in four ways.

First, such training promotes an open consideration of flaws in the current adaptation of a family system. Family members are required to present issues that they believe are problematic. Tensions experienced by any family member can be expressed. The power and communication structures of families have considerable inertia. Indeed, some families can become closed systems that are damaging to certain family members. This can result in the needs and stresses of some family members being suppressed. Family training can provide an important lever for getting the family to pay attention to suppressed needs. Family systems may be so rigid that such training has little effect. In such cases, other approaches are necessary.

Second, training in family problem solving *presupposes* that some change is useful. Once family members accept the idea of improving their problem solving, they have tacitly accepted the notion that they are going to change some things. Change is often threatening to family members, especially if it is imposed from outside the system. Problem solving training requires accepting no specific change imposed from outside—it is just a process for the family to try. In addition, if any changes are to occur, each family member will be involved in determining what they are. Family members typically see the potential of the process for producing changes that benefit them. In some families, circumstances may be so negative that family members readily acknowledge that some changes need to be made. In such cases, problem solving training can be quickly embraced.

Third, the hallmark of rational problem solving is the generation of alternative solutions. This is also the hallmark of adaptation dating back to Darwin. A family system must try *new* elements if it is to adapt to the changing internal and external environments. Problem solving training requires that alternative solutions be generated by as many family members as possible. These potential solutions are initially presented without immediate evaluation or criticism from other family members. This is important because new elements or changes often threaten the current family system and those who have a stake in keeping it the way it is. Such implicit "threats" often produce negative reactions and criticism of new approaches to family problems. Immediate criticism not only shoots down specific suggestions, but also inhibits future efforts to propose anything different from the current system.

Generating potential solutions through brainstorming can be a powerful source of beneficial change in rigid family systems. The participation of several family members in generating solutions encourages the feeling that "we" are solving this problem together. Active participation in the process promotes family cohesion and increases the likelihood that all family members will buy in to applying the ultimate solution.

Fourth, the training requires a specific plan for implementation of the solution and follow-up on how effective it is. Dysfunctional family systems typically resist any change, even if family members agree that it is needed. Problem solving training emphasizes that solutions must be applied after the discussion session is over if it is to do any good. A specific plan to evaluate the success of the solution is also put into place. In systems terminology, this completes the "feedback loop" that allows the system to adjust itself.

Family problem solving is not viewed as a short-term exercise to be used only while the program or treatment is under way. Ideally, families will continue to use the process on a regular basis. Family meetings on a weekly basis are usually recommended (Dinkmeyer & McKay, 1989; Forgatch & Patterson, 1989). Regular problem solving sessions allow small issues to be resolved before they get worse. They also allow updates and adjustments to past solutions that have been implemented. Problem solving training can, and should, also be used outside of the family meeting context. Family dyads may use elements of the process in dealing with difficulties that come up in relationships. The whole family need not always be brought into the picture.

It is important to emphasize that family problem solving training is not effective because it teaches troubled families to solve problems the way "normal" families do. Instead, it is effective because it provides a set of procedures that focus directly on improving the adaptation of family members to each other and their environment. Most families naturally find ways of adapting effectively that may or may not involve the rational model. It is not clear how these families accomplish this, though we can recognize that they have accomplished this through assessments of such characteristics as cohesion and adaptability.

Chronically troubled families have not created a system that adapts well enough to avoid negative outcomes for their members. Training in family problem solving seems to provide a process for making adjustments to the system to make it more effective. It is relatively nonthreatening and flexible. It can be applied as a component in treating a wide range of disorders and disabilities, and in a variety of family forms. Indeed, considering the wide range of disorders that have been treated with this training, it may be viewed in a manner similar to a broad-spectrum antibiotic.

Training in family problem solving is typically delivered in the psychoeducational context of learning some new skills. But the process of learning those skills often has powerful by-products that affect the core of the family system. The process can increase family cohesion as well as adaptability. Family members and the family unit itself can be empowered with new confidence in open communication and resiliency in the face of adversity. Family therapists, clinicians, and counselors have become skilled in effectively using and shaping the training process so that it can have the optimal beneficial effects for a given family situation. There are also indications that considerable benefits can be obtained from well-designed self-help programs without high levels of personal involvement with a therapist figure (e.g., Webster-Stratton, 1996).

Our review of applications in family problem solving focuses on three types of programs: treatments for child and adolescent mental health disorders, programs to prevent negative child outcomes, and parent education programs. Because such programs have been expanding over the past 20 years, it is impractical to attempt a comprehensive review. This review focuses on major trends. Most of the applications use some variation of the rational model of family problem solving and are based on the logic outlined in the previous section. Thus the aim in this book is to describe some of the details on how training in family problem solving is applied to achieve specific results.

Family Problem Solving and Mental Health Disorders

Training in family problem solving has most frequently been applied in the treatment of child and adolescent mental health disorders. Two different approaches have been most prominent. The behavioral family therapy approach has been used mostly in treating externalizing disorders (e.g., antisocial behavior, conduct disorder, oppositional disorder, attention deficit disorder). The cognitive approach has been used more often for treating both internalizing disorders (e.g., withdrawal, affective disorders, anxiety, phobias), as well as externalizing disorders. The behavioral family theory has focused on reinforcement contingencies and negative sequences in family interaction (Falloon, 1988; Patterson, 1982). The theory maintains that such sequences produce and maintain the child's aggressive, antisocial behavior. Such behavior patterns are often diagnosed as conduct disorder, oppositional disorder, or attention deficit disorder. The treatment approach seeks to stop the conflictual cycles by training parents and children to respond differently to each other. Part of that training includes rational family problem solving. The key is in changing *behaviors* in family interaction.

The second approach, reviewed in chapter 3, focuses on the dysfunctional thought processes of the diagnosed individual. The treatment emphasizes work with the child directly to use rational problem solving in dealing with their unpleasant troublesome feelings. These are linked to sadness in the case of depression, and anger in the case of conduct disorders. The key is changing how the child *thinks* about the feelings experienced. Other family members are enlisted in the treatment to help the child in learning to think and react differently to his or her feelings.

The use of rational problem solving techniques in strategic (Madanes, 1981), structural (Minuchin & Fishman, 1981), and functional (Morris, Alexander, & Waldron, 1988) family therapy is somewhat more complicated and does not easily yield to brief summary. The family therapy models of mental health disorders are not as simple as either the behavioral or cognitive theories. As we saw in chapter 3, family problem solving is at the core of strategic family therapy and serves a primary function in adaptation. However, the problem solving may not follow the rational model. From the strategic perspective, many different forms of problem solving may be effective as long as they avoid dysfunctional sequences or hierarchical misalignments (Haley, 1987; Madanes, 1981). Problem solving is less central to structural or functional theories but may be useful in reaching treatment objectives. As all these therapies evolve, there is an increasing tendency to merge components of treatment (Dodd, 1988; Robin & Foster, 1989). Treatments based on the behavioral and cognitive theories will be my focus because rational problem solving is a central part of their programs.

PROBLEM SOLVING IN BEHAVIORAL FAMILY THERAPY

In treating several child and adolescent disorders a primary concern is coercive parent–child interactions. Parents are viewed as a primary locus of treatment that is intimately involved in the coercive family interaction patterns. For younger diagnosed children the emphasis is on changing the behavior of parents so that it reinforces positive child behavior and discourages negative child behavior (e.g., Patterson, 1971). Inconsistent power-assertive discipline practices (e.g., yelling, hitting, threatening) are replaced by more consistent emphasis of the basis for rules and moderate discipline techniques such as time-outs. These procedures have proven to be successful in reducing the debilitating conflictual family interactions as well as the child's symptomatic aggressive behavior in many cases. This approach views young children as not being concerned with the complexities of defining complex family problems, generating alternatives, or evaluation. It operates on a simpler level, seeking largely to change the child's behavior by adjusting the parents' behavior. At one level, the therapy defines the child's misbehavior as the problem to be solved. But in an important twist, it defines changes in the parents' behavior as the basis for dealing with the problem. It assumes that once children are exposed to more effective parenting, their problematic behavior will naturally be reduced according to reinforcement principles. The child may also receive some individual therapy that may include drugs such as methylphenidate.

For diagnosed children older than 9 years and adolescents, however, changes in parental reinforcements and discipline practices are often less effective in reducing child symptoms. The behavior problems are often more serious and parents have less control over the contingencies to which the child or adolescent are exposed. To handle these issues, the behavioral therapies add training in family problem solving (e.g., Forgatch & Patterson, 1989; Robin & Foster, 1989). The treatment goal of this training is to replace coercive family sequences with use of a rational problem solving process. Such a process can be used on the spot when a conflict erupts or to defer the discussion of the conflict issue to another more appropriate time. Regular family meetings or family forums (e.g., Forgatch & Patterson, 1989) are often recommended as occasions for problem solving to take place, as has been discussed previously.

The delivery of family problem solving training can take place in several formats in the context of treatment. Of course such training can begin only after several important phases of the therapy process have already taken place. These include intake interviews, assessments, arrangements for financial responsibility, case planning, setting treatment goals, enlistment of family members to participate in the treatment, scheduling, and transportation. Any of these matters can create difficulties or constraints in how the treatment can proceed. For example, key parents or siblings may refuse to participate, insurance may cover only a limited number of sessions, additional disorders may be revealed in assessments, legal or ethical issues may surface, and so on. Such issues are conceptually separate from the treatment process itself. However, they may have a large role in determining how training for family problem solving can be delivered. Fortunately, the training can be delivered through several modalities, including detailed workbooks (Forgatch & Patterson, 1989) and videotapes (Webster-Stratton, 1996). The importance of these options will be addressed in chapter 7.

Perhaps the simplest format for delivery is through a series of family therapy sessions in which all relevant family members are present (e.g., Robin & Foster, 1989). But several other formats have been used. For example, several families at the same time may receive a number of weekly sessions of preliminary group instruction in family problem solving from a trainer who may not be a therapist. Such training covers the basics of the problem solving process and may include the use of videotapes (Webster-Stratton, 1996), workbooks (which include readings and exercises to be done at home), or other educational materials. Ideally, there are separate groups for parents and children, because training methods that are age appropriate can be much more effective (Vuchinich et al., 1996). Family members can learn what the basic stages of rational problem solving are and be exposed to examples of them. An advantage of this approach is that it is a cost-effective way of teaching the basic ideas of problem solving in a setting that is usually nonthreatening. This may also have some advantages often found in support groups, such as reducing the stigma of being a family in therapy. Once the group training is completed, families meet with a therapist to pursue problem solving in their families.

Robin and Foster (1989) provided perhaps the most detailed description of the use of family problem solving training from the therapist's point of view. Their complete therapy program includes elements of both behavioral and systems family therapy. I focus only on the behavioral component of their problem solving treatment. The therapist begins by giving a plan for the training, then proceeds to give direct instruction to the family on each phase of the problem solving process. Robin and Foster (1989, pp. 191–192) provide the following sample introduction.

> We are going to begin to work on a new way for you to solve your problems today. We will pick a problem to discuss, and I will suggest five steps to follow to solve it. I'll be like a "stage director," describing each step and guiding you to follow it. I'll stop you to comment on how you are doing. At future meetings we'll go through the five steps with other problems; eventually, you will solve the most important problems you have and also learn how to solve additional problems on your own. Any questions?

Some therapists explain the entire problem solving process in one session and immediately have the family use it on a problem of their choice (Robin & Foster, 1989). Others prefer to use each session to explain one or two phases and build up to the family applying them all to an actual problem. In either case, therapists use modeling, direct instructions, behavioral rehearsal, and feedback to involve family members in learning and practicing the problem solving stages. Families are given "homework," which can include instructions to implement a solution they reached during the session, written exercises that involve practice on vignette examples, or similar activities that promote generalization of what is learned in the sessions to the home setting. Robin and Foster provide families with the following outline (1989, pp. 193–194) of the problem solving process, which they refer to during the training. These items may seem a bit too familiar by now. However, it is useful to see how the theoretical descriptions of the problem solving process get translated into materials used by families in treatment.

I. Define the Problem.
   A. You tell the others what they are doing that is a problem and how it affects you.
   B. You each paraphrase the others' statements of the problem to check out your understanding of what they said.
II. Generate Alternative Solutions.
   A. You take turns listing possible solutions.
   B. You follow three rules for listing solutions.
      1. List as many ideas as possible.
      2. Don't evaluate the ideas.
      3. Be creative and freewheeling; suggest crazy ideas.
III. Decide on the Best Idea.
   A. You take turns evaluating each idea.
      1. Say what you think would happen if the family followed the idea.
      2. Give the idea a "plus" or "minus" and write the rating next to the idea.
   B. You Select the "Best" Idea.
      1. Look for the ideas rated "plus" by all.
         a. Select one idea.
         b. Combine several ideas.
      2. If none are rated "plus" by all, look for ideas rated "plus" by one parent and a teenager. Then negotiate a compromise.
IV. Plan to Implement the Selected Solution.
   A. You decide who will do what, where, and how.
   B. You write down the details on the bottom of the worksheet.

This outline highlights the directive nature of the training. Families are taught a specific set of behaviors to do in a specific sequence. Each phase is described in terms most people aged 9 years or older can understand.

Inherently complex phases are simplified by supplying a sequential procedure in advance. Thus, for example, evaluation is done by family members taking turns saying, "What would happen if the family followed that idea," then each person rates it as a "plus" or "minus." These ratings are the basis for selecting the best idea. A primary advantage of this directive approach is that it supplies a clear alternative to, and can completely replace, the dysfunctional sequences that are part of the disorder.

A typical therapy session may involve a family member selecting a problem that has bothered him or her, and then the family uses the problem solving method to try to resolve it (Robin & Foster, 1989). The therapist initially plays an active role in guiding the family through the process. This includes interrupting the discussion to praise good use of the process elements, to carefully correct errors, or to keep the discussion moving in a productive direction. This active coaching can be a considerable challenge in families with serious problems. The training may begin practice with the family role-playing a vignette sample problem whereby they act as if it was their family that had the problem. Next they graduate to trying to solve a minor problem in their household. Once they have learned the procedures, and other indications are favorable, they move to the more serious family problems they are having.

After such exercises, the therapist provides detailed feedback to the family on strengths and weaknesses of the session. Robin and Foster (1989, p. 193) provided the following feedback example, which would be used after a rather unsuccessful exercise that reached only a partial solution. The problem was that the teenager was breaking his curfew.

> You've really tried to solve the curfew problem. I can appreciate that it isn't easy to change your habits of talking to each other. The first step is often the most difficult to take, but you've started, and that's great. Of course, we have a long way to go. We will have to pay particular attention to the seemingly small swipes you take at each other. Tonight these zaps threatened several times to sidetrack you into angry arguments, but you managed to avoid these several times. That's the beginning of progress.

As the family becomes skilled at problem solving, more attention is focused on implementing solutions at home and how they deal with problems that come up between sessions. If treatment is successful, families become able to spontaneously use the problem solving techniques at home, and the dysfunctional interaction sequences slowly subside. Videotapes of families solving serious problems with no therapist present are useful in determining whether the family is using good problem solving methods. When substantial progress is made on the presenting problems that brought the family into therapy in the first place, the sessions move toward preparing the family for the termination of treatment.

In successful treatment, families are typically pleased about the changes they have made and may feel that the problem is solved. Therapists promote the idea that the family is "back on track," but must point out that it is important to continue using what they have learned. At the termination of treatment, the central success points of the therapy are reviewed and highlighted as keys to avoiding the recurrence of their problems. In addition, the weak points of the family's problem solving are specified and noted as areas that should be improved. Therapists give the family hints on how to anticipate new crises and plan strategies for how they should be handled. After the termination of therapy, follow-up visits or telephone calls are often used to monitor progress or as "booster shots" to help maintain treatment gains.

The treatment of troubled families involves many complexities beyond the scope of this book. Elements of strategic, structural, and functional family therapy are often applied along with behavioral therapy (Robin & Foster, 1989). One complex issue that requires some attention is the resistance of family members to treatment (see Robin & Foster, 1989, pp. 210–231). Some family members may not be willing to learn problem solving methods. Resistance can have many sources. For example, an antisocial adolescent may see therapy as yet another way for adults to unfairly try to control him. Or a father may deny that his child's suicide attempts have anything to do with family relationships, and thus consider family therapy as pointless. Therapists must be skilled in detecting resistance from the beginning of therapy. Several sessions may be required to overcome such resistance. Ultimately, training may have to work around a recalcitrant family member, with the extreme being excluding them from the training. Although this is undesirable, it is still possible to obtain benefits without all immediate family members participating. If the majority of family members change their behavior, the nonparticipator is likely to change some as well. Such individuals may well join the training after it is in progress.

The duration of treatments using family problem solving typically ranges from a minimum of 8 weeks to 16 weeks, with weekly sessions of 1 to 2 hours each. Of course, treatment success is more likely with a longer treatment period. Summarizing a series of evaluation studies of their training, Robin and Foster (1989) reported significant reductions in reported conflicts and disputes in one half to two thirds of families with adolescents, with treatment effects maintained from 6 to 15 weeks following termination. Other studies evaluating similar problem solving treatments report similar success rates (Barton, Alexander, Waldron,

Turner, & Walburton, 1985; Blechman, 1977; Klein, Alexander, & Parsons, 1976). In the clinical realm, such results are considered promising because the antisocial and conduct disorder diagnoses have been known for years to be notoriously difficult to treat, with low success rates being common. However, it is clear that problem solving training by itself is not effective in many cases. Whether that is a result of fundamental flaws in the theory it is based on or attributable to practical difficulties with implementing the treatment is not known. In either case, as we shall see, success rates are better when problem solving training is combined with other treatment components.

Cognitive–Behavioral Problem Solving in Therapy

As described in chapter 3, the cognitive approach to treatment sees the primary basis of disorders as residing in the way the diagnosed person thinks (e.g., Shure & Spivack, 1991). Many recent applications of this approach focus first on how the person perceives his or her own extreme emotions, such as fear, sadness, anger, rage, and anxiety. These reactions are often based on cognitive deficiencies or distortions (Kendall, 1991). The person either does not attend to essential parts of actions and events they are exposed to (i.e., deficient cognition) or creates cognitions of them that are distorted in a way that promotes inappropriate emotion or action. Internal processes such as self-talk exacerbate the reaction to such cognitions. Thus a minor disapproving look from a mother may inappropriately result in the child's distorted perception that the mother is going to kill him. The child's reaction to that cognition could be exacerbated by the child telling himself that, "Mom hates me," "Mom is reaching for the butcher knife," or other fear-provoking statements.

The cognitive approach has had considerable success in treating a wide range of disorders, including clinical depression, phobias, antisocial behavior, conduct disorder, attention deficit disorder, learning disabilities, and mental retardation (Kendall, 1991) in both children and adults. Family problem solving is more often a part of treatment of child disorders, in part because children are so dependent on parents and because they are often available and willing to help with the treatment. However, unlike the behavioral therapies, the cognitive approach typically does not place the family unit at the core of the disorder or treatment. Instead, the focus is on the distorted thinking and feelings of the diagnosed child. As in the early work (Shure & Spivack, 1991), the basic steps in rational problem solving are used to help the individual child develop less distorted thinking about emotions and appropriate behavioral responses to them. Thus changing the individual's, not the family's, problem solving practices is the primary focus of the cognitive approach.

Although a pure cognitive approach is still frequently applied, the merging of cognitive and behavioral principles begun by D'Zurilla and Goldfried (1971) has become increasingly influential in work with families. Current cognitive–behavioral therapies use one set of procedures to change individual thinking and a different set of procedures to attach new thinking patterns with appropriate behavior (Brasswell & Bloomquist, 1991; Kendall, 1991). The rational problem solving model is usually used in two ways. First, the diagnosed child is trained to use it in his individual thinking. This takes place in individual or child group sessions, or combinations of them. Parents are typically not present. Second, the rational model is used to train families to more effectively manage the difficulties that they have been associating with the child disorder. Applying it at the family level also helps model and maintain cognitive changes in the diagnosed child. The family training is similar to that used in the behavioral model.

After the initial steps of getting therapy underway a detailed assessment determines the nature and extent of the disorder. This allows a treatment plan to be formulated. The early sessions often focus on affective education (e.g., Stark, Rouse, & Livingston, 1991). A child learns the names of emotions and that emotions are experienced on a continuum (e.g., from happy to sad to so sad it hurts). Children learn to identify the different emotions and behavioral cues that often accompany them in themselves and in others. This process may reveal important deficits that require immediate attention in therapy. Some children do not experience the full range of emotions, some experience them but cannot recognize them when they do, some do not recognize them in others. Detailed games and exercises have been developed to deal with these often subtle matters. For some disorders in which emotions produce physical tension (e.g., phobias, conduct disorder), relaxation training is applied (Kendall, 1991). This provides a way to short-circuit physical–cognitive stress cycles in which a physical reaction to an emotional experience tends to elicit more extreme emotions.

Such procedures may seem quite removed from family problem solving. However, I have maintained from the outset that family problems are based on tensions and unmet needs perceived by family members. These cognitive approaches focus directly on some emotions that create those tensions and perceptions of unmet needs. Indeed, when one or more family members' perceptions of emotions are seriously distorted it may be difficult for them to participate in effective problem solving.

The next part of the treatment begins cognitive restructuring (Kendall, 1991). This seeks to remove misinterpretation of environmental events and to build strategies for coping with extreme emotions and situations. Many different techniques are applied in accomplishing this, depending on the disorder and client characteristics. They include instruction in self-monitoring, self-evaluation, and self-reinforcement (Stark et al., 1991). The main goals are to show the children that their initial perceptions of some situations may be incorrect, that people should pay attention to their reactions to situations just to see where they stand, and that initial reactions can be changed into coping thoughts. It may take several sessions of training and practice for a child to learn these skills.

The next stage of treatment focuses on the application of cognitive restructuring through the use of individual problem solving. Although cognitive restructuring is important, it does not extend the impact of the treatment effects to influence the child's adaptation to the environment. The child is taught to recognize intense emotional responses or impulses to do extreme things as potential problems that should be solved. Children are taught to ask themselves the following four questions in order, and to answer each in turn (Braswell & Bloomquist, 1991, p. 296):

1. Stop! What is the problem?
2. What are some plans?
3. What is the best plan?
4. Do the plan.
5. Did the plan work?

There are a number of variations on the techniques used to teach this process to the child (e.g., Kendall, 1991; Stark et al., 1996). Therapists must adjust to each client in terms of how to approach each stage and how much time is needed. For many children it is useful to role-play the problem solving process, with the therapist playing the role of the child using the stages and the client playing the role of another child making trouble. The following is a brief example of what the therapist would say (Braswell & Bloomquist, 1991, p. 151).

> In this situation, you are sitting behind me in class and you are kicking my chair. Okay, start kicking my chair. [The child pretends to kick the chair.]
> Stop! *What is the problem?* The problem is he is kicking my chair and I am getting mad. *What are some plans?* I could turn around and kick his chair, I could tell the teacher, or I could ignore him. *What is the best plan?* If I turn and kick him he might really get mad at me or just keep kicking

me. If I tell the teacher, he might stop kicking me, but he might call me a tattletale. If I ignore him, he may stop kicking me. I think I'll try ignoring him. *Do the plan.* Okay, now I need to ignore him because that was my best plan. [The therapist models ignoring while the child kicks his chair.]

Did my plan work? Yes it did. I thought about it; came up with some plans; did the best one, which was to ignore him; and he stopped kicking my chair.

The training continues by similar exercises in which the therapist plays the role of the troublemaker and the child applies the problem solving process. School-age children usually learn to use the stages in four or five sessions, after which they can begin to be applied to actual situations between sessions (Braswell & Bloomquist, 1991, p. 151). The cognitive therapy can include several different techniques depending on the specific disorder, severity of the case, and other factors. The most significant of these is the increasing use of components that train parents or the whole family in problem solving.

Throughout the history of therapy, parents have been given some education on the nature of their child's disorder and things they could do at home to facilitate the therapy the child received. But more recently, the active involvement of parents during therapy is seen as an essential part of cognitive–behavioral treatment. The following comment is representative of the current view.

> For cognitive–behavioral therapy to succeed with clinically referred children, it must be taught to the primary caregivers (parents, teachers, etc.) of these children who, on a daily basis, in myriad contexts and social exchanges, encounter and manage the impulsive, disinhibited, inattentive, and poorly regulated behavior for which ... [attention deficit disorder] children are notorious. (Barkley, 1991, p. viii)

Part of what parents are taught are basic parenting skills, which are usually derived from behavioral parent training techniques that have been used for some time (e.g., Patterson, 1971). This includes making careful observations of the child's behavior, positively reinforcing good behavior, setting clear and consistent rules, and providing consequences for noncompliant or inappropriate behavior (Braswell & Bloomquist, 1991; Stark et al., 1996; Webster-Stratton, 1996). Increasingly, parents and their children are also taught to do family problem solving as a group (e.g., Anastopoulos et al., 1996; Braswell & Bloomquist, 1991; Kendall, 1991; Lewinsohn et al., 1996; Robin et al., 1996; Vuchinich, Wood, & Angelelli, 1996; Webster-Stratton, 1996). The basic parent training techniques provide a solid foundation for parent–child relations. But they were initially developed to provide treatment for families with young, antisocial children. Their emphasis on reinforcement and discipline practices does not promote the more complex cooperation, negotiation, and adaptive patterns that are needed by families dealing with a wide range of disorders or families with older children. These are provided by the training in family problem solving.

An additional benefit of family problem solving in cognitive–behavioral therapy is that the same problem solving steps the child is taught to use individually are also applied by the family as a whole. This helps generalize the individual training into the home setting and also increases the likelihood that the problem solving process will continue to be used after the termination of treatment. A variety of methods are used to encourage maintenance of treatment effects. These vary from mailing families brochures or newsletters, to telephone checkups, to "booster" follow-up sessions.

Evaluations of cognitive–behavioral therapy for child disorders have generally shown that it is usually effective in reducing symptoms (e.g., Hibbs & Jensen, 1996; Kazdin, 1996). Treatment success, of course, depends on a number of factors. For example, some disorders are innately more recalcitrant than others, some clients have much more severe expressions of the disorder than others, clients vary in how long they have had the disorder, and so on. Although significant reduction in symptoms is an indication of success, a stricter criterion is whether the symptoms are reduced below the clinical level. That is usually a score (or range) on an assessment instrument that separates individuals for whom treatment is usually recommended from those for whom it is not recommended. One quantitative goal of treatment is to have clients score below the clinical level. Cognitive behavioral therapy has had success with this criterion. But with more severe disorders, the proportion of treated cases below clinical levels is sometimes low, in the 10% to 30% range (e.g., Anastopoulos et al., 1996).

Because cognitive–behavioral therapy often includes several components, it is difficult to evaluate the distinct contribution that the problem solving portions make to success. Research designs to test this are complex and expensive. But some studies have examined the role of problem solving components in cognitive–behavioral therapy (Kazdin, 1996; Kazdin et al., 1992). Kazdin et al. (1992), for example, treated 97 children (ages 7 to 13) who had been clinically diagnosed with conduct disorder or oppositional disorder. Three separate treatment conditions were used: parent management training alone (PMT), child problem solving skills training alone (PSST), and a combination of both PMT and PSST that included some family problem solving. They found that all

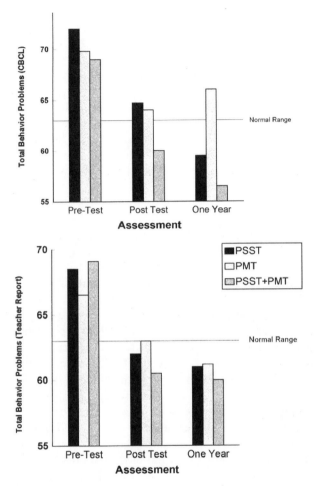

Figure 6.1. Pretest, Posttest, and Follow-up Behavior Problems Scores for Kazdin, Siegel, and Bass Treatment Programs (Kazdin, Siegel, & Bass, 1992). © 1992 by the American Psychological Association. Reprinted with permission.

NOTE: PSST = Problem Solving Skills Training; PMT = Parent Management Training; PSST + PMT = Both Types of Training

three treatments reduced symptoms on the parent-reported Child Behavior Checklist, a standard assessment instrument. But only the combination treatment (PMT *and* PSST) reduced average scores below the clinical level, and maintained that improvement for 1 year after treatment. Figure 6.1 graphically depicts these reductions in Total Behavior Problems at home (Child Behavior Checklist, CBCL) and at school (Child

Behavior Checklist–Teacher Report Form, CBCL–TRF). These findings are especially noteworthy because the disorders are notoriously difficult to treat.

Because the use of family problem solving components in cognitive–behavioral therapy is relatively new, it will be some time before its contribution can be fully evaluated in a quantitative way. What is clear is that therapists dealing with a variety of child disorders are using it. Bringing families into any therapy program adds logistical and inter-personal complexity to the treatment process. The fact that therapists outside of the family therapy realm are willing to accept these additional burdens suggests that the benefits of family-based components are clini-cally pervasive.

Family Problem Solving in Prevention Programs

It has been known for some time that there is an association between negative adolescent outcomes (e.g., mental illness, juvenile delinquency, teenage pregnancy, drug use) and family experience (e.g., Glueck & Glueck, 1950; Henggeler, 1989; McCord, 1991). The potential benefits of preventing such negative outcomes before they occur are well-known (e.g., Bogenschneider, 1996; Dryfoos, 1990). Once mental illness, crime, drug use, or teenage pregnancy have occurred, a substantial amount of damage has already been done to the individuals involved. Typically, these outcomes are not one-time, short-term events. For many, they begin a developmental path of similar negative events. Additional damage is done to those affected by the outcomes, such as crime victims, family members who must cope with mental illness and drug use, children of inadequate teenage parents, and so on. The costs of coping with these outcomes are immense, as society has to deal with individuals who become dangerous to others or are unable to support themselves. Police services, mental health facilities, social service agencies, legal services, child protective service agencies, and drug treatment facilities all are very costly to all of society.

The logic of prevention programs is to avoid these personal and financial costs by interrupting the processes that create the negative outcomes, thus preventing them from occurring. The prevention model is most widely applied in medicine and public health in which the development of certain diseases and other conditions is well understood. For example, infants are given inoculations of substances that prevent the development of childhood diseases such as diphtheria. An essential prerequisite for a prevention program is that the developmental course of the negative outcome be understood. Research over the past 20 years has expanded our understanding of how mental illness, delinquency, drug use, and teenage pregnancy develop. Thus there is increasing interest in applying that knowledge to prevent these outcomes (e.g., Bogenschneider, 1996; Dryfoos, 1990).

But the developmental course of these outcomes is not as strictly determined as the development of physical diseases. In addition, many of the conditions contributing to these negative outcomes cannot be controlled (e.g., poverty). Thus the prevention programs for negative psychological and social outcomes are unlikely to be as successful as those with a simple physical basis. But as the costs of these negative outcomes to society become more apparent, there is an emerging consensus that, even with a lower success rate, such prevention programs offer a better alternative than dealing with the outcomes after they have occurred. This view has been buoyed by several social prevention programs that have recently been proven to be effective. For example, one such program focusing on preventing child abuse was shown to reduce the rate of child abuse by about one half (Olds, Henderson, Chamberlin, & Tatelbaum, 1986; Olds et al., 1997). The field of prevention science is developing new strategies that are being applied to a number of public health issues such as the prevention of underage smoking, alcohol use, and pregnancy.

I will focus on how training in family problem solving is used in some of these prevention programs. The logic behind family problem solving components in prevention is similar to that for treatment. Ineffective family functioning is known to be a contributing cause for negative adolescent outcomes. Family conditions such as child abuse, alcoholism, drug use, child neglect, and inadequate parenting are linked to those outcomes. These conditions impair the ability of the family to adapt in such a way that the needs of children are met. Training in family problem solving provides a way of improving this adaptation.

As in the case of treatment applications, family problem solving is one of a set of components used in prevention. These may include school-based education, community-based education, home-visiting programs by social workers or nurses, brochures or booklets, videotapes, films, and so on. In addition to improving family functioning, home-based problem solving increases the likelihood that beliefs and behavior patterns learned in other modalities generalize to the home setting. It helps mobilize the family to support the goals of the overall prevention program.

There are three types of prevention programs that are distinguished by the extent to which the negative outcome has developed and the population involved. Primary prevention seeks to eliminate a negative outcome by exposing an entire population to the prevention program. Inoculation of all infants to prevent chicken pox is an example of this.

Because the program must be delivered to so many people, low cost is a major consideration. Secondary prevention delivers the program only to an at-risk segment of the population. These are individuals who have social, psychological, or physical characteristics that predispose them to the negative outcome. This is typically determined from studies of the characteristics of those who have experienced the negative outcome. Unwed teenage mothers who were victims of child abuse have high rates of abusing their own children. Thus such mothers could be targeted as an at-risk group for a secondary prevention program.

Primary and secondary prevention are both delivered to individuals who have not yet developed the negative outcome. Tertiary prevention programs focus on preventing the recurrence or expansion of effects in individuals who have already experienced the negative outcome. Drug treatment for a teenager who has already used drugs is an example of this. Tertiary prevention overlaps with treatment but emphasizes the prevention of specific outcomes rather than curing an ongoing disorder.

Training in various types of family problem solving has been used in all three types of prevention work. These components are usually less intensive than those used in treatment programs. The goals for the family problem solving component are similar in treatment and prevention applications, and the rational model is used as a foundation. But cost limits require that scaled-down problem solving components be applied. The treatment norm of one highly trained therapist working with one family on their problem solving is simply not feasible in most prevention programs. Less expensive options for delivery (e.g., group training, print material, videotapes) have been developed. A comprehensive review of the prevention programs that use family problem solving is not practical. Instead, I will provide one example for each of the three types of prevention: primary, secondary, and tertiary. Some programs can be adapted for use across these types.

The logic of prevention is flawless. But prevention requires that time and money be spent on individuals who have not yet developed the negative outcome, and ultimately may never develop it. Individual families typically believe that such negative outcomes will probably not happen to their children. Thus they see investing time and money in prevention as wasteful. Schools, churches, and governments are painfully aware that those outcomes will develop in a considerable proportion of those families. They are most interested in the benefits of prevention. But unless the rates of the negative outcome are alarmingly high, public support for funding prevention programs has always been limited. As a result, there has not yet been adequate funding to apply high quality prevention programs except in limited experiments. But even with limited funding, schools, churches, communities, and all levels of government are becoming more involved in prevention efforts.

FAMILY PROBLEM SOLVING IN PRIMARY PREVENTION

One program that has been used for the primary and secondary prevention of adolescent drug use is Preparing for the Drug Free Years (Hawkins, Catalano, & Kent, 1991). This is a five-session, 10-hour multimedia program designed for families with children in fifth and sixth grades. The children attend only one session on peer pressure resistance. The parents attend the four other sessions, which include training in identifying risk factors for adolescent substance abuse, effective child management, and positive involvement of children. Family conflict management and the use of family meetings are two key elements in the training. These modules use part of the rational problem solving model to help parents reduce conflict and increase cohesion. The principle is that when adolescents are part of adaptive families, they are less likely to turn to drug use.

Research has been done on factors contributing to the success of this prevention program (Spoth, Redmond, Haggerty, & Ward, 1995). This is a low-cost program with a clear focus, which makes it feasible as primary prevention. Because the program has not been fully evaluated in large populations, it is not yet clear how effective it is. It is unlikely that any 10-hour program can prevent all adolescent drug abuse. But in conjunction with other efforts, such programs may make a significant contribution compared with no program at all. My main concern is how family problem solving is being used in prevention programs, rather than the issues associated with evaluation.

Many middle and high schools are implementing programs to prevent drug use, violence, teenage pregnancy, and other negative outcomes. When delivered to all students these can be considered as primary prevention programs. Some schools implement problem solving programs for the school to help reduce difficulties with peer conflict and student–teacher conflict. Although some of these bring parents into the picture, most focus on problem solving in the school context. Even though such programs do not include family problem solving, they typically promote the rational model that may generalize to the home. Because most children attend schools over a long period of time the school setting is perhaps the most reasonable place for any primary prevention program. Involving all parents in active participation in primary prevention programs is a challenge and may be a limiting factor in applying family problem solving components (Dumka et al., 1995).

FAMILY PROBLEM SOLVING IN SECONDARY PREVENTION

Because secondary prevention focuses on a relatively small at-risk segment of the population, it can provide a more extensive program. Elements of family problem solving are included in a variety of secondary prevention efforts (e.g., Conduct Problems Prevention Research Group, 1992; Wasik, Bryant, & Lyons, 1990). One example is the Metropolitan Area Child Study family intervention (Tolan & McKay, 1996) designed to prevent antisocial delinquent behavior in inner-city, low-income, minority neighborhoods in and around Chicago. Because very high delinquency rates have always been associated with these factors, children in these neighborhoods are considered to be at risk. This prevention program involves families of children 7 to 13 years old in a 22-week program that includes elements of family therapy as well as cognitive behavioral training. The third phase of the program (weeks 4 and 5) involves two sessions on "problem definition" (Tolan & McKay, 1996, p. 151). The bulk of the program (weeks 6–20) addresses other family relationship issues, including specific training in family problem solving and family meetings.

This program is noteworthy because it is the first relatively large study ($N = 4,125$) of delinquency prevention in an inner-city minority population. Early reports from this research emphasize the challenges associated with delivering a systematic family program in this environment (Tolan & McKay, 1996). The evaluation of such preventions requires years of follow-up, however, and results are not yet available.

FAMILY PROBLEM SOLVING IN TERTIARY PREVENTION

It is well-known that once any negative outcome occurs, the likelihood of recurrence or the occurrence of related difficulties increases. Perhaps the best example is prison incarceration. After a person has been in prison once, the chances of future crime and incarceration greatly increase. A similar pattern holds for residence in mental health institutions, as well as several negative child and adolescent outcomes. For example, children diagnosed with conduct disorder are at higher risk for dropping out of school, drug use, delinquency, and so on later in their lives (Patterson, Reid, & Dishion, 1992). The reasons for this pattern depend on the outcomes involved. In some cases, institutionalization, prison, or a mental health diagnosis tend to create a self-identity that promotes continued problem behavior. The social labeling or stigma associated with these life events can similarly shape behavior in negative ways. In other cases, recurrence can be part of the natural course of a mental health disorder such as depression or schizophrenia.

For individuals experiencing these events, the family can be an important source of support in recovery from a challenging life event. But at the same time, such events disrupt family organization and can reduce its ability to function as a source of support. Such events and their aftermath can increase conflict and family stress. In this frame of reference, family problem solving can be beneficial in facilitating the family's positive adaptation to a negative life event for one of its members. Of course, as we have seen, family processes may have been involved in creating the negative outcome in the first place. In such cases, problem solving training can address some of the causes of the events.

An example of the use of problem solving in tertiary prevention is the family-based program to prevent relapse of severe schizophrenia symptoms and return to residential mental health care (e.g., Falloon, 1988). As noted earlier, a linkage between family processes and schizophrenia has been recognized for some time (e.g., Bateson et al., 1956). More recently, the clearest empirical connections have been found with the concept of "expressed emotion," a subtle pattern of family interaction in which family members have excessive affective involvement that also carries a negative message (Mueser et al., 1993). Several schizophrenia treatment programs include components that use variations of family problem solving to avoid the expressed emotion pattern. It is known that schizophrenia often has a genetic basis, and that drug therapy can be effective. In combinations with the latest drug and individual therapies, the family-based problem solving components seem to contribute to treatment success (Falloon, 1988).

Given this background, it is clear that there is a solid basis for problem solving in tertiary prevention in schizophrenia. Schizophrenia is a chronic disorder that requires long-term care. A major issue in this care is how frequently and for what durations the patient requires hospitalization in a residential care facility. Such hospitalization is common in most cases, and is a costly, often traumatic event. The Falloon program focuses on preventing the recurrence of symptoms severe enough to require rehospitalization (Falloon, 1988). The family component follows a psychoeducational format. While the patient is still hospitalized, family members are given instruction in the nature of schizophrenia and the kinds of symptoms to expect when the patient returns home. In addition, they receive training in family problem solving to promote open communication and the resolution of the inevitable problems. This training combats the subtle nagging intertwined conflict forms produced by high levels of expressed emotion. Family training may also include the patient before and after returning home. As with most applications, problem solving is one of several components. Falloon's program is recognized as one of the best success stories in mental health prevention. It has been shown to prevent or delay rehospitalization in most cases. Patients are able to spend much less time in mental hospitals. For example, in a 2-year follow-up after hospital discharge, 83% of patients in the family program had no recurrence of substantial clinical episodes of schizophrenia. But only 17% of patients in an individual program avoided the recurrence of such symptoms (Falloon et al., 1988). The family problem solving program promotes adaptation to home and community environments and drastically cuts the cost of long-term care by avoiding rehospitalization.

Another example of family problem solving in tertiary prevention is the multisystemic therapy developed by Henggeler and colleagues (Henggeler, 1992; Henggeler & Borduin, 1990). One focus of this therapy is previously incarcerated juvenile offenders (Henggeler, 1992). A goal is to prevent reincarceration by using a family preservation approach. This program is especially sensitive to the social ecology of the juvenile and includes a wide variety of components depending on the social and psychological resources in the immediate environment. An eclectic therapeutic approach is needed, and training in family problem solving is one component that is useful in several of these contexts. Indeed, the concept of adaptive problem solving is a fundamental pillar in this program.

Family Problem Solving in Parent Education

Parent education refers to any program designed to improve parenting behavior. All of the family treatment and prevention programs outlined previously include elements of parent education. But parent education is not limited to such programs designed to cure or prevent negative outcomes. In some contexts, parent education is done as family enrichment. No disorder is present or expected. The goal is to provide ways for parents and children to get more out of their family life. In recent years, the sale of self-help books on parenting has exploded. Parenting experts flood conferences, the lecture circuits, television, and now the Internet. Using books as guides to parenting has been widely accepted since Spock's classic child care manual (1946).

But the recent volume of sales of books and other media on parenting suggests that parents are more interested than ever before in receiving information on parenting. It is easy to speculate on the reasons for this increase. It may be a result of rapid changes in American family structure, the increase in knowledge about parenting and child development, or technological changes that reduce the costs of publication and other forms of media. It is not known whether this material is having any effect on the quality of parenting in America. These are questions that do not have answers. What is clear, however, is that family problem solving has taken a place, or a market share if you will, in this expansion.

As was noted in chapter 2, family problem solving has been included as part of parent education for half a century. Dreikurs's (1948) detailed manual for parents integrated guidelines for discipline and support with explicit instructions on problem solving during family meetings. His work has had a wide following over the years, especially in family counseling. One of the most popular current parent education books for parents was written by Dreikurs's disciples, who have translated and extended his ideas for use in the modern era (Dinkmeyer & McKay, 1989). The needs of American society have produced a veritable explosion in the amount of parent education materials available in various forms. Dreikurs's ideas have had a major impact on much of that material. Dreikurs is of interest not only because of the extent of his influence, but from the beginning he emphasized the importance of families solving problems together. His parenting system advocates a more "democratic" approach with emphasis on reasoning in discipline and restraint in consequences of disobedience. His model posits that effective parenting involves much more than discipline. The development of the child requires interaction with parents to learn to see the other person's viewpoint, to move beyond a selfish ethical standard, and to negotiate solutions that are fair to all family members. Dreikurs proposed regular family council meetings as a way of accomplishing this (1948). In modern terms, this is family problem solving.

There are many different forms of parent education that apply problem solving. I focus briefly on the popular Dinkmeyer and McKay (1989) program, Systematic Training for Effective Parenting. The program integrates Dreikurs's approach with several more recent approaches, including the cognitive and behavioral models described previously. It includes modules on understanding the child's misbehavior, self-esteem, parent–child communication, and discipline. *The Parent's Handbook* (Dinkmeyer & McKay, 1989) is a highly effective manual that describes the key elements of parenting in laypersons' terms. This a very polished book that is clear and compelling in describing the necessary principles, and in giving well-conceived examples and practical worksheets. The years of experience in parent education that went into this product are apparent. The material is engaging and even fun to read, with summary tear-out charts and clever cartoon drawings of family situations that ring true to any parent.

One chapter is devoted to exploring alternatives and expressing ideas. This chapter instructs the parent in showing the child how to use the stages of rational problem solving to deal with a problem he or she is having. This follows the individual problem solving training given by therapists in the cognitive behavioral treatment. Another chapter is devoted to family meetings. It includes instructions for using the problem solving stages in the group setting. But it also covers a host of practical issues that are important in actually doing regular family meetings. For example, it emphasizes the importance of including positive activities at every family meeting. Family meetings do not work if they become just gripe sessions. It gives specific recommendations on how to get family members to participate, how to include children of different ages, handling meetings when all family members are not present, and so on. These practical matters are critical to actually creating a regular niche in the family ecosystem when family problem solving can take place. Knowing the stages of family problem solving will have little benefit if situations are not available for using them.

Evaluations of parent education programs have indicated that they have some beneficial effects along with limitations (see Thomas, 1996, for a review). Programs for parents with younger children often do not include family problem solving training. Those that do include it have not sought to assess the distinct contribution of problem solving components. Funding for research is more readily available for programs that seek to prevent or treat specific disorders or negative outcomes. Thus the role of problem solving in parent education may not be empirically established for some time. Be that as it may, its role has been practically established by its continued inclusion in parent education programs.

Summary

The past 20 years has seen a steady increase in the use of family problem solving components in treatment, prevention, and parent education. Much of this has been a result of theoretical applications combined with trial and error in finding techniques that are effective. The role of the family in many negative outcomes has been apparent for decades. But pinning down exactly what can be done with the family to help matters has proven to be more elusive. Trying to develop practical and effective techniques for working directly with such vague concepts as adaptability, cohesion, family relationships, double binds, expressed emotion, and the like has been a difficult challenge.

One way of interpreting the increased application of family problem solving techniques is that the rational model uniquely provides two essential features. On the one hand, it is made up of a clear, straightforward set of stages. There are only about five of them and they make sense to most family members. Thus the advantage is that family members can learn them rather easily. They are not complex to describe, and they do not involve intense psychodynamic experiences. They can be taught in the guise of useful skills and do not presume that any family member is diseased or deficient. It may not always be easy to follow through with them, however. But family members do not know that as the training gets underway. As indicated in chapter 5, rational problem solving is consistent with a cultural value of rationality in America. This streamlines the acceptance of the ideas as well as the learning of them. For most family members, the stages of problem solving have a familiar ring from the beginning.

The second feature is that the rational problem solving model provides a lever into the core of adaptive family functioning. It does not directly change many characteristics of a family system. But by providing a format for unmet needs to be expressed, and for family members to jointly create ways of getting those needs met, it taps into perhaps the most fundamental function of the family—meeting the needs of its members. Insofar as that is true, it stands as evidence in favor of Dewey's theory on the adaptive function of rational problem solving (Dewey, 1910/1982, 1938). Rational problem solving apparently helps individual and family systems adapt to their environments.

The adaptation principle appears again and again across the 100 years of work on problem solving (e.g., Dewey, 1910/1982, 1938; D'Zurilla & Goldfried, 1971; Haley, 1987; Reiss, 1981; Tallman, 1961; Vuchinich et al., 1996; Weakland, 1976). The principle continues to find new applications as evidenced in recent work in human development (Lewis, 1997), cognitive science (Pinker, 1997), and evolutionary psychology (Barkow et al., 1992). It is in terms of adaptation that family problem solving fits into general theories of family systems. Ultimately, progress in family applications using problem solving will depend on this theoretical connection. Most prior work has begun with an abstract concept of problem solving and applied it to the family. Much may be gained by reversing the emphasis to consider how family structures and patterns constrain the way problem solving occurs. That is what David Reiss's family paradigm concept introduced to the problem solving field (1981). It is also the basis for the positions developed here in chapters 4 and 5. Bringing more family into family problem solving may offer an avenue for further improvements in treatment and prevention programs.

7

Recent Advances in
Family Problem Solving

This book has sought to provide some measure of integration to the family problem solving field in three ways. First, most work on this topic can be understood in terms of an interplay between rational models and irrational behavior in family systems. Second, we showed how research, theory, and applications in diverse fields have been converging as a result of a continuous series of empirical studies and applications over the past 50 or so years. This convergence has centered on the rational model and efforts to supplement it. Third, the principle of adaptation has been at the foundation of work on family problem solving across all the scientific disciplines.

The past decade has shown especially encouraging signs of convergence. For example, elements of structural family therapy and cognitive–behavioral therapy are being merged in several applications that use family problem solving (e.g., Robin & Foster, 1989; Tolan & McKay, 1996). Relevant findings in developmental psychology are being applied in clinical psychology (Conduct Problems Prevention Research Group, 1992). Sociological methods have been applied to prevention efforts (Rueter & Conger, 1995). Although these connections are exciting, the emergence of a unified theory of family problem solving is not imminent. Disciplinary paradigms are still separated by theoretical and methodological barriers that are difficult to overcome. Nevertheless, the research results and applications are driving toward integration. As this trend continues, a theoretical unification becomes increasingly likely. This could yield extended benefits for all types of applications. The prospects for such a unification depend largely on the direction taken by future research.

In this chapter, the focus turns to three recent advances that hold great promise for improving theory, research, and practice in family problem solving. Then I describe two challenges with which future work in this area must come to grips. The advances reviewed reflect the perspective on problem solving presented in this book. No attempt is made to review all the important streams of ongoing work in the field—there are too many. The advances selected include research findings, theoretical developments, and technological innovations that have emerged over the past two decades. Some of these advances have been briefly discussed in earlier chapters, though their special significance for future work was not addressed. The three advances are in the areas of (a) understanding the natural course of development of family problem solving, (b) an expanding interest in qualitative research and constructionist theory applied to the family, and (c) technological tools available for improving family problem solving in a large segment of society.

The Natural Course of
Development of Family Problem Solving

All family members start out as children. Their problem solving proclivities do not suddenly appear in adolescence, at the age of 21, or when they have their own children. Most work on family problem solving has funneled attention on the formidable task of capturing the elusive process in the family group. Perhaps that has been necessary in establishing the viability of the concept and applying it in beneficial ways. But an adequate model of family problem solving will ultimately require an understanding of how these processes develop in the individual. Indeed, efforts at improving family problem solving can gain tremendously from knowledge about its natural course of development in individuals and in families.

There are factors that have inhibited work on this topic. One is that it adds a layer of temporal complexity to an already complex phenomenon. Inevitably, developmental studies require longitudinal research that is difficult and expensive to conduct. Despite such factors, the recent successes in treatment programs for child and adolescent disorders have given a new motivation to pursue such work. Deficits in interpersonal problem solving skills are associated with negative child and adolescent outcomes. Treating those deficits yields beneficial results. Thus understanding the developmental sources of those deficits can provide insights for better treatment and prevention.

In the past 10 years, there has been an increase in interest in how individual problem solving comes about. This research has produced a fragmentary set of images of how interpersonal problem solving emerges through the first 18 years of life (e.g., Ellis & Siegler, 1994). This includes some findings on how the interpersonal problem solving maps onto family problem solving. Although there are still many gaps in the developmental sequence, the fact that research has begun serious efforts to put together these pieces represents a major advance for understanding family problem solving.

As indicated in chapter 3, much of the psychological research on problem solving has addressed individuals trying to solve problems of logic or mathematics. Work on the cognitive approach to child adjustment (e.g., Spivack et al., 1976) stimulated interest in interpersonal problem solving and the more general concept of social competence. Developmental psychologists began providing measures for these aspects of cognition and behavior. This allowed studies of what factors were associated with development in these domains (Ellis & Siegler, 1994). Experimental paradigms have pushed the analysis of interpersonal problem solving to the age of 2 years and beyond (e.g., Ellis & Siegler, 1994; Frankel & Bates, 1990). Some of these studies include parents, and thus introduce a family component. The mother–toddler experiments study how the mother and child jointly work to solve puzzles involving toys. Problem solving is measured by the extent to which the puzzles are solved. Problem solving was linked to mother–child attachment in infancy and child temperament. Such studies do not easily mesh with the most prevalent paradigms in family problem solving. But they provide a starting point for making connections.

As indicated in chapter 3, Selman and colleagues (e.g., Selman et al., 1986; Yeates et al., 1991) have proposed a comprehensive individual developmental model for Interpersonal Negotiation Strategies (INS). Their model merges the rational problem solving stages with developmental theory. Unlike much of the work on child and adolescent problem solving, this model seeks to provide a general description of how problem solving develops in "normal" individuals. This theoretical model, the methods used to test it, and the research that has shown evidence for it must all be considered as important recent advances. Even if major flaws are found, their basic premise elevates the analysis of problem solving to an entirely new dimension of inquiry: Interpersonal problem solving has a natural course of development similar to basic individual characteristics as intelligence or personality.

The INS work has only begun to consider the question of what factors shape an individual's development through the INS levels and the role of the family in that process (e.g., Beardslee, Schultz, & Selman, 1987; Selman et al., 1986). It is likely that family factors have a considerable impact on this development. There is already considerable overlap between the INS interview coding system and those currently used to assess family problem solving observationally (e.g., Vuchinich et al.,

1996). But additional work is needed to merge the INS research with ongoing work on family problem solving.

Although a model of the development of problem solving abilities in individuals is a significant advance, it may be only one part of the picture. Perhaps the family's contribution to problem solving skills can be subsumed within an individual model as merely a contributing factor. Perhaps family problem solving is simply some function of the individual problem solving skills of each family member. But it is also possible that family problem solving has a life of its own, and that the whole is more than the sum of its parts (e.g., Reiss, 1981). There is considerable support for such a systems view. Little is known about the extent to which the problem solving of individual family members is related to their family's problem solving.

Linking individual and family models of problem solving creates challenges. But some research is already taking the position that it is important to understand how exposure to certain kinds of family problem solving may influence child development (e.g., Cummings & Davies, 1994; Vuchinich et al., 1996). This work reflects a growing trend of developmental studies to increasingly take family factors into account. Advances in knowledge about how individuals acquire problem solving abilities will make a positive contribution to our understanding of family problem solving.

Addressing complex developmental questions has stimulated more rigorous approaches to measuring family problem solving. In recent studies, such techniques as factor analysis, multiple family informants, and structural equation models (see Appendixes F and G; Rueter & Conger, 1995; Vuchinich & DeBaryshe, 1997; Vuchinich et al., 1993) have been used. This work has found that a variety of measures of family problem solving do have solid psychometric properties. Although no single measure has yet emerged as being universally superior, there has been convergence on what aspects of family behavior signal effective problem solving. Combinations of observational and questionnaire reports seem to provide the most comprehensive assessment (e.g., Rueter & Conger, 1995; see Appendix F), though it is somewhat expensive. Adequate measurement of family problem solving has never been a major scientific obstacle. But the use of advanced statistical techniques is providing a new level of precision in those measures. Such precision is especially important in longitudinal studies of problem solving.

Considering the natural course of development of individual and family problem solving provides a potentially valuable approach to understanding the phenomena of interest. Those phenomena, as we have seen, are quite complex. Previous chapters have shown that it is not easy to isolate exactly what should be studied. But some discrete parts of the family problem solving puzzle are relatively easy to isolate and examine. For example, episodes of verbal family conflict can be located and examined in detail (e.g., Gottman, 1979; Patterson, 1982; Vuchinich, 1987). Understanding how these episodes unfold can provide empirically based insights on how families deal with their problems. Recent research has shed new light on the natural history of family conflict episodes.

One way of viewing this new approach is to consider a verbal family conflict as an important type of microlevel family problem. Any time a family conflict erupts it may be considered as a "problem." The disagreements, oppositions, threats, and the like that make up family conflicts can be seen as reactions to blocked goals (Tallman, 1988). Consider a mother arguing with her son about his refusal to do his chore of taking out the trash. The son is blocking her goal of getting the trash taken out, and perhaps also a secondary goal of teaching her son responsibility through assignment of chores. Taking out the trash could also block the son's goal of watching his favorite television show. In this manner, any family conflict can be conceptualized in terms of blocked goals, and thus as a "problem" in terms of the problem solving literature. The way the family handles the conflict may be viewed as an indication of its problem solving process. The research on how family conflicts end or "resolve" their conflicts provides the best available window on how the micro-problems are handled.

In a series of studies, I addressed the question of how families end their conflict episodes from a different perspective (Vuchinich, 1986, 1987, 1990; Vuchinich, Emery, & Cassidy, 1988). Rather than presupposing the traditional problem solving paradigm, I examined how families ended conflicts from a data-driven sociolinguistic perspective. Sociologists had been inductively analyzing natural units of conversation for some time (e.g., Sacks, Schegloff, & Jefferson, 1974). Goffman had demonstrated a classical foundation for such analysis from ethology and sociology (Goffman, 1971, 1981). The conversation analysis movement had already established conflicts as units of analysis (Goodwin, 1981; Maynard, 1985), as well as a framework for understanding how such units end (Schegloff & Sacks, 1973). In essence, I pursued a more inductive approach to family behavior sequences, as suggested in chapter 4.

I began by collecting several hundred conflict episodes from video-tapes of 52 diverse families having dinner at home with no researchers present (Vuchinich, 1986, 1987). As with all studies of interaction since Bales (1950), conflict episodes were easily located. Using inductive procedures and previous work on conflict, four recurrent social arrangements for ending family conflicts were identified: submission, compromise, withdrawal, and standoff (Vuchinich, 1987, 1990). In the standoff, the disputants simply drop the conflict with no apparent resolution. Standoffs ended more than 60% of the conflicts, with submissions ending about 20%, and compromise ending about 15%. Although there are glaring limitations to this study (e.g., generalizability and the potential of family reactivity to being videotaped), it provided new information on how families manage their conflicts in an ecologically valid family situation. This is especially pertinent to the link between family conflict and family problem solving. If the study is an approximate reflection of "normal" families, it means that most conflicts are not resolved at all. But about half of those that are resolved *do* involve some compromise, and about half are resolved on the basis of power relations in the family.

Because the study was descriptive, implications for theory must be based on interpretation. The presence of compromise solutions clearly suggests that resolutions consistent with the problem solving literature do occur in routine family interactions, though they account for a small proportion of conflict endings. In addition, the role of power relations in problem solving has been acknowledged since Strodtbeck's early work (1954), and the family therapists' demonstration of the importance of hierarchy (Haley, 1987; Madanes, 1981). The high frequency of standoff endings, however, has an implication for considering family conflict episodes as family problem solving. Families are either unable to, or not concerned with, resolving most of their conflicts. Unresolved conflicts seem to be accepted as normal. This diverges from the problem solving literature that emphasizes creating a single best "solution" to every problem—essentially a miniresolution for every problem. However, that literature, dating back to Dewey, does acknowledge that any given solution may not work and needs to be tried and reevaluated. Families may be unwilling to push for resolution of conflict episodes if no workable resolution seems to be forthcoming. The proportion of conflicts that get resolved could be an indication of family functioning.

The high frequency of unresolved conflicts led me to consider other mechanisms that constrain conflicts. Again drawing from sociolinguistics, I considered the possibility that family conflicts are constrained by a social regulation mechanism that governs conversational conflict units in a manner similar to the way other aspects of social interaction are governed. Bales's early studies of the distribution of participation in problem solving groups led Mishler to study the length of question–answer sequences during problem solving (Mishler, 1975). He found that an exponential law accurately described how long question–answer episodes were sustained. The turn-at-talk was the unit of analysis. The exponential law says that the probability of continuing the question–answer activity for one more turn is constant throughout the questioning sequence. A questioning sequence was conceptualized as a sociolinguistic unit. It was already well-known that an exponential law governed the length of linguistic units such as words and sentences (e.g., Miller, Newman, & Friedman, 1958).

My colleagues and I surmised that a similar "law" might apply to conflict sequences, because most conflicts did not have a rational resolution to close them off (Vuchinich, 1986, 1987). Perhaps the duration of family conflicts was organized in terms of a sociolinguistic unit. Patterson (1982) had examined the probability of continuing conflict in his sequential analysis of reinforcement contingencies in coercive family interactions, but did not consider how conflicts ended. Reid (1986) had found differences in conflict duration in families in which child abuse had occurred. Thus it was clear that length of family conflicts was pertinent to troubled families. But there was no principled theory for what determined how long conflicts should last in nondistressed families.

We posited (Vuchinich, 1986, 1987) that family members learn how to do conflicts as cultural speech activities (Gumperz, 1982). They should continue long enough to accomplish the functions of conflict (e.g., boundary maintenance, reaffirming hierarchy, emotional expression), but not enough to be redundant or excessively damaging to family bonds. A constant probability of continuing conflict (i.e., an exponential law) would serve to regulate conflict duration consistent with these criteria. Such a law would provide a sociolinguistic answer to the question, "How long do families continue to fight?"

Using videotapes of family dinners made in the homes of 52 families, we located conflict episodes and counted how many conversational turns were taken in each episode. We found that conflict duration, measured as the number of turns-at-talk in the conflict in an episode, was consistent with an exponential law once the conflict was underway (Vuchinich, 1987). The Markov chain provides a way of mathematically representing an exponential law (e.g., Vuchinich, 1986). If an exponential law is operating, the following equation should hold in any sample of conflict episodes.

$$F_u = ntc^{\frac{1}{u-r}}$$

In this equation n is the total number of conflict episodes in the sample, t is the probability of terminating the episode in the next turn, and c is the constant probability of continuing a conflict episode for one more turn. The values for t and c can be estimated using regression (Vuchinich, 1986); n is simply the sample size. Figure 7.1 shows the values of these terms for data on 318 conflict episodes. The predicted and the observed frequency of conflicts of each length from 1 through 12 turns are also

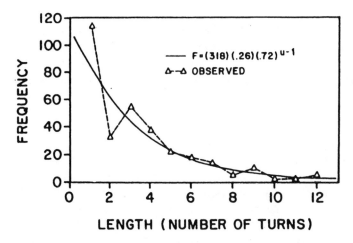

Figure 7.1. Frequency of Family Conflicts by Length of Conflict (Vuchinich, 1986)

shown. The model provides an adequate fit to the data. But it is clear that it does not fit as well for one- and two-turn conflicts. Pursuing the basic exponential law required the inclusion of one-turn conflicts. But conceptually, a single verbal attack without a counterattack is not really a conflict. A true conflict is only fully initiated after an initial attack is followed by a counterattack. That might explain why an exponential law is so accurate for conflict episodes three or more turns long (Vuchinich, 1987).

It is surprising how close a very simple principle could come to explaining a key feature (length) of such a complex family phenomenon (conflict). These results provided some general support for the idea that the shape of family conflicts is influenced by some systematic features of social interaction. From this perspective, constraints on something as potentially volatile and destructive as family conflict cannot be left to the whims of individual family members with various motives, skills, and levels of emotional stability. Such criteria often would not lead to beneficial decisions about when to stop or regulate family conflicts. So some patterns of interaction may be learned as a part of family life that more consistently regulates conflict episodes. Of course, people do not think about such things as exponential laws during family conflicts. But their behavior seems to follow such a pattern nevertheless. If the duration of family conflicts was based on the capriciousness of individual emotional dispositions and personalities, a more random distribution of conflict lengths would be observed.

Although the length of family conflicts as turns in a sociolinguistic unit is interesting, it does not reflect the amount of time family members actually spend in conflict episodes. A turn may last a few seconds or for minutes. Elapsed time may capture features of family conflicts not apparent when analyzing episode length in terms of turns-at-talk. We later examined exact conflict durations in seconds using hazard models in two larger independent samples of family conflicts (Vuchinich & Teachman, 1993; Vuchinich, Teachman, & Crosby, 1991).

Although an exponential law may provide a structured "envelope" for regulating conflicts, some systematic variations within that envelope would be expected. Indeed, because long conflict episodes typically become more unpleasant as they are extended, their likelihood of ending might well be expected to increase with elapsed time. The increasing unpleasantness, and the decreasing likelihood of anything beneficial emerging, suggests that the utility of the conflict for the family should decline as the conflict drags on. We predicted that because of this decreasing utility (i.e., cost–benefit ratio), there should be an increasing likelihood of a conflict ending as it is extended in real time. Such a pattern would not be captured by an analysis of the number of turns in conflict episodes. We proposed that within the structural constraints of the exponential law, there should be a second layer of constraints to conflict duration based on decreasing utility of longer conflicts.

To test for this second type of constraint, we used hazard models. The hazard rate is a mathematical indicator of how likely a conflict is to end at any time once it is underway. We found evidence for increasing hazard rates in two independent samples of family conflict episodes. (Vuchinich & Teachman, 1993; Vuchinich et al., 1991). The link between utility and conflict duration was also examined in samples of wars, strikes, and riots (Vuchinich & Teachman, 1993). Hazard rates for wars and strikes were predicted to decrease because nations and unions typically stockpiled resources in preparation for conflict, and stood to win discrete benefits if they can outlast their opponents. That prediction was also confirmed (Vuchinich & Teachman, 1993). In wars and strikes, there is no family bond to be eroded by extended conflict, so fights are more likely to continue "to the death."

The hazard model studies also demonstrated that the likelihood of continuing a conflict episode varied systematically according to the social context. More participants resulted in longer conflicts. Parent–child conflicts tended to last longer (Vuchinich, 1986, 1987; Vuchinich et al., 1991). This was consistent with the kind of variation in conflict sequences found by Patterson (1982) and Reid (1986). Further research showed that the shape of the conflict hazard function varied across different types for families. Families with a child who had been referred

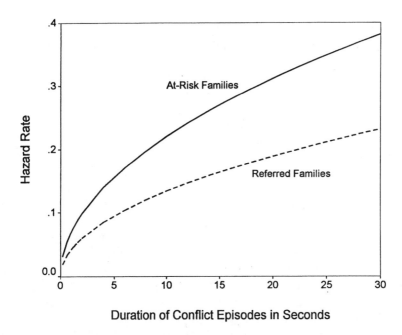

Figure 7.2. Hazard Curves for Referred and At-Risk Families

for treatment of antisocial behavior had significantly higher conflict hazard rates than comparable at-risk families whose child had never been referred to treatment (see Figure 7.2). Such research may help isolate when and how the conflicts of dysfunctional families diverge from those in comparison families.

Sequential analysis was also applied to the formation and functioning of alliances during family conflicts (Vuchinich et al., 1988). The course of conflict was found to be influenced by coalitions of two family members against a third. Family roles (e.g., mother, son) constrained how coalitions were formed and how interventions were done. The results demonstrated systematic features of how family members intervened in conflicts to extend or mediate them. The analysis showed how triadic family structures function in the resolution of conflicts.

Although these studies did not focus directly on problem solving activities as such, they provide a valuable description of the natural history of family conflicts and an approach to explaining how conflicts are terminated or resolved. Family conflicts are apparently constrained in systematic ways that can be expressed in family-level mathematical parameters, such as the probability of continuing conflict. These are similar to the kinds of parameters that have emerged from Gottman's analytic perspective (e.g., Cook, Tyson, White, Rushe, & Gottman, 1995). Like Reiss's concept of family paradigms (Reiss, 1981), such analyses do not fit well into the rational model of problem solving. They posit family-level processes beyond the rational action of individuals. Such processes specify discrete limits to how families can socially construct their problems and the ways they deal with them. Such social constructions can take many forms, but they must function within layers of constraints. The specific implications these processes have for prevention and treatment have not yet been fully developed. They will become more important as more comprehensive models of family problem solving are pursued.

The research on family conflict episodes has been complemented by new work on specific aspects of problem solving. An important strand of that work focused on what factors predicted good problem solving by the family as a group. This has come to be assessed by coder ratings of such features of the discussions as how many possible solutions were brought up, the quality of the solutions, and the extent to which the problem was solved (e.g., Forgatch, 1989; Rueter & Conger, 1995; Vuchinich et al., 1993). These are key features of family interaction that emerge in the context of conflict about a family problem.

One series of studies examined the affective interchanges between family members that tended to produce better problem solving outcomes. Rueter and Conger (1995; see Appendix F), for example, found expressions of positive affect (e.g., warmth) promoted better problem solving. Such studies added to earlier findings that expression of negative affect hindered problem solving (Forgatch, 1989). These results are not surprising. Families that tend to complain, argue, fight, and show little support for each other do not make much progress in solving problems. But these results are important for two reasons. First, they raise the possibility that adjustments in the *affective* tone of family interactions may lead to improved problem solving, regardless of the family's level of problem solving skill. Second, they suggest that "open" communication, usually considered a beneficial feature in families, can be carried too far when family members share their negative feelings too much. In a similar vein, agreement between parents should enhance family problem solving. But when that agreement takes the form of an alliance against a child, the family problem solving deteriorates (Vuchinich et al., 1993).

These methods were used to consider the contribution of other factors to problem solving. In a longitudinal study (Vuchinich et al., 1996), we found that family problem solving (see Appendix D2 for description of the scale) deteriorated during the child's preadolescence (ages 10 to 12) because of the increase in the child's autonomy striving. Thus the quality of family problem solving is tied to the course of the child's development.

The study further found evidence that conflict between the father and preadolescent was responsible for much of the decline. The special difficulties between fathers and adolescents had been noted in previous research (e.g., Steinberg, 1981). But this study showed that such difficulties may subvert the problem solving of the family as a whole.

The analysis also showed that problem solving was significantly worse when a parent, rather than the preadolescent, selected the problem to be discussed. This echoed a similar result from the marital problem solving literature in which problem solving is much less effective when the wife, rather than the husband, selects the problem to be discussed (Heavey et al., 1993). The common thread is that parents in the family context, and wives in the marital context, tend to be the ones who initiate discussions about "problems." It is not clear why there is poorer problem solving when the more frequent discussion initiator selects the topic. Perhaps the more frequent initiator's complaints are taken less seriously because there are so many of them and they often prove to be insubstantial. For example, a spouse might use complaints as a way of getting attention. Over time, such complaints may be seen as "crying wolf"—that is, a false alarm that turns out to have little basis. This cry wolf hypothesis would suggest that other family members may be less sincere about pursuing solutions because they have seen too many false alarms from that person.

These studies suggest that family problem solving is shaped by several factors beyond the rational phases of problem solving. They have empirically demonstrated that family problem solving is systematically sensitive to the developmental status of children, the ecological context of the problem solving, the affective style of the family, the structure of family coalitions, and the logic of conflict episodes. These are important factors to consider in understanding why one family solves problems effectively, and another family cannot. The developmental approach opens up new ways of thinking about family problem solving.

A second strand of developmental work tested whether good family problem solving predicted other variables of developmental concern. In a longitudinal study, Coughlin and Vuchinich (1996) found that better family problem solving when the child was 10 significantly reduced the risk of arrest by age 17 in stepfamilies. Better problem solving in a structured problem solving task was linked with shorter parent–preadolescent conflict episodes in spontaneous conflicts that occurred at home (Vuchinich et al., 1991). Better family problem solving in such structured tasks was also associated with lower levels of reported sibling conflict (Brody et al., 1992). Further work on outcomes tied to the child's interpersonal problem solving skills has been pursued. One series of studies showed that these problem solving skills helped children cope with stressful life events and reduced negative outcomes associated with those events (DuBow & Tisak, 1989; DuBow et al., 1991; Elias et al., 1986; Glyshaw, Cohen, & Towbes, 1989). Taken together, this recent work is establishing a core research base on family problem solving from a developmental perspective. It has made progress in understanding how problem solving develops in family discussions, through the individual's developmental trajectory, and through the family life course.

Taking the Social Construction
of Family Problem Solving Seriously

This book has sought to stretch the reader's paradigmatic perspective and isolate some points of convergence across paradigms. Such efforts lead to the question of where knowledge on family problem solving currently stands. Answers to such questions have their own biases and oversimplify the complex body of ongoing work. But they are worthwhile to pursue in the course of planning the most beneficial direction for future work.

It is hardly debatable that the rational model has dominated work on family problem solving for decades. That is perhaps an altogether fitting and proper happenstance. Research has flourished and beneficial applications have resulted. But in my view, that model is beginning to have diminishing returns. It may be time to consider that the rational paradigm has made most of the contributions to family problem solving that it can make. If further progress is to be made, it may require a different paradigm.

In the positivist scientific tradition, aging dominant paradigms are usually not replaced until empirical evidence shows that a different paradigm provides a superior explanation for important phenomena. In the case of family problem solving, that has not happened—yet. However, there have been some compelling conceptual challenges to the rational model (e.g., Aldous, 1971; Reiss, 1981; Weick, 1971). Many predictions from the rational model simply do not hold in families, and recent applications have found the need to supplement the rational model with systemic family theory (e.g., Robin & Foster, 1989; Tolan & McKay, 1996). These are all signs of an inadequate paradigm.

The flaws in the rational paradigm are slowly becoming more of a concern to researchers. The most prevalent tactic is to add and patch correcting features while retaining the main rational elements. This is perhaps the most astute short-term approach, but more fundamental revisions may be necessary. It would be unwise to discard the rational model. However, it may be time to acknowledge that much of the rational paradigm has focused on a limited range of family problem solving behavior. Thus, knowledge about family problem solving may be expanded by opening up the range of phenomena that is examined and by opening up the way it is conceptualized. Such efforts may well find that the rational model still offers the best explanation of the most phenomena. What is important is that we be empirical—and simply observe.

A variety of alternate ways of observing or looking are available. As described in chapters 4 and 5, a reasonable approach is to take a qualitative tactic that focuses on the social construction of family problem solving. The advantage of qualitative analysis for the issue at hand is that it takes an inductive approach to the phenomena under study. In simplified terms, this opens the conceptualization of what data is relevant, and uses this process to inform the analysis about what is important. This is especially pertinent as an alternative to the rational model because that paradigm deductively creates and shapes data in an effort to test a limited hypothesis. It is in this context that we see the third important recent advance with implications for family problem solving. That advance is the emergence of qualitative and social constructionist research in family studies over the past 10 years.

The social constructionist perspective is not new in the study of family problem solving. Reiss's (1981) most penetrating analysis of the topic was, after all, titled *The Family's Construction of Reality*. But as is often the case with work outside of the dominant paradigm, it was not quickly assimilated (Reiss & Klein, 1989). Its complex merging of psychiatric and rational paradigms with the constructionist perspective appeared well ahead of its time. There is a long and esteemed history of more straightforward qualitative work on family life (for reviews, see Ambert et al., 1995; Gilgun et al., 1992). In recent years, there has been increasing concern that there are strict limits to the quantitative analysis of family life. Ambert et al. (1995) pointed out that fewer than 3% of all publications in *Journal of Marriage and the Family* between 1989 and 1994 were qualitative. Such an overwhelming dominance by quantitative family studies publications raises the likelihood that the current understanding of the family is biased toward those features that can be easily quantified. Such concerns have stimulated more interest in a qualitative approach (e.g., Gubrium & Holstein, 1990) and efforts to consolidate past qualitative family research (Ambert et al., 1995). In addition, an active social constructionist movement has emerged in psychology (e.g., Gergen, 1985).

The rise of the feminist perspective has given additional motivation to use qualitative and social constructionist methods (e.g., Ferree, 1990; Thompson & Walker, 1995). Although there are many strands of feminist work, several of them share a concern over the dominance of quantitative methods and call for reconceptualizations of family relationships and family life (e.g., Thompson & Walker, 1995). A qualitative constructionist approach is often recommended. Qualitative work is becoming increasingly influential as is evidenced in Hochschild's (1989) widely hailed use of interviews and other methods in *The Second Shift*. Corresponding to the renewed interest in this approach, new computer tools to facilitate qualitative analysis have been made widely available (e.g., Non-Numerical Unstructured Data-Indexing, Searching, and Theorizing—or NUDIST).

We consider these developments important advances because they provide a supportive intellectual climate and expanded methodological foundations for pursuing a social constructionist analysis of family problem solving. A substantial contribution could be made by simply doing a sustained constructionist analysis of family problem solving at home. There are some fragments of past work that help provide a starting point. Weick's (1971) classic paper frames some conceptual issues. Aldous (1971; Aldous & Ganey, 1989) as well as Klein and Hill (1979) provides some key observations. My home observations (Vuchinich, 1987, 1990; Vuchinich et al., 1988; 1991) offer some methodological technique and analytic leverage. Such studies point the direction toward a potentially useful analysis—an analysis that could step out of the shadow of the rational paradigm and see if anything else is there. The recent advances in qualitative family studies provide guidelines for how that can be done.

Technology and Family Problem Solving

The idea that technology influences family life is one of the oldest in all realms of family studies (e.g., Morgan, 1877). This interest expanded through the twentieth century as new technologies stimulated economic transformations through industrialization and the information age (Aulette, 1996). Family systems have adapted in many ways, including reduced family size, emphasis on nuclear rather than extended kin ties, geographic mobility, dual-career households, and so on. Whether such changes have been for the better or the worse is a matter of ongoing debate. However, what is not disputed is the fact that technology is increasingly seeping into family life. This technology has several implications for family problem solving. I focus on impacts for research in the field and on two specific recent advances: videotapes for training families and the Internet resources for promoting family problem solving.

It should be noted that the general question of how technological tools influence family problem solving is of interest in itself. In certain segments of the population, cellular telephones, cable television, e-mail, beepers, video games, headphone audio players, and computer games are part and parcel of family life. Family problems are negotiated on cell phones during commutes and at recess in the school yard. The availability of more diverse and compelling cable television programming (e.g., in stereo on a 4-foot screen) creates new opportunities for parent–child isolation and conflict as well as for bonding. With Mom checking her e-mail, Dad hypnotized by the ball game on the 4-foot screen, Billy in a chatroom on the Internet, and Susan slaying dragons on her video game, there may be little time to have a family meeting to bond or resolve a family problem. Of course, the fundamental family issues (e.g., teenage rebellion, sibling rivalry, maintaining order) are probably the same as they ever were. But they get acted out in a different environment that can enhance or inhibit an effective adaptation. This general issue is beyond our purview. But the increasing familiarity and use of these technologies has some very positive implications for doing research on and disseminating applications in family problem solving.

I have claimed that it is important to learn more about how family problem solving takes place at home. There are a variety of techniques for doing that. But several of them involve audiotaping or videotaping family behavior in the home and related locations. This can be done either by taping long segments of what families normally do or in structured exercises. In either case, the potential reactivity of the family to taping procedures is a primary concern. Lower reactivity results in more valid data. New technology allows for lower reactivity in two ways: It has produced smaller, better equipment, and families are more familiar with audio and video equipment in the home.

Audio and video equipment is increasingly smaller, and produces increasingly better quality recordings without additional (and intrusive) lighting. Smaller size is important in limiting reactivity because it makes it possible for the taping equipment to recede into the background of the situation so that more normal family processes can take place. Family members are more likely to forget it is there. Better sound and video quality is critical for simply being able to capture what family members say in the local social ecologies of their kitchens, living rooms, and dining rooms. Observational coding or transcriptions require a minimal threshold of audio clarity. Video is often needed to identify who is saying what, because family voices are often similar. Videotaping also tracks physical movements, which facilitates interpretation of what is said. Home taping is still a long way from producing tapes that can be used to code facial gestures or subtle intonation contours. But the quality of home taping available today is an order of magnitude better than it was a decade ago. In addition, the mass production of consumer audio and video equipment has substantially reduced the costs associated with home taping.

Twenty years ago it was rare to find an audio- or videotape recorder in an American home. Today, it is more rare *not* to find one. The idea of videotaping a family at home was once a foreign concept. Today, it is commonplace. Indeed, one can see such tapes played on national television on a weekly basis, as we have discussed before. Many family members have been videotaped at one time or another and many even have their own video camera. These facts have a substantial impact on how families react to home taping research. In an environment where home taping is often done just for the fun of it, such research can be interpreted in more relaxed terms. This is important in getting a family's permission to do such research in the first place. And once underway, it increases the likelihood of the taping receding into the background. This limits any reactivity of family members to the procedure.

There are a variety of strategies for increasing the effectiveness of home taping data collection. Many are tactical rather than technological. These include such things as leaving the equipment in the home for an extended period, consulting with family members on which rooms to use and the most advantageous microphone or camera placements, the timing of taping, enlisting family cooperation in taping, and so on.

VIDEOTAPES FOR TRAINING IN FAMILY PROBLEM SOLVING

Focused training in family problem solving has been part of treatment programs for more than two decades. As a result of this, books, pamphlets, workbooks, brochures, and other materials to facilitate that training have already gone through several generations of improvements. These products have had the benefit of trial, error, and feedback about what works with families (Dinkmeyer & McKay, 1989; Forgatch & Patterson, 1989). Such products are available for use as part of therapy, prevention, parent education programs, or as self-help materials for parents to read on their own. Though extensive empirical evaluations of such materials have not been done, most professionals in the field acknowledge that they can have a substantial impact on the success of any family program.

Over the past 10 years, several videotapes for training in family problem solving have been developed (e.g., Kavanaugh, Frey, & Larsen, 1991; Popkin, 1991; Webster-Stratton, 1996). There are two reasons why these products represent a major new advance in efforts to improve family problem solving in America: The video medium can display interactive family processes, and viewing videotapes has become a normal part of American life.

Films and videotapes have been used for educational purposes for many years. So the mere machine technology is not the basis for the advances involved here. It has been said that if one picture is worth a thousand words, then one video is worth a million words. There is substantial communication and education theory that provides explanations for the effectiveness of video media in teaching about any topic. These advantages all accrue to video applications in the area of concern. But the added value for teaching about family problem solving is that family members can see family problem solving in action. This can activate the powerful psychological mechanisms of identification and modeling (Bandura, 1969) in the service of learning. A father can read 50 pages on how to do brainstorming and be able to write a definition of it. But seeing a father in a videotape restrain himself from rejecting a silly adolescent proposal can push his understanding of how to do it to a much higher level. Although workbooks can have written transcripts of such interactions, they cannot capture the immediacy and subtle emotional cues that can be displayed on video.

Video training tapes are most effective when used in conjunction with other materials in a program of instruction. Ideally, a trainer, teacher, or therapist provides live interactive instruction in conjunction with readings, exercises, and other techniques over several meeting periods. Videotapes fit well into this instructional format. But live instruction is expensive and it is often difficult to get families who need training to attend such programs. These facts make the work of Webster-Stratton (1996) especially significant. In controlled longitudinal designs, she carefully tested whether there were any beneficial effects on parents who used parent education videos (including a workbook) at home without live instruction. She found that there were substantial significant effects. Her initial findings were for parents with children aged 6 to 8 years and focused on the behavioral parent training model (Patterson, 1982).

She has extended the work to include videotapes on individual and family problem solving and found improved significant effects in families with children with conduct disorders (Webster-Stratton, 1996). She has included comparisons of different delivery methods, including therapist-led parent discussion groups and videotape modeling. Her work has also been extended to producing training videos for children that include problem solving training (Webster-Stratton, 1996). Her research provides convincing empirical evidence of the effectiveness of video materials for training in parenting and family problem solving. These successes are stimulating efforts to produce even better video products.

The availability of proven videotaped training materials is significant in itself. But what amplifies their significance is the vast expansion of availability of video players in American homes and increases in the use of videotapes. Reduced costs of the video equipment, as a result of better manufacturing technology, have made this expansion possible. Americans have embraced these machines and videotape players are now considered just another home appliance.

This has spawned new industries in videotape sales and rentals. Videotapes are available for entertainment, but more important, for self-improvement and education. There is an ever expanding market in several areas: exercise videos to trim and tone any part of the body, motivational videos to improve attitude, sports videos to improve one's golf game, health videos to help one stop smoking, and so on. Slowly, videos on parenting and those that include family problem solving are beginning to appear. They will never dominate the selections at the local video store. But they ultimately may reach more people and have a more immediate impact than the best-written book on the library shelf. This use of such materials is promoted by the corresponding increases in parenting television shows or discussion of parenting issues on variety talk shows.

Of course, the video medium is a double-edged sword. Many popular television shows and videos model dysfunctional family problem solving. The negative impact of such material is an ongoing issue of public policy. Whatever the outcome of such debates, the presence of both negative and positive video material will continue. The recent advances in effective parenting and family problem solving video material can make a substantial contribution on the positive side.

The applications that take advantage of the video medium are not limited to videotape or television. Compact disc (CD) technology provides state-of-the-art video quality and the added capability of using it to create compelling interactive learning experiences. Television shows and videotapes play the program as the viewer typically sits and watches. The viewer has no control over what comes next—unless she turns it off. The videotape or television does not take into account how the viewer is responding to the material: It is a one-way process. CD technology allows a program to receive input from the viewer and play video segments that "respond" to that input: It is an interactive process. Children's video games are so engaging to them because they are finely tuned interactive devices. The game responds to the child's input, and the child reacts in turn, thus completing an interactive loop. Such games show that interactivity can stimulate excited and continued involvement with a computer, even though the child learns nothing except how to play the game better.

But such excited and continued involvement can be invaluable in learning about any topic. CD educational products that accomplish this are now widely available and are increasing in their effectiveness. The use of Computer Based Training (CBT) in the business world is expanding the acceptance of CD applications. Because of the unique value of video material for training in family problem solving, the CD medium has great potential for educating families in this domain. As CD players become more available in the home, such applications are inevitable.

FAMILY PROBLEM SOLVING AND THE INTERNET

Any text, photo, video, or CD family problem solving media that is created can be placed on the Internet. Thus it might initially appear that the Internet would provide few advantages beyond the other technologies already discussed. Such a conclusion, however, would underestimate the significance of the interactive access to millions of other people that the Internet allows.

Consider what a parent has to do to get to a parenting book or video. He or she has to travel somewhere, probably stand in line and pay money, return home, then use the product. If it was checked out of the library or video rental store, it must then be returned. Taking a parent education class or receiving family therapy involves much more effort and money. Compare that with the relatively little time, effort, and cost required to get on the Internet through the telephone line and click the browser a few times to receive comparable parenting material.

Of course one has to have, or have access to, a computer of some kind (Web television units currently cost less than $200) and a telephone line. One has to know how to use Internet. One has to be able to locate the most effective parenting sites. Many parents do not meet these criteria, so the Internet does not eliminate access as an issue. But it offers incredible potential for access to parenting material. Hundreds of Internet sites dedicated to parenting issues already exist. These range from support-group style chatrooms to photo-rich parenting Internet magazines. Streaming video techniques and Java-style programming allow interactive modules similar to those available on CDs.

Low costs of creating such Internet sites mean that there are many options from which to choose. In such a context, the issue of quality control looms large. Some sites may provide misleading or even damaging information. The Web-surfing parent must be cautious. However, professional organizations in the family field are beginning to consider recommendations. Some universities already offer parent education material on the Internet. As with video technology, what makes the Internet such an important advance is the increase of its use in American homes.

Another part of the access issue is the quality of interaction available through the Internet. Getting access to effectively prepared text, graphic, photo, or video material is of major importance in itself. But the Internet also provides new ways of interacting with other individuals or groups. At the most basic level, topical newsgroups provide an effective forum in which one can see other people's views in a given subject area. Messages are posted in a bulletin board format. Individuals can respond to messages previously posted or raise a new topic or question for discussion. Several ongoing parenting newsgroups are already popular and anyone can join in for free. These "groups" can serve some functions similar to support groups in the sense of expressing their problems and learning that they are not the only ones with that problem. Advice is often sought and given in newsgroups. But the quality of the advice varies widely. With individuals from around the country and world participating, responses are often "interesting."

The process of posting a message on a newsgroup and receiving feedback can take hours or days. Immediate response is not expected. Chatrooms are essentially subject-specific newsgroups in which the technology allows almost immediate response. Thus a textual analogy to a telephone conference call is created. These interactions approximate some elements of a sequential group conversation. With many participants, this can become unwieldy. Some chatrooms limit the number of participants.

Similar technology is used in the business world to allow meetings involving people in distant locations. Such meetings can be enhanced by group "white boards," which is a graphic display to which different participants can contribute. This allows geographically separated individuals to jointly work on diagrams, blueprints, photo layouts, text documents, and so on. These meetings can also be enhanced by video displays of each person in the meeting. This videoconferencing simulates the eye contact and other intangibles of a group meeting. Videoconferencing is already being applied in the medical and business worlds. Physicians and psychiatrists can conduct some examinations and consultations at a distance. No one claims such interactions are equivalent to face-to-face meetings. But the physical location of the person with the most appropriate expertise and the person needing that expertise may be hundreds or thousands of miles apart. Because time and costs of physical transport are often prohibitive, videoconference meetings are proving to be more useful than no meetings at all.

As the costs of such tools as videoconferencing decline, they become relevant for family problem solving. At the simplest level such technologies can help families separated by distance to maintain their relationships and even do problem solving. They can facilitate distance parent education, which makes it possible for excellent instructors to reach more students. They can allow engaging, interactive parenting support-group meetings without any of the members leaving their homes. They could even allow effective family therapy to be conducted without the family leaving the home. Ultimately, the primary advance of the Internet is increased, low-cost access of families to training and support services in parenting and family problem solving.

Summary

Access to support services and training in the area of family problem solving can only be worthwhile if those services and training are based on a solid foundation of understanding. This book has claimed that much is already known about family problem solving and that there may be much more to be learned. I have shown that enough has been discovered to produce beneficial applications. One of the greatest challenges to future progress is to avoid "resting on our laurels" in the area of family problem solving. A brief survey of applications in the field could easily lead to the conclusion that family problem solving is essentially a closed case. The impression is that it is rather well understood. The rational model explains most of its important features, and what is left to do is to clear up some of the relatively minor details.

This impression is fostered in part by an understandable need for writings on applications to be optimistic and confident about the basis of programs and their prospects for success. It should be acknowledged that no one has ever explicitly claimed that the rational model explains most of what we need to know about family problem solving. But after a couple of decades of numerous studies based on that model, and few based on any other model, the prevalence of that conclusion seems implicit.

As noted earlier, it is possible that the rational model provides the best possible explanation for family problem solving. But it is impossible to test that unless other paradigms are seriously examined. One challenge for the future of family problem solving is to explore other models of family problem solving. Science promotes exploration of alternative explanations. But when paradigms become entrenched and have some proven applications, such exploration tends not to be encouraged.

If other models are tested and found to be useful, a second challenge presents itself. How can the useful features of the rational model be reconciled with the useful features of the alternate model? Alternate paradigms may have quite diverse conceptual foundations. The applications literature already provides examples of some of these issues. How can the irrational concepts in strategic (e.g., paradox) and structural (e.g., triangulation) family therapy be reconciled with the rational premises of the cognitive–behavioral models? In applications, therapists or trainers can simply be instructed to apply them in tandem (e.g., Robin & Foster, 1989; Tolan & McKay, 1996). That might well serve to cover the bases, and may yield some good results. But it is likely to be inefficient, and diverse components may cancel each other out. Such approaches are entirely appropriate in efforts to try to make progress with what is available. But in the long run, the challenge is to integrate these perspectives conceptually and theoretically.

A final challenge for the future of family problem solving is to use the available technologies to apply what is known, and what will be known, to help families prevent and cope with trouble. The family problem solving materials and programs reviewed in this book are the product of years of work by dedicated professionals in several fields. The proven benefits of those products offer a significant contribution to efforts to help families. But for a host of reasons, families who can most benefit from these products do not have access to them. Emerging technologies have the potential to increase access and thus expand the benefits. But technology is not equally distributed to the members of a society. Thus the challenge here is two-fold: to translate what we know about family problem solving into dissemination technologies and to make sure those technologies get distributed to populations that most need it. John Dewey would have had no way of foreseeing the Internet. But he would have completely understood why training in problem solving should be on it.

Dewey (1910/1982) believed that education was a mechanism that could improve rational thinking and societal well-being in large populations. His basic reasoning was that better problem solving would produce better adaptations, fewer unmet needs, and less social conflict. His logic was clear, but he provided no empirical evidence for these speculations. In any event, this is an important line of thinking when considering the future prospects of family problem solving. Is it possible to improve the family problem solving in a large population such as the United States? The skeptic would argue that families have always had their problems, and always will have their problems. And furthermore, the existential conditions of family life necessarily generate primal problems and conflicts that often cannot be solved, regardless of problem solving ability.

Thus it would be folly to expect any meaningful improvements in how well family problems are actually solved. There may be little reason to expect that family problem solving will be any better in the year 2000 than it was in 1950 or in 1900.

Although the skeptic's position has a certain appeal, the assumption that families necessarily have insoluble problems is not based on fact. Indeed, there is an entire literature on how adaptive families overcome the most challenging problems imaginable (e.g., Klein & Aldous, 1988). Furthermore, there is convincing clinical research that shows substantial improvements in problem solving are possible in even the most troubled families (see chapters 3 and 6). Research on prevention is beginning to show that such gains can be made in families across a broader spectrum of the population. With emerging improvements in educational technology and increasing societal commitment to parent education, widespread gains in family problem solving appear to be quite feasible. The next question is, "What impact would such gains have?"

Entertain the following hypothetical situation. What if the problem solving ability of all American families doubled overnight? Would that produce any changes of significance? From the perspective presented in this book, the answer is a resounding yes! Families would more effectively adapt to their circumstances. More basic human needs would be met and there would be less destructive family conflict. Interpersonal family relationships would improve. Children would be exposed to more healthy family environments, and fewer of them would fall prey to negative outcomes such as delinquency, mental health disorders, substance abuse, and sexual problems. There would still be poverty, crime, hunger, wars, discrimination, and so on. But families would be able to provide their members in any circumstance with a more supportive primary group for growth, development, and adaptation throughout the life span. This is an optimistic vision. But 100 years of work on family problem solving suggests that it is possible.

Appendix A
Description of Group
Discussion Task in Bales and Slater (1955)

All of the groups in this sample were composed of paid male under-graduates at Harvard, recruited through the student employment office. Every effort was made to ensure that none of the participants knew one another, but there were a few pairs where this condition was not met. The subjects were not introduced to each other by name, and no leader was appointed by the experimenter. The aim was to start the members on as equal a footing as possible, and leave them to solve all of their problems of social organization by themselves. We wanted to observe the development of role differentiation from some minimum starting point.

The task given to each group was the same. They were told we were interested in group discussion and decision making and that the physical facilities had been designed to make our observations as easy as possible. Microphones were pointed out, the participants were told a sound recording would be made, and that they would be observed from an observation room divided from the discussion room by a one-way mirror, in order to avoid distracting them with observers. Each participant was given a five-page written summary of facts about an administrative problem of the sort familiar in college case-discussion courses. They were asked not to show these summaries to each other. The summaries were collected after they had been read by the participants individually.

The subjects were asked to consider themselves as members of the administrative staff of the central authority in the case. They had been asked by their superior to consider the facts and return a report to him that would give their opinion as to why the persons involved in the case were behaving as they did, and their recommendation about what he should do about it. They were to take 40 minutes for the discussion, and in the final one or two minutes to dictate their decisions for the sound record. They were asked for a "group decision" without further specification as to what this meant or how they were to arrive at it.

Appendix B
Interaction Profiles From Bales (1950)

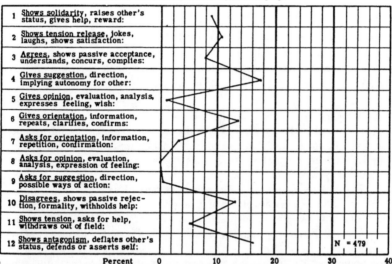

Chart 8. Interaction profile of a preschool gang.*

* Protocol by Alma Perry Beaver, "A Preliminary Report on a Study of a Preschool Gang"; Thomas, Dorothy Swain, and associates, Some New Techniques for Studying Social Behavior, Chap. VI, Bureau of Publications, Teacher's College, Columbia University, New York, N. Y., 1929, 99-117.

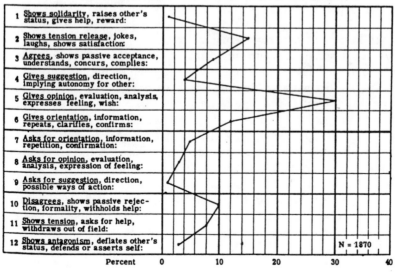

Chart 9. Pooled interaction profile for five four-person groups of 9th grade boys.

Appendix C
Family Interaction Task
From Strodtbeck (1954)

Our procedure for obtaining a sample discussion between a father, mother, and adolescent son was, very briefly, as follows: Each family is visited at home. We explain that we are interested in the way a family considers questions that relate to the son's selection of his occupation. To help the family recall specific topics that they may have previously discussed, we ask the father, mother, and son to check independently one of two alternatives to 47 items of the following type:

(a) A teenagers' hobby club plans to enter their models in a statewide contest. Some of the boys want to put the models up under the club's name and win honor for the club as a whole. Others want to put the models up under each boy's name so that each can gain individual honor. Which plan should they adopt?

(b) Two fathers were discussing their boys, one of whom was a brilliant student and the other an athlete of great promise. In general, some people feel one father was more fortunate and some the other. Do you think the father with the *athletic* son or the father with the *studious* son was most fortunate?

(c) Some people believe that a father should be prepared to speak to a son as a father and direct the son's behavior so long as the son lives; others believe the son should be accepted as completely independent of his father's direction after 18 or 21. Which would you tend to agree to with regard to a boy in his late 20s?

While our introductory remarks are being made in the home, we request permission to set up our portable tape recorder. After the 47-item questionnaire has been checked, we have the family fill out still another similar questionnaire so that we will have time to sort through their responses. We select three items that represent a potential coalition of the type in which the mother and father have taken one alternative and the son another; three with mother–son paired against the father; and three with father–son paired against the mother. We then present the family successively with these nine disagreements rotating the isolate role. They are asked to talk the question over, understand why each person chose the alternative he or she did, and, if possible, select one alternative that best represents the thinking of the family as a whole. While this discussion takes place, the experimenter withdraws to another room, operates the controls on the sound equipment, and tries to keep any other member of the family from overhearing or interrupting the interaction. During May and June of 1953 we obtained 48 cases in this manner.

Appendix D1
List of Issues Family Members Chose From,
Used by Vuchinich, Angelelli, and Gatherum (1996)

Family Issues List

Family ID_____
Date _____

Below is a list of issues that sometimes get talked about at home. Please read this list to help you come up with a topic to discuss in your discussion. Note that you may choose another topic.

1. Telephone calls
2. Time for going to bed
3. Cleaning up bedroom
4. Doing homework
5. Putting away clothes
6. Using the television
7. Cleanliness (showers, etc.)
8. Which clothes to wear
9. How neat clothing looks
10. Making too much noise at home
11. Table manners
12. Fighting with brothers/sisters
13. Cursing
14. How money is spent
15. Picking books or movies
16. Allowance
17. Going places without parents
18. Playing stereo or radio too loud
19. Turning off lights in house
20. Drugs
21. Taking care of possessions/pets
22. Drinking beer or other liquor
23. Buying records, games, toys, etc.
24. Going on dates
25. Amount of time parents spend with child
26. Who should friends be
27. Coming home on time
28. Getting to school on time
29. Getting in trouble at school
30. Lying
31. Helping out around the house
32. Talking back and arguing with parents
33. Getting up in the morning
34. Bothering parents when they want to be alone
35. Bothering child when child wants to be alone
36. Putting feet on furniture
37. Messing up the house
38. What time to have meals
39. How to spend free time
40. Smoking
41. Earning money away from house
42. What child eats
43. Child taking things not belonging to him/her
44. Parents setting consequences
45. Going places with family
46. Bad behavior/attitude
47. Social activities
48. Parents favoring other children
49. Other

(Originally from Forgatch, 1989)

Appendix D2
Observational Problem Solving Measure From Vuchinich,
Angelelli, and Gatherum (1996)

Coding Family Problem Solving Sessions

Videotapes of the problem solving sessions were coded by a team of five coders. One 10-min session was coded at a time. Coders made their ratings once after viewing the 10-min session. Coders were trained for about 100 hours to attain reliability. Intercoder reliability was tested on 20% of the data. Coding discrepancies were reconciled by both coders reviewing the session together.

The measure of the effectiveness of *family problem solving* was based on the multiple indicator instrument initially developed by Forgatch (1989) and later adapted for other applications (e.g., Vuchinich et al., 1993). The present measure did not include coding for the total number of solutions proposed or a sequential measure of parental problem solving responses to children that the Forgatch (1989) measure included. The global measure used here was found to be highly correlated with the Forgatch measure (mean correlation in 20 comparisons was 0.75). Global coding systems (i.e., rating aspects of problem solving on 7-point scales) similar to this have been used to assess social problem solving in several recent studies (Brody et al., 1992; Buhrmester, Camparo, Christensen, Gonzalez, & Hinshaw, 1992; DuBow, Tisak, Causey, Hryshko, & Reid, 1991), including observational assessments in tasks similar to the one applied here (Brody et al., 1992; Buhrmester et al., 1992). The external and ecological validity of the observational assessments have been acknowledged as being especially good (e.g., Brody et al., 1992).

In this study, family problem solving effectiveness was rated on three separate 7-point scales. The first was the *quality of the solutions proposed,* which ranged from "no solutions proposed" (1) to "excellent solutions proposed" (7). This measure assessed whether any potential solutions were brought up and how practical, inventive, integrative, or realistic they were. The second was the *extent of resolution,* which ranged from "no resolution/total disagreement" (1) to "problem resolved" (7). This score represents an overall assessment of how close the family came to a final solution to the problem, regardless of how much agreeing or disagreeing went on in the discussion.

The third component of the problem solving effectiveness score was an overall score that assessed more global aspects of the problem solving sessions. This included how well the family members took the perspective of each other during the sessions, considered others' views and feelings (Selman et al., 1986), promoted group participation, and cooperated. This was labeled the *perspective-taking* score. Ratings on this scale ranged from "extremely poor" (1) to "extremely good" (7).

The three components (i.e., quality of solutions, extent of resolution, and perspective taking) were combined to provide a more comprehensive assessment of different key elements of family problem solving than is possible with any single item. This measure captures specific features of the family discussions which have been shown to promote the resolution of family problems (e.g., generating high-quality potential solutions, engagement of the problem rather than avoidance, making sustained progress toward resolution, open participation, and taking the viewpoints and needs of others into consideration).

The *family problem solving* score was calculated by summing the quality of solutions-proposed rating, the extent of resolution rating, and the perspective-taking rating (possible range of scores, 3–21). Cronbach's alpha for this composite score was 0.88. Test–retest reliability correlations for this measure have been shown to be about 0.70 for short-term comparisons (5 min between sessions), and about 0.50 for long-term (2-year) comparisons (Vuchinich et al., 1993). For the present data the corresponding short-term test–retest reliability for three-person sessions was 0.73, and 2-year test–retest correlations were 0.55. This level of reliability is similar to that found for family problem solving scores in previous studies (Brody et al., 1992; Buhrmester et al., 1992; DuBow et al., 1991; Forgatch, 1989).

In the present study, family problem solving scores were calculated for four sessions (two parent-selected, two preadolescent-selected problems) at each wave of assessment.

Appendix E
Some of the Brief Vignettes Given to Families
by Aldous and Ganey (1989)

Sometimes when one of the family members uses the car, the gas tank does not get filled.

The husband sometimes complains about the amount of money the wife and teenager spend on clothes.

The teenager and one of the other children argue a lot. They do not cooperate when they are asked to do things around the house.

Your family has received this invitation to an informal wedding in the park. Dress as you like.

The wife tried out a recipe that the husband is not very fond of.

This is a copy of the teenager's report card. It contains 3 Cs, 2 Bs, 2 Ds. Comment: "Poor workmanship."

An FBI agent asked you some questions about your neighbors. He said it was a routine background investigation.

One of the family's relatives wants your family to be legally responsible for her children in case she and her husband die.

The wife was not able to go out with friends for 2 weeks due to an increased workload at home.

This is part of a letter from the teenager's friend: "Things have gotten really bad since we moved from Minnesota. Mom and Dad are getting a divorce. I'm supposed to stay with Mom. I wonder sometimes if that means that Dad doesn't like me."

Photograph of an interracial couple. (The man is black, the woman is white. The woman is holding a black baby on her lap.)

The Internal Revenue Service in its random check of income tax returns is going over your returns for 1969–72 and will need your records from those years.

For the last two days, the teenager in the family has left for school without speaking to any other family member and says little after coming home from school. This is the third or fourth time that this happened.

Reprinted by permission.

This announcement came from your local school. "Due to rising food costs, we are forced to increase the present school lunch program by 50 cents per week to begin the first of next month."

Last week the wife did not agree with her husband on what to do when they had some free time together.

This is an article from your newspaper about a recent series of crimes in the north side of your city. Some people have moved because of the crimes. Others can't because people are afraid to buy their houses.

The husband learns that a new person has been appointed head of his department starting the 15th of next month.

Your family has come across this poster. (The poster says, "A, B, Cs of Birth Control")

The teenager sometimes leaves for school without eating breakfast.

Someone sitting in a car has been watching your house for a week.

The family uses a certain washing detergent. One night the teenager reports that his ecology class teacher said that water pollution could be cut down if every household would use a nonpolluting detergent.

This notice came from your local school. Students in the 7th, 8th, and 9th grades will have the opportunity next year to participate in a special school program without grades. Students will take the subjects they want and set their own standards of accomplishment. Counselors will be available to give students advice.

Your next-door neighbors are away. You all hear a loud crash near their house that sounds like glass breaking.

The teenager is not happy with the amount he is receiving for his allowance.

This is an article from your newspaper about an 11% rise in hospital costs in a year.

The wife will be away for 3 days next week visiting relatives.

A teacher told the teenager the other day that he didn't think s/he was a very good worker.

Appendix F
Structural Model of Family Problem Solving
From Rueter and Conger (1995)

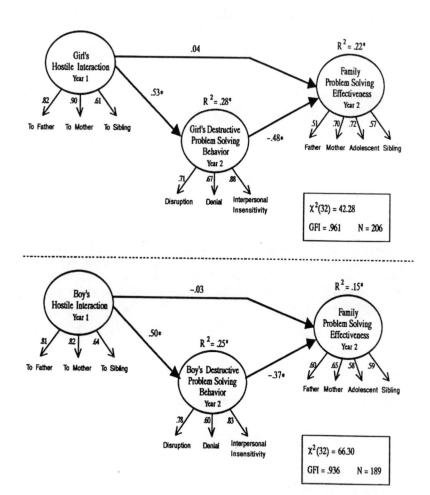

Appendix G
Measurement Models for Family Ratings of Problem Solving
(Vuchinich & DeBaryshe, 1997)

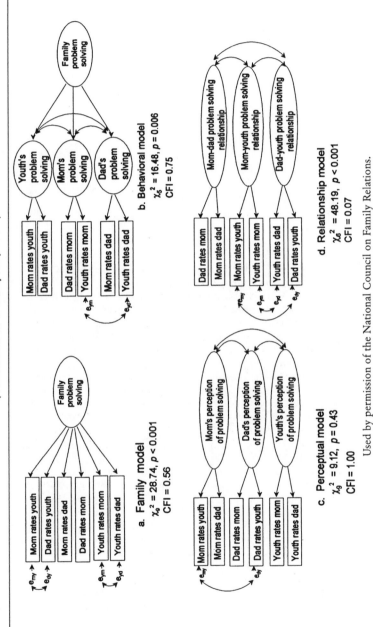

a. Family model
$\chi_9^2 = 28.74$, $p < 0.001$
CFI = 0.56

b. Behavioral model
$\chi_5^2 = 16.48$, $p = 0.006$
CFI = 0.75

c. Perceptual model
$\chi_9^2 = 9.12$, $p = 0.43$
CFI = 1.00

d. Relationship model
$\chi_6^2 = 48.19$, $p < 0.001$
CFI = 0.07

Used by permission of the National Council on Family Relations.

References

Abbott, A. (1995). Sequence analysis. *Annual Review of Sociology, 21*, 93–113.

Ackerman, N. (1937). The family as a social and emotional unit. *Bulletin of the Kansas Mental Hygiene Society, 2*, 1–6.

Ackerman, N. W. (1958). *The psychodynamics of family life.* New York: Basic Books.

Adler, A. (1930). *The education of children.* New York: Greenberg.

Aldous, J. (1971). A framework for the analysis of family problem solving. In J. Aldous, T. Condon, R. Hill, M. Straus, & I. Tallman (Eds.), *Family problem solving: A symposium on theoretical, methodological, and substantive concerns.* Hinsdale, IL: Dryden Press.

Aldous, J. (1975). The search for alternatives: parental behaviors and children's original problem solutions. *Journal of Marriage and the Family, 37*, 711–722.

Aldous, J., & Ganey, R. (1989). Families' definition behavior of problematic situations. *Social Forces, 67*, 871–897.

Alexander, J. F., & Parsons, B. V. (1973). Short term behavioral intervention with delinquent families: Impact on family process and recidivism. *Journal of Abnormal Psychology 81*, 219–225.

Ambert, A., Adler, P. A., Adler, P., & Detzner D. F. (1995). Understanding and evaluating qualitative research. *Journal of Marriage and the Family, 57*, 879–893.

Anastopoulos, A. D., Barkley, R. A., & Sheldon, T. L. (1996). Family based treatment: Psychosocial intervention for children and adolescents with attention deficit hyperactivity disorder. In E. D. Hibbs & P. S. Jensen (Eds.), *Psychosocial treatments for child and adolescent disorders: Empirically based strategies for clinical practice* (pp. 267–284). Washington, DC: American Psychological Association.

Aulette, J. R. (1996). *Changing families.* Belmont, CA: Wadsworth.

Bales, R. F. (1950). *Interaction process analysis.* Cambridge, MA: Addison-Wesley.

Bales, R. F., & Slater, P. E. (1955). Role differentiation in small decision-making groups. In T. Parsons & R. F. Bales (Eds.), *Family Socialization and interaction process* (pp. 259–306). Glencoe, IL: Free Press.

Bales, R. F., & Strodtbeck, F. L. (1951). Phases in group problem solving. *Journal of Abnormal and Social Psychology, 46*, 485–495.

Bandura, A. (1969). *Principles of behavior modification.* New York: Holt, Rinehart & Winston.

Barkley, R. A. (1991). Foreword. In L. Braswell & M. L. Bloomquist, *Cognitive-behavior therapy with ADHD children: Child, family and school interventions* (pp. vii–xi). New York: Guilford Press.

Barkow, J., Cosmides, L., & Tooby, J. (1992) *The adapted mind: Evolutionary psychology and the generation of culture.* New York: Oxford University Press.

Barnard, C. I. (1938). *The functions of the executive.* Cambridge, MA: Harvard University Press.

Barton, C., Alexander, J. F., Waldron, H., Turner, C. W., & Walburton, J. (1985). Generalizing treatment effects of functional family therapy: Three replications. *American Journal of Family Therapy, 13,* 16–26.

Bateson, G., Jackson, D. D., Haley, J., & Weakland, J. (1956). Toward a theory of schizophrenia. *Behavioral Science, 1,* 251–264.

Baumrind, D. (1991). The influence of parenting style on adolescent competence and substance use. *Journal of Early Adolescence, 11,* 56–95.

Beardslee, W. R., Schultz, L. H., & Selman, R. L. (1987). Level of social-cognitive development, adaptive functioning, and DSM-III diagnoses in adolescent offspring of parents with affective disorders: Implications for the development of the capacity for mutuality. *Developmental Psychology, 23,* 807–815.

Becker, G. (1981). *A treatise on the family.* Cambridge, MA: Harvard University Press.

Bell, D. C., Chafetz, J. S., & Horn, L. (1980). Marital conflict resolution: A study of strategies and outcomes. *Journal of Family Issues, 6,* 111–113.

Berger, J. B., Cohen, P., & Zelditch, M. (1972). Status characteristics and social interaction. *American Sociological Review, 37,* 241–255.

Berger, P., & Luckmann, T. (1966). *The social construction of reality.* Norwich, UK: Penguin.

Bernstein, B. (1960). Language and social class. *British Journal of Sociology, 2,* 271–276.

Bernstein, B. (1961). Social class and linguistic development: A social learning theory. In A. H. Halsey, J. Floud, & C. A. Anderson (Eds.), *Education, economy and society.* Glencoe, IL: Free Press.

Billings, A. (1979). Conflict resolution in distressed and nondistressed married couples. *Journal of Consulting and Clinical Psychology, 47,* 368–376.

Billingsley, A. (1968). *Black families in white America.* Englewood Cliffs, NJ: Prentice Hall.

Bishop, Y. M., Fienberg, S. E., & Holland, P. W. (1975). *Discrete multivariate anaylsis.* Cambridge: MIT Press.

Blechman, E. A. (1977). Objectives and procedures believed necessary for the success of a contractual approach to family intervention. *Behavior Therapy, 8,* 275–277.

Blechman, E., & McEnroe, M. J. (1985). Effective family problem solving. *Child Development, 56,* 429–437.

Bogenschneider, K. (1996). An ecological risk/protective theory for building prevention programs, policies, and community capacity to support youth. *Family Relations, 45,* 127–137.

Bossard, J. H., & Boll, E. S. (1950). *Ritual in family living.* Philadelphia: University of Pennsylvania Press.

Bowen, M. A. (1960). Family concepts of schizophrenia. In D. D. Jackson (Ed.), *The etiology of schizophrenia.* New York: Basic Books.

Brasswell, L., & Bloomquist, M. L. (1991). *Cognitive–behavioral therapy with ADHD children: Child, family and school interventions.* New York: Guilford Press.

Brim, O. G. (1959). *Education for child rearing.* New York: Russell Sage Foundation.

Brody, G. H., Stoneman, Z., McCoy, J. K., & Forehand, R. (1992). Contemporaneous and longitudinal association of sibling conflict with family relationship assessments and family discussions about sibling problems. *Child Development, 63*, 391–400.

Bronfenbrenner, U. (1979). *The ecology of human development.* Cambridge, MA: Harvard University Press.

Brown, P. M., & Shalett, J. S. (1997). *Cross-cultural practice with couples and families.* Binghamton, NY: Haworth Press.

Buhrmester, D., Camparo, L., Christensen, A., Gonzalez, L. S., & Hinshaw, S. P. (1992). Mothers and fathers interacting in dyads and triads with normal and hyperactive sons. *Developmental Psychology, 28*, 500–509.

Burgess, E. W. (1916). *The function of socialization in social evolution.* Chicago: University of Chicago Press.

Burgess, E. W., & Cottrell, L. S. (1939). *Predicting success or failure in marriage.* New York: McGraw-Hill.

Burman, B. Margolin, G., & John, R. S. (1993). America's angriest home videos: Behavioral contingencies observed on home reenactments of marital conflict. *Journal of Consulting and Clinical Psychology, 61*, 28–39.

Capaldi, D. M., Forgatch, M. S., & Crosby, L. (1994). Affective expression in family problem solving discussions with adolescent boys: The association with family structure and function. *Journal of Adolescent Research, 9*, 28–49.

Chagnon, N. (1983) *Yanomamo: The fierce people.* (3rd ed.). New York: Holt, Rinehart & Winston.

Cheal, D. (1991). *Family and the state of theory.* Toronto: University of Toronto Press.

Christensen, A., & Hazzard, A. (1983). Reactive effects during naturalistic observation of families. *Behavior Assessment, 5*, 349–362.

Conduct Problems Prevention Research Group. (1992). A developmental and clinical model for the prevention of conduct disorder: The FAST Track program. *Development and Psychopathology, 4*, 509–527.

Cook, J., Tyson, P., White, J., Rushe, R., & Gottman, J. (1995). Mathematics of marital conflict: Qualitative dynamic mathematical modeling and marital interaction. *Journal of Family Psychology, 9*, 110–130.

Cooley, C. H. (1902). *Human nature and the social order.* New York: Scribner.

Coughlin, C., & Vuchinich, S. (1996). Family experience in preadolescence and the development of male delinquency. *Journal of Marriage and the Family, 58*, 491–501.

Crick, N. R., & Dodge, K. A. (1996). Social information-processing mechanisms in reactive and proactive aggression. *Child Development, 67*, 993–1002.

Cummings, E. M., & Davies, P. T. (1994). *Children and marital conflict: The impact of family dispute and resolution.* New York: Guilford Press.

Cummings, E. M., Iannotti, R. J., & Zahn-Waxler, C. (1985). Influence of conflict between adults on the emotions and aggression of young children. *Developmental Psychology, 21*, 495–507.

Cyert, R. M., & March, J. G. (1963). *A behavioral theory of the firm.* Englewood Cliffs, NJ: Prentice Hall.

Daly, K. J. (1996). *Families and time: Keeping pace in a hurried culture.* Thousand Oaks, CA: Sage.

Darwin, C. (1871). *The descent of man and selection in relation to sex.* New York: Appleton.

Dashiell, J. F. (1935). Experimental studies of the influence of social situations on the behavior of individual human beings. In C. Murchison (Ed.), *Handbook of social psychology* (pp. 1097–1158). Worcester, MA: Clark University.

De Waal, F. (1989). *Peacemaking among primates.* Cambridge, MA: Harvard University Press.

De Waal, F. (1996). *Good natured: The origins of right and wrong in humans and other animals*. Cambridge, MA: Harvard University Press.

Dewey, J. (1910/1982). *How we think*. Lexington, MA: Heath.

Dewey, J. (1938). *Logic: The theory of inquiry*. New York: Henry Holt.

Dinkmeyer, D., & McKay, G. D. (1989). *The parent's handbook* (3rd ed.). Circle Pines, MN: American Guidance Service.

Dodd, T. C. (1988). Behavioral and systemic family therapy: A comparison. In I. R. H. Falloon (Ed.), *Handbook of behavioral family therapy* (pp. 449–460). New York: Guilford Press.

Dodge, K. A. (1980). Social cognition and children's aggressive behavior. *Child Development, 51*, 162–170.

Dodge, K. A. (1993). The future of research on the treatment of conduct disorder. *Development and Psychopathology, 5*, 311–320.

Dornbusch, S. M., Ritter, P. L., Liederman, P. H., Roberts, D. F., & Fraleigh, M. J. (1987). The relation of parenting style to adolescent school performance. *Child Development, 58*, 1244–1257.

Dreikurs, R. (1948). *The challenge of parenthood*. New York: Hawthorne.

Dreikurs, R. (1964). *Children: The challenge*. New York: Hawthorne.

Dryfoos, J. G. (1990). *Adolescents at risk: Prevalence and prevention*. New York: Oxford University Press.

DuBow, E. F., & Tisak, J. (1989). The relation between stressful life events and adjustment in elementary school children: The role of social support and social problem-solving skills. *Child Development, 60*, 1412–1423.

DuBow, E. F., Tisak, J., Causey, D., Hryshko, A., & Reid, G. (1991). A ten-year longitudinal study of stressful life events, social support, and social problem-solving skills: Contributions to behavioral and academic adjustment. *Child Development, 62*, 583–599.

Dumka, L. E., Roosa, M. W., Michaels, M. L., & Suh, K. (1995). Using research and theory to develop prevention programs for high risk families. *Family Relations, 44*, 78–86.

Dunnette, M. D., Campbell, J., & Jaastad, K. (1963). The effect of group participation on brainstorming effectiveness for two industrial samples. *Journal of Applied Psychology, 47*, 30–37.

Durkheim, E. (1926). *Elementary forms of the religious life*. New York: Macmillan.

D'Zurilla, T. J., & Goldfried, M. R. (1971). Problem solving and behavior modification. *Journal of Abnormal Psychology, 78*, 107–126.

Elias, M. J., Gara, M., Ubriaco, M., Rothman, P. A., Clabby, J. F., & Schuyler, T. (1986). Impact of a preventive social problem solving intervention on children's coping with middle school stressors. *American Journal of Community Psychology, 14*, 259–276.

Ellis, S., & Siegler, R. S. (1994). Development of problem solving. In R. J. Sternberg (Ed.), *Thinking and problem solving* (pp. 334–367). San Diego, CA: Academic Press.

Emery, R. E. (1982). Interparental conflict and the children of discord and divorce. *Psychological Bulletin, 92*, 310–330.

Falloon, I. R. H. (1988). Prevention of morbidity in schizophrenia. In I. R. H. Falloon (Ed.), *Handbook of behavioral family therapy* (pp. 316–349). New York: Guilford Press.

Ferree, M. M. (1990). Beyond separate spheres: Feminism and family research. *Journal of Marriage and the Family, 52*, 866–884.

Fiese, B. H. (1992). Dimensions of family rituals across two generations: Relation to adolescent identity. *Family Process, 31*, 151–162.

Forgatch, M. S. (1989). Patterns and outcomes in family problem solving: The disrupting effect of negative emotion. *Journal of Marriage and the Family, 51*, 115–124.

Forgatch, M. S., & Patterson, G. R. (1989). *Parents and adolescents living together, Part 2: Family problem solving*. Eugene, OR: Castalia.

Frake, C. (1964). How to ask for a drink in Subanun. *American Anthropologist, 66,* 127–132.

Frankel, K., & Bates, J. (1990). Mother–toddler problem solving: Antecedents in attachment, home behavior and temperament. *Child Development, 61,* 810–819.

Freedman, J. L., Carlsmith, J. M., & Sears, D. O. (1970). *Social psychology.* Englewood Cliffs, NJ: Prentice Hall.

Freud, S. (1923). *The ego and the id.* London: Hogarth Press.

Freud, S. (1930). *Civilization and its discontents.* London: Hogarth Press.

Fromm-Reichmann, F. (1948). Notes on the development of treatment of schizophrenia by psychoanalytic psychotherapy. *Psychiatry, 11,* 263–273.

Galvin, K. M., & Brommel, B. J. (1996). *Family communication: Cohesion and change* (4th ed.). New York: HarperCollins.

Garfinkel, H. (1967). *Studies in ethnomethodology.* Englewood Cliffs, NJ: Prentice Hall.

Geertz, C. (1970). *Agricultural involution.* Berkeley: University of California Press.

Gergen, K. G. (1985). The social constructionist movement in psychology. *American Psychologist, 40,* 266–275.

Gergen, K. G. (1994). *Realities and relationships: Soundings in social construction.* Cambridge, MA: Harvard University Press.

Gilgun, J. F., Daly, K. J., & Handel, G. (1992). *Qualitative methods in family research.* Newbury Park, CA: Sage.

Glaser, B. G., & Strauss, A. L. (1967). *The discovery of grounded theory: Strategies for qualitative research.* Chicago: Aldine.

Glueck, S., & Glueck, E. (1950). *Unraveling juvenile delinquency.* New York: Commonwealth Fund.

Glyshaw, K., Cohen, L. H., & Towbes, L. C. (1989). Coping strategies and psychological distress: Prospective analyses of early and middle adolescents. *American Journal of Community Psychology, 17,* 607–623.

Goffman, E. (1967). *Interaction ritual.* New York: Anchor Books.

Goffman, E. (1971). *Relations in public.* New York: Harper and Row.

Goffman, E. (1981). *Forms of talk.* Philadelphia: University of Pennsylvania Press.

Goodwin, C. (1981). *Conversational organization: Interaction between speakers and hearers.* New York: Academic Press.

Goodwin, M. H. (1982). Processes of dispute management among urban black children. *American Ethnologist, 9,* 76–96.

Gottman, J. M. (1979). *Marital interaction: Experimental investigations.* New York: Academic Press.

Gottman, J. M. (1991). Chaos and regulated change in families: A metaphor for the study of transitions. In P. A. Cowan & E. M. Hetherington (Eds.), *Family transitions* (pp. 247–274). Hillsdale, NJ: Erlbaum.

Gottman, J. M. (1993). The roles of conflict engagement escalation, and avoidance in marital interaction: A longitudinal study of five types of couples. *Journal of Consulting and Clinical Psychology, 61,* 6–15.

Gottman, J. M. (1994). *What predicts divorce: The relationships between marital processes and marital outcomes.* Hillsdale, NJ: Erlbaum.

Gottman, J. M., & Krokoff, L. J. (1989). Marital interaction and satisfaction: A longitudinal view. *Journal of Consulting and Clinical Psychology, 57,* 47–52.

Gottman, J. M., & Roy, A. K. (1990). *Sequential analysis: A guide for behavioral researchers.* New York: Cambridge University Press.

Graesser, A. C., Singer, M., & Trabasso, T. (1994). Constructing inferences during narrative text comprehension. *Psychological Review, 101,* 371–395.

Grotevant, H. D., & Cooper, C. R. (1984). Individuation in family relationships: A perspective in individual differences in the development of role-taking skill in adolescence. *Human Development, 29,* 82–100.

Gubrium, J. F., & Holstein, J. A. (1990). *What is family?* Mountain View, CA: Mayfield.

Gubrium, J. F., & Holstein, J. A. (1993). Phenomenology, ethnomethodology, and family discourse. In P. Boss, W. Doherty, R. LaRossa, W. Schumm, & S. Steinmetz (Eds.), *Sourcebook of family theories and methods: A contextual approach* (pp. 651–672). New York: Plenum Press.

Guerin, P. J. (1976). Family therapy: The first twenty-five years. In P. J. Guerin (Ed.), *Family therapy: Theory and practice* (pp. 2–22). New York: Gardner Press.

Gumperz, J. J. (1982). *Discourse strategies.* New York: Cambridge University Press.

Gurman, A. S., & Kniskern, D. P. (1991). *Handbook of family therapy.* New York: Brunner/Mazel.

Haley, J. (1987). *Problem-solving therapy* (2nd ed.). San Francisco: Jossey-Bass.

Hauser, S. T., Powers, S., Noam, G., Jacobsen, A., Weiss, B., & Follansbee, D. (1984). Familial contexts of adolescent ego development. *Child Development, 55,* 195–213.

Hawkins, J. D., Catalano, R. T., & Kent, L. A. (1991). Combining broadcast media and parent education to prevent teenage drug abuse. In L. Donohew, H. E. Sypher, & W. J. Bukoski (Eds.), *Persuasive communication and drug abuse prevention* (pp. 283–294). Hillsdale, NJ: Erlbaum.

Hazelrigg, M. D., Cooper, H. M., & Borduin, C. M. (1987). Evaluating the effectiveness of family therapies: An integrative review and synthesis. *Psychological Bulletin, 101,* 428–442.

Heavey, C. L., Larson, B. M., Zumtobel, D. C., & Christensen, A. (1996). The Communication Patterns Questionnaire: The reliability and validity of a constructive communication subscale. *Journal of Marriage and the Family, 58,* 796–800.

Heavey, C. L., Layne, C., & Christensen, A. (1993). Gender and conflict structure in marital interaction. *Journal of Consulting and Clinical Psychology, 61,* 16–27.

Henggeler, S. W. (1989). *Delinquency in adolescence.* Newbury Park, CA: Sage.

Henggeler, S. W. (1992). Family preservation using multisystemic therapy: An effective alternative to incarcerating serious juvenile offenders. *Journal of Consulting and Clinical Psychology, 60,* 953–961.

Henggeler, S. W., & Borduin, C. M. (1990). *Family therapy and beyond: A multisystemic approach to treating the behavior problems of children and adolescents.* Pacific Grove, CA: Brooks/Cole.

Hibbs, E. D., & Jensen, P. S. (1996). *Psychosocial treatments for child and adolescent disorders: Empirically based strategies for clinical practice.* Washington, DC: American Psychological Association.

Hochschild, A. (1989). *The second shift: Working parents and the revolution at home.* New York: Viking.

Hoffman, L. R. (1965). Group problem solving. In L. Berkowitz (Ed.), *Advances in experimental social psychology* (Vol. 2). New York: Academic Press.

Hoffman, L. R., & Maier, N. R. F. (1961). Quality and acceptance of problem solutions by members of homogeneous and heterogeneous groups. *Journal of Abnormal and Social Psychology, 62,* 401–407.

Hoffman, L. R., & Smith, C. G. (1961). Some factors affecting the behavior of members of problem-solving groups. *Sociometry, 23,* 273–291.

Hughes, J. N., & Hall, R. J. (1989). *Cognitive-behavioral psychology in the schools: A comprehensive handbook.* New York: Guilford Press.

Imber-Black. E., Roberts, J., & Whiting, R. A. (1988). *Rituals in families and family therapy.* New York: Norton.

Jacobson, N. S. (1977). Training couples to solve their marital problems: A behavioral approach to relationship discord. *International Journal of Family Counseling, 5,* 22–31.

Jahoda, M. (1953). The meaning of psychological health. *Social Casework, 34,* 349–354.

Jahoda, M. (1958). *Current concepts of positive mental health.* New York: Basic Books.

James, W. (1890). *Principles of psychology.* New York: Henry Holt.

Janis, I. L. (1967). *Victims of groupthink.* Boston: Houghton Mifflin.

Jones, E. E., & Gerard, H. B. (1967). *Foundations of social psychology.* New York: John Wiley.

Kavanaugh, K., Frey, J., & Larsen, D. (1991). *Growing opportunities guide for parents of school-age children: A video-based family enrichment program, Part 3, Problem solving.* Eugene, OR: Northwest Family and School Consultants.

Kazdin, A. E. (1996). Problem solving and parent management in treating aggressive and antisocial behavior. In E. D. Hibbs & P. S. Jensen (Eds.), *Psychosocial treatments for child and adolescent disorders: Empirically based strategies for clinical practice* (pp. 377–408). Washington, DC: American Psychological Association.

Kazdin, A. E., Siegel, T. C., & Bass, D. (1992). Cognitive problem solving skills training and parent management training in the treatment of antisocial behavior in children. *Journal of Consulting and Clinical Psychology, 60,* 733–747.

Kendall, P. C. (1991). *Child and adolescent therapy: Cognitive-behavioral procedures.* New York: Guilford Press.

Kenkel, W. F. (1959). Traditional family ideology and spousal role in family decision-making. *Journal of Marriage and the Family, 21,* 334–339.

Kieren, D. K., Maguire, T. O., & Hurlbut, N. (1996). A marker method to test a phasing hypothesis in family problem-solving interaction. *Journal of Marriage and the Family, 58,* 442–455.

Klein, D. M., & Aldous, J. (Eds.). (1988). *Social stress and family development.* New York: Guilford Press.

Klein, D. M., & Hill, R. (1979). Determinants of family problem solving effectiveness. In W. R. Burr, R. Hill, F. I. Nye, & I. L. Reiss (Eds.), *Contemporary theories about the family: Vol. 1.* New York: Free Press.

Klein, D. M., & White, J. M. (1996). *Family theories: An introduction.* Thousand Oaks, CA: Sage.

Klein, N. C., Alexander, J. F., & Parsons, B. V. (1976). Impact of family systems intervention on recidivism and sibling delinquency. *Journal of Consulting and Clinical Psychology, 45,* 759–768.

Kohlberg, L. (1969). Stage and sequence: The cognitive developmental approach to socialization. In D. A. Goslin (Ed.), *Moral development and behavior.* Chicago: Rand McNally.

Kuhn, T. (1970). *The structure of scientific revolutions* (2nd ed.). Chicago: University of Chicago Press.

Kurdek, L. A. (1995). Predicting change in marital satisfaction from husbands' and wives' conflict resolution styles. *Journal of Marriage and the Family, 57,* 153–164.

Larson, R., & Richards, M. H. (1995). *Divergent realities: The emotional lives of mothers, fathers, and adolescents.* New York: HarperCollins.

Leadbeater, B. J., Hellner, I., Allen, J. P., & Aber, J. L. (1989). The assessment of interpersonal negotiation strategies in multiproblem youth. *Developmental Psychology, 25,* 465–472.

Leik, R. K. (1963). Instrumentality and emotionality in family interaction. *Sociometry, 26,* 131–145.

Levenson, R. W., & Gottman, J. M. (1985). Physiological and affective predictors of change in relationship satisfaction. *Journal of Personality and Social Psychology, 49*, 85–94.

Lewinsohn, P. M., Clark, G. N., Rohde, P., Hops, H., & Seeley, J. R. (1996). A course in coping: A cognitive-behavioral approach to the treatment of adolescent depression. In E. D. Hibbs & P. S. Jensen (Eds.), *Psychosocial treatments for child and adolescent disorders: Empirically based strategies for clinical practice* (pp. 109–136). Washington, DC: American Psychological Association.

Lewis, J. D., & Smith, R. L. (1980). *American sociology and pragmatism: Mead, Chicago sociology, and symbolic interaction.* Chicago: University of Chicago Press.

Lewis, M. (1997). *Altering fate: Why the past does not predict the future.* New York: Guilford Press.

Madanes, C. (1981). *Strategic family therapy.* San Francisco: Jossey-Bass.

Malinowski, B. (1927). *Sex and repression in savage society.* New York: Humanities Press.

March, J. G., & Simon, H. A. (1958). *Organizations.* New York: Wiley.

Maynard, D. W. (1985). On the functions of conflict among children. *American Sociological Review, 50*, 207–223.

McCord, J. (1991). Long-term perspectives on parental absence. In L. Robins & M. Rutter (Eds.), *Straight and devious pathways from childhood to adulthood* (pp. 116–134). Norwood, NJ: Ablex.

McHugh, P. (1968). *Defining the situation: The organization of meaning in social interaction.* New York: Bobbs-Merrill.

Mead, G. H. (1934). *Mind, self, and society.* Chicago: University of Chicago Press.

Mead, M. (1928). *Coming of age in Samoa.* New York: Morrow.

Miller, G. A., Newman, E. B., & Friedman, E. A. (1958). Length-frequency statistics for written English. *Information and Control, 1*, 370–389.

Minuchin, S., & Fishman, H. C. (1981). *Family therapy techniques.* Cambridge, MA: Harvard University Press.

Minuchin, S., Rosman, B. L., & Baker, L. (1978). *Psychosomatic families.* Cambridge, MA: Harvard University Press.

Mishler, E. (1975). Studies in dialogue and discourse: An exponential law of successive questioning. *Language in Society, 4*, 31–51.

Morgan, L. H. (1877). *Ancient society.* Chicago: Charles S. Kerr.

Morris, S. B., Alexander, J. F., & Waldron, H. (1988). Functional family therapy. In I. R. H. Falloon (Ed.), *Handbook of behavioral family therapy* (pp. 107–127). New York: Guilford Press.

Moynihan, D. P. (1965). *The Negro family: The case for national action.* Washington, DC: Office of Policy Planning and Research, U.S. Department of Labor.

Mueser, K. T., Bellack, A. S., Wade, J. H., & Sayers, S. L. (1993). Expressed emotion, social skill and response to negative affect. *Journal of Abnormal Psychology, 102*, 339–351.

Murdock, G. P. (1949). *Social structure.* New York: Macmillan.

Napier, A. Y., & Whitaker, C. A. (1978). *The family crucible: One family's therapy—An experience that illuminates all our lives.* New York: Harper & Row.

Newell, A., & Simon, H. A. (1972). *Human problem solving.* Englewood Cliffs, NJ: Prentice Hall.

Olds, D. L., Eckenrode, J., Henderson, C. R., Kitzman, H., Powers, J., Cole, R., Sidora, K., Morris, P., Pettitt, L. M., & Luckey, D. (1997). Long-term effects of home visitation on maternal life course and child abuse and neglect. *Journal of the American Medical Association, 278*, 637–643.

Olds, D. L., Henderson, C. R., Chamberlin, R., & Tatelbaum, R. (1986). Preventing child abuse and neglect: A randomized trial of nurse home visitation. *Pediatrics, 78*, 16–28.

Olson, D. L. (1986). Circumplex model IV: Validation studies and FACES III. *Family Process, 25*, 337–351.

O'Rourke, J. (1963). Field and laboratory: The decision-making behaviors of family groups in two experimental conditions. *Sociometry, 26*, 422–435.

Parsons, T. (1951). *The social system.* Glencoe, IL: Free Press.

Parsons, T., & Bales, R. F. (Eds.). (1955). *Family socialization and interaction process.* Glencoe, IL: Free Press.

Patterson, G. R. (1971). *Families: Applications of social learning to family life.* Champaign, IL: Research Press.

Patterson, G. R. (1974). Intervention for boys with conduct problems. *Journal of Consulting and Clinical Psychology, 42*, 471–481.

Patterson, G. R. (1982). *Coercive family process.* Eugene, OR: Castalia.

Patterson, G. R., Reid, J. B., & Dishion, T. J. (1992). *Antisocial boys.* Eugene, OR: Castalia.

Patterson, G. R., Reid, J. B., Jones, R. R., & Conger, R. E. (1975). *A social learning approach to family prevention, Vol. 1: Families with aggressive children.* Eugene, OR: Castalia.

Pecora, P. J., Fraser, M. W., & Haapala, D. A. (1992). Intensive home-based family preservation services: Update from the FIT Project. *Child Welfare, LXXI*, 177–188.

Pettit, G. S., Dodge, K. A., & Brown, M. M. (1988). Early family experience, social problem solving patterns, and children's social competence. *Child Development, 59*, 107–120.

Piaget, J. (1932). *The moral judgment of the child.* London: Kegan Paul, Trench & Trubner.

Pinker, S. (1994). *The language instinct.* New York: Morrow.

Pinker, S. (1997). *How the mind works.* New York: W. W. Norton.

Popkin, M. (1991). *Active parenting for families.* Atlanta, GA: Active Parenting.

Pukui, M. K., Haertig, E. W., & Lee, C. A. (1972). *Nana I Ke Kumu* (Vol. 1). Honolulu, HI: Auxiliary of Queen Liliuokalani Children's Center.

Reid, J. B. (1986). Social interactional patterns in families of abused and nonabused children. In C. Zahn-Waxler, M. Cummings, & R. Iannotti (Eds.), *Altruism and aggression: Social and biological origins* (pp. 238–255). New York: Cambridge University Press.

Reid, J. B. (1993). Prevention of conduct disorder before and after school entry: Relating interventions to developmental findings. *Development and Psychopathology, 5*, 243–262.

Reiss, D. (1967). Individual thinking and family interaction, I: An introduction to an experimental study of problem solving in families of normals, character disorders and schizophrenics. *Archives of General Psychiatry, 16*, 80–93.

Reiss, D. (1981). *The family's construction of reality.* Cambridge, MA: Harvard University Press.

Reiss, D., & Klein, D. (1989). Paradigm and pathogenesis: A family-centered approach to problems of etiology and treatment of psychiatric disorders. In T. Jacob (Ed.), *Family interaction and psychopathology: Theories, methods and findings* (pp. 203–258). New York: Plenum Press.

Riecken, H. W. (1958). The effect of talkativeness on ability to influence group solutions to problems. *Sociometry, 21*, 309–321.

Robin, A. L., Bedway, M., Siegel, P. T., & Gilroy, M. (1996). Therapy for adolescent anorexia nervosa: Addressing cognitions, feelings and the family's role. In E. D. Hibbs & P. S. Jensen (Eds.), *Psychosocial treatments for child and adolescent disorders: Empirically based strategies for clinical practice* (pp. 239–262). Washington, DC: American Psychological Association.

Robin, A. L., & Foster, S. L. (1989). *Negotiating parent-adolescent conflict: A behavioral-family systems approach.* New York: Guilford Press.

Roethlisberger, F. J., & Dickson, W. J. (1939). *Management and the worker.* Cambridge, MA: Harvard University Press.

Rosenbaum, C. P., & Beebe, J. E. (1975). *Psychiatric treatment*. New York: McGraw-Hill.

Rosenthal, R. (1966). *Experimenter effects in behavioral research*. New York: Appleton-Century-Crofts.

Rubin, K. H., Bream, L. A., & Rose-Krasnor, L. (1991). Social problem solving and aggression in childhood. In D. J. Pepler & K. H. Rubin (Eds.), *The development and treatment of childhood aggression* (pp. 219–248). Hillsdale, NJ: Erlbaum.

Rubin, K. H., & Krasnor, L. R. (1986). Social-cognitive and social behavioral perspectives on problem solving. In M. Perlmutter (Ed.), *Cognitive perspectives on children's social and behavioral development* (pp. 1–68). Hillsdale, NJ: Erlbaum.

Rueter, M. A., & Conger, R. D. (1995). Interaction style, problem-solving behavior, and family problem solving effectiveness. *Child Development, 66,* 98–115.

Sacks, H., Schegloff, E., & Jefferson, G. (1974). A simplest systematics for the organization of turn-taking in conversation. *Language, 50,* 696–735.

Schegloff, E., & Sacks, H. (1973). Opening up closings. *Semiotica, 8,* 289–327.

Scott, F. G. (1962). Family group structure and patterns of social interaction. *American Journal of Sociology, 68,* 214–228.

Selman, R. L., Beardslee, W., Schultz, L. H., Krupa, M., & Podorefsky, D. (1986). Assessing adolescent interpersonal negotiation strategies: Toward the integration of structural and functional models. *Developmental Psychology, 22,* 450–459.

Selman, R. L., & Demorest, A. P. (1984). Observing troubled children's interpersonal negotiation strategies: Implications for a developmental model. *Child Development, 55,* 288–304.

Shure, M. B., & Spivack, G. (1978). *Problem-solving techniques in child rearing*. San Francisco: Jossey-Bass.

Shure, M. B., & Spivack, G. (1982). Interpersonal problem solving in young children: A cognitive approach to prevention. *American Journal of Community Psychology, 10,* 341–356.

Shure, M. B., & Spivack, G. (1991). Interpersonal cognitive problem solving. In L. E. Beutler & M. Crago (Eds.), *Psychotherapy research: An international review of programmatic studies* (pp. 69–82). Washington, DC: American Psychological Association.

Sim, H., & Vuchinich, S. (1996). The declining effects of family stressors on antisocial behavior from childhood to adolescence and early adulthood. *Journal of Family Issues, 17,* 408–427.

Simmel, G. (1950). *The sociology of Georg Simmel* (Kurt Wolff, Trans.). Glencoe, IL: Free Press.

Simon, H. A. (1945). *Administrative behavior: A study of decision-making processes in administrative organization*. New York: Free Press.

Simon, H. A. (1956). *Models of man*. New York: Wiley.

Skinner, B. F. (1953). *Science and human behavior*. New York: Macmillan.

Smetana, J. G. (1989). Adolescents' and parents' reasoning about actual family conflict. *Child Development, 60,* 1052–1067.

Spivack, G., Platt, J. J., & Shure, M. B. (1976). *The problem-solving approach to adjustment*. San Francisco: Jossey-Bass.

Spock, B. (1946). *The common sense book of baby and child care*. New York: Duell, Sloan & Pearce.

Spoth, R., & Redmond, C. (1996). A theory-based parent competency model incorporating intervention attendance effects. *Family Relations, 45,* 139–147.

Spoth, R., Redmond, C., Haggerty, K., & Ward, T. (1995). A controlled parenting skills outcome study examining individual difference and attendance effects. *Journal of Marriage and Family Issues, 17,* 408–464.

Stack, C. (1974). *All our kin: Strategies for survival in the black community*. New York: Harper & Row.

Stark, K. D., Rouse, L. W., & Livingston, R. (1991). Treatment of depression during childhood and adolescence: Cognitive-behavioral procedures for the individual and family. In P. C. Kendall (Ed.), *Child and adolescent therapy: Cognitive-behavioral procedures* (pp. 165–209). New York: Guilford Press.

Stark, K. D., Swearer, S., Kurowski, C., Sommer, D., & Bowen, B. (1996). Targeting the child and the family: A holistic approach to treating child and adolescent depressive disorders. In E. D. Hibbs & P. S. Jensen (Eds.), *Psychosocial treatments for child and adolescent disorders: Empirically based strategies for clinical practice*. Washington, DC: American Psychological Association.

Steinberg, L. (1981). Transformations in family relations at puberty. *Developmental Psychology, 17*, 833–840.

Steinberg, L., & Silverberg, S. B. (1986). The vicissitudes of autonomy in early adolescence. *Developmental Psychology, 57*, 841–851.

Steinhauer, P. D. (1989). The family as a small group: The process model of family functioning. In T. Jacob (Ed.), *Family interaction and psychopathology: Theories, methods and findings* (pp. 67–116). New York: Plenum Press.

Sternberg, R. J. (1994). *Thinking and problem solving*. San Diego, CA: Academic Press.

Straus, M. A. (1968). Communication, creativity and problem solving ability of middle and working class families in three societies. *American Journal of Sociology, 73*, 417–430.

Straus, M. A. (1972). Family organization and problem solving ability in relation to societal modernization. *Journal of Comparative Family Studies, 3*, 70–83.

Strodtbeck, F. L. (1954). The family as a three person group. *American Sociological Review, 19*, 23–29.

Tallman, I. (1961). Adaptability: A problem solving approach to assessing childrearing practices. *Child Development, 32*, 651–668.

Tallman, I. (1980). Social structure, family socialization and children's achievement goals. In J. Trost (Ed.), *The family in change* (pp. 75–87). Vasteras, Sweden: International Library.

Tallman, I. (1988). Problem solving in families: A revisionist view. In D. M. Klein & J. Aldous (Eds.), *Social stress and family development* (pp. 102–128). New York: Guilford Press.

Tallman, I. (1993). Theoretical issues in researching problem solving in families. *Marriage and Family Review, 18*, 155–186.

Tallman, I., Leik, R. K., Gray, L. N., & Stafford, M. C. (1993). A theory of problem solving behavior. *Social Psychology Quarterly, 56*, 157–177.

Tallman, I., & Miller, G. (1974). Class differences in family problem solving: The effects of verbal ability, hierarchical structure, and role expectations. *Sociometry, 37*, 13–37.

Taylor, F. K., Berry, P. C., & Block, C. H. (1958). Does group participation when using brainstorming facilitate or inhibit creative thinking? *Administrative Science Quarterly, 3*, 23–47.

Taylor, F. W. (1911). *Scientific management*. New York: Harper & Row.

Terman, L. M. (1938). *Psychological factors in marital happiness*. New York: McGraw-Hill.

Thomas, D. S., and associates. (1950). *Some new techniques for studying social behavior*. New York: Bureau of Publications, Teacher's College.

Thomas, R. (1996). Reflective dialogue parent education design: Focus on parent development. *Family Relations, 45*, 189–201.

Thomas, W. I., & Thomas, D. S. (1928). *The child in America: Behavior problems and programs*. New York: Knopf.

Thompson, L., & Walker, A. J. (1995). The place of feminism in family studies. *Journal of Marriage and the Family, 57*, 847–866.

Thorndike, R. L. (1920, January). Intelligence and its uses. *Harpers Monthly Magazine*, 227–235.

Tolan, P. H., & McKay, M. M. (1996). Preventing serious antisocial behavior in inner-city children: An empirically based family prevention model. *Family Relations, 45*, 148–155.

Tooby, J., & Cosmides, L. (1997). *Evolutionary psychology: A primer.* Unpublished manuscript, University of California, Santa Barbara. (Available at Internet site: www.psych. ucsb.edu/research/cep/primer.html)

Torrance, E. P. (1955). Some consequences of power differences on decision making in permanent and temporary three-man groups. In A. P. Hare, E. F. Borgatta, & R. F. Bales (Eds.), *Small groups: Studies in social interaction* (pp. 482–491). New York: Knopf.

Triplett, N. (1898). The dynamogenic factors in pacemaking and competition. *American Journal of Psychology, 2*, 507–533.

Ullmann, L. P., & Krasner, L. A. (1969). *A psychological approach to abnormal behavior.* New York: Holt, Rinehart & Winston.

Urbain, E. S., & Kendall, P. C. (1980). Review of social-cognitive problem solving interventions with children. *Psychological Bulletin, 83*, 109–143.

Vuchinich, S. (1984). Sequencing and social structure in family conflict. *Social Psychology Quarterly, 47*, 217–234.

Vuchinich, S. (1986). On attenuation in verbal family conflict. *Social Psychology Quarterly, 49*, 281–293.

Vuchinich, S. (1987). Starting and stopping spontaneous family conflict. *Journal of Marriage and the Family, 49*, 591–601.

Vuchinich, S. (1990). The sequential organization of closing in verbal family conflict. In A. D. Grimshaw (Ed.), *Conflict talk: Sociolinguistic investigations* (pp. 118-138). New York: Cambridge University Press.

Vuchinich, S., & Angelelli, J. (1995). Family interaction during problem solving. In M. A. Fitzpatrick & A. L. Vangelisti (Eds.), *Explaining family interaction* (pp. 177–206). Thousand Oaks, CA: Sage.

Vuchinich, S., Angelelli, J., & Gatherum, A. (1996). Context and development in family problem solving with preadolescent children. *Child Development, 67*, 1276–1288.

Vuchinich, S., & DeBaryshe, B. (1997). Factor structure and predictive validity of questionnaire reports of family problem solving. *Journal of Marriage and the Family, 59*, 915–927.

Vuchinich, S., Emery, R. E., & Cassidy, J. (1988). Family members as third parties in dyadic family conflict: Strategies, alliances and outcomes. *Child Development, 59*, 1293–1302.

Vuchinich, S., Hetherington, E. M., Vuchinich, R. A., & Clingempeel, G. (1991). Parent–child interaction and gender differences in early adolescents' adaptation to stepfamilies. *Developmental Psychology, 27*, 618–626.

Vuchinich, S., & Teachman, J. (1993). Influences on the duration of wars, strikes, riots, and family arguments. *Journal of Conflict Resolution, 37*, 544–568.

Vuchinich, S., Teachman, J., & Crosby, L. (1991). Families and hazard rates that change over time: Some methodological issues in the study of transitions. *Journal of Marriage and the Family, 53*, 898–912.

Vuchinich, S., Vuchinich, R. A., & Coughlin, C. (1991). Family talk and parent–child relationships: Toward integrating deductive and inductive paradigms. *Merrill-Palmer Quarterly, 38*, 69–94.

Vuchinich, S., Vuchinich, R. A., & Wood, B. (1993). The interparental relationship and family problem solving with preadolescent males. *Child Development, 64,* 1389–1400.

Vuchinich, S., Wood, B., & Angelelli, J. (1996). Coalitions and family problem solving in the psychosocial treatment of adolescents. In E. D. Hibbs & P. S. Jensen (Eds.), *Psychosocial treatments for child and adolescent disorders: Empirically based strategies for clinical practice* (pp. 497–520). Washington, DC: American Psychological Association.

Vuchinich, S., Wood, B., & Vuchinich, R. A. (1994). Coalitions and family problem solving with preadolescents in referred, at-risk, and comparison families. *Family Process, 33,* 409–428.

Wasik, B. H., Bryant, D., & Lyons, C. (1990). *Home visiting: Procedures for helping families.* Newbury Park, CA: Sage.

Watson, J. B. (1928). *Psychological care of infant and child.* New York: Norton.

Watzlawick, P., Weakland, J., Fisch, R., & Bodin, A. (1974). Brief therapy: Focused problem resolution. *Family Process, 13,* 141–167.

Weakland, J. (1976). Communication theory and clinical change. In P. J. Guerin (Ed.), *Family therapy: Theory and practice* (pp. 111–128). New York: Gardner Press.

Webster-Stratton, C. (1996). Early intervention with videotape modeling: Programs for families of children with oppositional defiant disorder or conduct disorder. In E. D. Hibbs & P. S. Jensen (Eds.), *Psychosocial treatments for child and adolescent disorders: Empirically based strategies for clinical practice.* Washington, DC: American Psychological Association.

Weick, K. E. (1971). Group processes, family processes, and family problem solving. In J. Aldous, T. Condon, R. Hill, M. A. Straus, & I. Tallman (Eds.), *Family problem solving: A symposium on theoretical, methodological and substantive concerns* (pp. 3–32). Hinsdale, IL: Dryden Press.

Weiss, B., Dodge, K. A., Bates, J. E., & Pettit, G. S. (1992). Some consequences of early harsh discipline: Child aggression and a maladaptive social information processing style. *Child Development, 63,* 1321–1335.

Westermarck, E. (1891/1922). *The history of human marriage.* New York: Allerton Books.

Williams, T. (1955). *Cat on a hot tin roof.* New York: New Directions Books.

Wilson, E. O. (1975). *Sociobiology: The new synthesis.* Boston, MA: Harvard University Press.

Wolin, S. J., Bennett, L. A., & Noonan, D. L. (1979). Family rituals and the recurrence of alcoholism across generations. *American Journal of Psychiatry, 136,* 589–593.

Yeates, K. O., Schultz, L. H., & Selman, R. L. (1991). The development of interpersonal negotiation strategies in thought and action: A social-cognitive link to behavioral adjustment and social status. *Merrill-Palmer Quarterly, 37,* 369–406.

Zajonc, R. (1969). Cognitive theories in social psychology. In G. Lindzey & E. Aronson (Eds.), *The handbook of social psychology* (Vol. I, 2nd ed., pp. 320–411). Menlo Park, CA: Addison-Wesley.

Zvonkovic, A., Schmiege, C., & Hall, L. (1994). Influence strategies used when couples make work-family decisions and their importance for marital satisfaction. *Family Relations, 43,* 182–188.

Index

Adaptational model, 28-29, 61-63, 91,
    97-98
  and treatment, 158-161, 183
Administrative Behavior (Simon), 39
Affective component. *See* Emotional
    expression
Anthropological perspective, 6-7
Applied approach, 8-10
  and cultural variations, 9
  and divorce, 9
  and gender roles, 9-10
  and social policy, 8-9
  and societal trends, 9
  See also Treatment
Audiotapes, 199-200

Bales, Robert, 44-51
Beeper sampling, 141-142
Behavior profiles, 48, 209
Behavioral family therapy, 155-156,
    161-168
  cognitive-behavioral approach, 77-79,
    169-174
  problem solving in, 162-168
Behaviorism, 65-66
Biblical perspective, 1-2
Breach of responsibility structure, 114-115

Cat on a Hot Tin Roof (Williams), 4-6
Closure, family paradigms and, 70, 71
Coding:
  and emotional expression, 78-79

and home observation, 138
and verbal behavior, 138, 146-147
Cognitive-behavioral family therapy,
    77-79, 169-174
Cognitive processes, 17-18
  and social competence, 72
  and theory, 1950-1990, 71-77
  and treatment, 155, 161, 162, 168-
    169
  Interpersonal Negotiation Strategies
    (INS), 74-77, 186-187
Compact discs (CDs), 202-203
Complaint ritual, 124-125
Configuration, family paradigms and, 70,
    71
Conflict:
  and developmental perspective,
    188-194, 211
  and marital relationship, 80-82, 195
  and theory, 1950-1990, 79-82
Control phase, small groups, 50-51, 145
Coordination, family paradigms and, 70,
    71
Cross-complaining ritual, 124
Cultural values, 130-131, 183
Cultural variations, 9
  and SIMFAM (SIMulated FAMily
    game), 54-56
  and theory, 1950-1990, 53-57
  ethnicity, 53, 57
  Hawaiian, 6
  social class, 53-57
  Western perspective, 1-6

Darwin, Charles, 25-26, 28, 34
Decision making, 98-99
Deductive strategy, 93
Delinquency treatment, 178
Democratic parenting model, 40-41, 181
Developmental perspective, 185-196
    and conflict, 188-194, 211
    and interpersonal problem solving,
        185-187
    studies on, 187-196, 212-213, 216, 217
Dewey, John, 25-30, 54, 61, 66, 71-72,
    90-91, 97-98, 132-133
Divorce, 9
Drug abuse treatment, 177-178
    Preparing for the Drug Free Years, 177
Drug therapy, 156-157, 158

Emotional expression, 18
    and schizophrenia, 79, 179
    and theory (1900–1950), 28
    and theory (1950–1990), 78-79
    and treatment, 152-155, 169
    Specific Affective Coding System,
        78-79
Ethnicity, 53, 57
Evaluation phase, small groups, 50-51,
    128, 145
Evolutionary psychology, 35-36
Experimenter effect, 143
External threat structure, 115-116
External validity, 58-59

Family cohesion, 118-122, 134
Family council model, 40-41
Family dinners, 139
Family interaction, 107-111
    and treatment, 157
Family interaction task, 49, 210
Family meetings, 128-129
Family paradigms:
    and schizophrenia, 68
    and theory, 1950-1990, 68-71
    closure, 70, 71
    configuration, 70, 71
    coordination, 70, 71
Family participation, 157-158
Family problems defined, 11
    and problem solving strategies,
        105-112

and theory, 1900-1950, 28-29
Family problem solving defined, 10-16
Family problem solving strategies:
    and family cohesion, 118-122, 134
    and family interaction, 107-111
    and family social skills, 118-122
    and family system, 94, 117-118, 129
    and rational model, 94, 129
    and solving processes, 92-93
    and uncertainty absorption, 98-99
    breach of responsibility structure,
        114-115
    complaint ritual, 124-125
    cross-complaining ritual, 124
    decision making, 98-99
    deductive strategy, 93
    examples of, 95-96, 99-102, 103-105,
        110-113, 114-115, 120-121,
        125-127
    external threat structure, 115-116
    family meetings, 128-129
    family problem construction, 107-116
    family problems defined, 105-112
    garbage can model, 99-102
    inductive strategy, 93-94, 129
    negotiated consent, 117
    preceding defined problem, 103-105
    problem structures, 112-116
    qualitative strategy, 93-94, 129,
        197-198
    retrospective, 102-103
    ritual, 94, 122-129
    rule violation structure, 112-113
    scapegoat structure, 115
    selection ritual, 125-128
    unfair rule structure, 113-114
    validation ritual, 125
    See also Rational model; Small group
        processes; Social constructionism;
        Treatment
Family social skills, 118-122
Family system, 94, 117-118, 129
Family therapy:
    and external validity, 58-59
    and schizophrenia, 58
    and theory (1900–1950), 41-42
    and theory (1950–1990), 57-64
    behavioral, 155-156, 161-168
    cognitive-behavioral, 77-79, 169-174
    strategic, 59-64, 67-68, 162
    See also Treatment

Freud, Sigmund, 30-33

Garbage can model, 99-102
Gender roles, 9-10
Goal attainment:
    blockage of, 11-12, 13f, 28
    of theory, 23-25
    process of, 12-16
Group discussion task, 48, 208
Groups. *See* Small group processes
Groupthink, 133

Hawaiian culture, 6
Hawthorne study (Chicago), 38-39
Hazard model, 192-194
Home observation:
    and rational model, 138-142, 151
    and subject reactivity, 140-141
    and verbal behavior coding, 138
    beeper sampling, 141-142
    family dinner, 139
How We Think (Dewey), 29-30, 71-72

Incest, 6
Inductive strategy, 93-94, 129
Instinct, 34-37
Integrative approach, 7-10, 21
    and applied approach, 8-10
    and rational model, 135-136, 151,
        184
    and theory, 7-8
    and treatment, 156-157
Interaction Process Analysis (IPA), 44-51
Intergenerational differences, 19-20
Internet, 203-205
Interpersonal Negotiation Strategies (INS):
    and developmental perspective,
        186-187
    and theory, 1950-1990, 74-77
    collaborative level, 75
    impulsive level, 75
    reciprocal level, 75
    unilateral level, 75
Irrational model, 30-33, 34, 36, 38-39

James, William, 34-37

Leadership:
    social-emotional leader, 46-47, 49-50
    task leader, 46-47, 49-50
Literary perspective:
    American, 4-6
    Greek, 2-3

Marital relationship, 19-20
    and conflict, 80-82, 195
    and cross-complaining ritual, 124
    and divorce, 9
Markov model, 150
Mental health:
    and schizophrenia, 58, 68, 79
    and theory, 1950-1990, 65-68
Mental health treatment, 155-156,
        161-174
    and cognitive processes, 155, 161,
        162, 168-169
    and rational model, 156, 159-160,
        162, 168-169
    behavioral family therapy, 155-156,
        161-168
    cognitive-behavioral therapy, 169-174
    parent education, 171-172
    parent management training (PMT),
        172-174
    problem solving skills training (PSST),
        172-174
    role play, 170-171
    schizophrenia, 179-180
    strategic family therapy, 162
    success rates, 167-168, 172
Metropolitan Area Child Study, 178

Negotiated consent, 117

Objective analysis, 8, 106
Oedipus Rex (Sophocles), 2-3
Orientation phase, small groups, 50-51, 145

Parent education:
    and theory, 1900-1950, 40-41
    and treatment, 171-172, 180-182
    and treatment success rates, 182
    democratic parenting model, 40-41,
        181

Systematic Training for Effective
      Parenting, 181
Parenting characteristics, 86-87
Parent management training (PMT),
      172-174
Parent's Handbook, The (Dinkmeyer &
      McKay), 181-182
Phase model:
      and consensus building, 146
      and phasing rationality, 145, 148
      and rational model, 25-30, 66,
            132-134, 144-150
      and sequential model, 145, 148-150
      and theory, 1900-1950, 25-30
      small group control phase, 50-51, 145
      small group evaluation phase, 50-51,
            128, 145
      small group orientation phase, 50-51,
            145
      See also Rational model
Phasing rationality, 145, 148
Preparing for the Drug Free Years, 177
Prevention programs, 174-180
      for delinquency, 178
      for drug abuse, 177-178
      for schizophrenia, 179-180
      Metropolitan Area Child Study, 178
      Preparing for the Drug Free Years, 177
      primary, 175-176, 177-178
      secondary, 176, 178
      success rates, 175, 180
      tertiary, 176, 178-180
      See also Treatment
Problem defined, 26-29
Problem solving skills training (PSST),
      172-174
Problem structures:
      breach of responsibility, 114-115
      external threat, 115-116
      rule violation, 112-113
      scapegoat, 115
      unfair rule, 113-114
Psychoanalysis:
      and theory, 1900-1950, 31-33, 41-42,
            60
      transference process, 31, 41

Qualitative strategy, 93-94, 129, 197-198

Rational model:
      alternatives to, 131-132, 151, 197-198
      and cultural values, 130-131, 183
      and home observation, 138-142, 151
      and model integration, 135-136, 151,
            184
      and phasing rationality, 145, 148
      and problem solving strategies, 94, 129
      and sequential model, 145, 148-150
      and theory, 1900-1950, 26, 28, 30,
            34, 36, 38-39
      and time-limited problem solving,
            137-138, 143, 144, 151
      and treatment, 156, 159-160, 162,
            168-169, 183
      and verbal behavior coding, 138,
            146-147
      limitations of, 133-136, 137-138,
            142-144, 148, 196-197
      scope of, 136-137
      vs. irrational model, 30-33, 34, 36,
            38-39
      See also Phase model
Relationship endurance, 18-19
Ritual, 94, 122-129
      complaint, 124-125
      cross-complaining, 124
      family meetings, 128-129
      selection, 125-128
      validation, 125
Role differentiation, 47, 49-50
Role play, 170-171
Rule violation structure, 112-113

Scapegoat structure, 115
Schizophrenia:
      and emotional expression, 79, 179
      and family paradigms, 68
      and family therapy, 58
      and theory, 1950-1990, 58, 68, 79
      treatment for, 179-180
      treatment success rates, 180
School system, 29-30
Selection ritual, 125-128
Sequential model, 145, 148-150
      and Markov model, 150
SIMFAM (SIMulated FAMily game), 54-56
Simon, Herbert, 39
Small group processes, 17-18
      and theory (1900–1950), 37-39

and theory (1950–1990), 44-53
behavior profiles, 48, 209
control phase, 50-51, 145
evaluation phase, 50-51, 128, 145
experimental paradigm for, 37-39,
    51-53
family interaction task, 49, 210
group discussion task, 48, 208
Hawthorne study (Chicago), 38-39
Interaction Process Analysis (IPA),
    44-51
leadership, 46-47, 49-50
orientation phase, 50-51, 145
phase model for, 50-51, 128, 145
role differentiation, 47, 49-50
social-emotional leader, 46-47, 49-50
task leader, 46-47, 49-50
Social class, 53-57
Social competence, 72
Social constructionism, 94, 95-105,
    107-129
and complaint ritual, 124-125
and cross-complaining ritual, 124
and decision making, 98-99
and family cohesion, 118-122
and family interaction, 107-111
and family meetings, 128-129
and family problems defined, 105-112
and family social skills, 118-122
and family system, 94, 117-118, 129
and garbage can model, 99-102
and negotiated consent, 117
and problem solving solutions,
    116-118
and qualitative analysis, 197-198
and ritual, 94, 122-129
and selection ritual, 125-128
and uncertainty absorption, 98-99
and validation ritual, 125
breach of responsibility structure,
    114-115
examples of, 95-96, 99-102, 103-105
external threat structure, 115-116
family problem construction, 95-98,
    107-116
problem structures, 112-116
retrospective problem solving, 102-103
rule violation structure, 112-113
scapegoat structure, 115
social nature of problems, 98-103

strategies preceding defined problem,
    103-105
unfair rule structure, 113-114
Social-emotional leader, 46-47, 49-50
Social learning theory, 65-68, 77-78
Social policy, 8-9
Societal trends, 9
Sociobiology, 36
Sophocles, 2-3
Specific Affective Coding System, 78-79
Strategic family therapy, 59-64, 67-68, 162
Structural-functionalism, 39-40
Subject reactivity, 140-141
Substance abuse treatment, 177-178
Subsystem differences, 19
Symbolic interactionism, 44
Systems theory, 7
    and theory, 1900-1950, 28-29

Task leader, 46-47, 49-50
Technology, 198-205
    audiotapes, 199-200
    compact discs (CDs), 202-203
    internet, 203-205
    video-conferences, 204-205
    videotapes, 198-203
Theory, 7-8
    and objective analysis, 8, 106
    goals of, 23-25
Theory, 1900-1950:
    adaptational model, 28-29, 61-63, 91,
        97-98
    and school system, 29-30
    democratic parenting model, 40-41,
        181
    emotional expression, 28
    evolutionary psychology, 35-36
    family council model, 40-41
    family problems defined, 28-29
    family therapy, 41-42
    goal attainment blockage, 28
    instinct, 34-37
    irrational model, 30-33, 34, 36, 38-39
    John Dewey, 25-30, 54, 61, 66, 71-72,
        90-91, 97-98, 132-133
    overview of, 25f
    parent education, 40-41
    phase model, 25-30
    problem defined, 26-29
    psychoanalysis, 31-33, 41-42, 60

rational model, 26, 28, 30, 34, 36, 38-39
Sigmund Freud, 30-33
small group processes, 37-39
sociobiology, 36
structural-functionalism, 39-40
systems theory, 28-29
transference process, 31, 41
William James, 34-37
Theory, 1950-1990:
    and conflict, 79-82
    and cultural variations, 53-57
    and schizophrenia, 58, 68, 79
    behaviorism, 65-66
    cognitive-behavioral family therapy, 77-79
    cognitive processes, 71-77
    emotional expression, 78-79
    external validity, 58-59
    family paradigms, 68-71
    family problem solving, 82-84
    family therapy, 57-64
    Interaction Process Analysis (IPA), 44-51
    Interpersonal Negotiation Strategies (INS), 74-77
    overview of, 25f, 43, 84-91
    parenting characteristics, 86-87
    small group processes, 44-53
    social learning theory, 65-68, 77-78
    Specific Affective Coding System, 78-79
    strategic family therapy, 59-64, 67-68, 162
    symbolic interactionism, 44
Theory, post-1990, 85-91
    and audiotapes, 199-200
    and compact discs (CDs), 202-203
    and conflict, 188-194, 211
    and internet, 203-205
    and technology, 198-205
    and video-conferences, 204-205
    and videotapes, 198-203
    developmental perspective, 185-196
    developmental studies, 187-196, 212-213, 216, 217
    interpersonal problem solving, 185-187
    parenting characteristics, 86-87
    qualitative strategy, 93-94, 129, 197-198

Time-limited problem solving, 137-138, 143, 144, 151
Transference process, 31, 41
Treatment:
    and adaptational model, 158-161, 183
    and negative emotions, 152-155, 169
    and rational model, 156, 159-160, 162, 168-169, 183
    and unmet needs, 152-155, 159, 169
    behavioral family therapy, 155-156, 161-168
    cognitive approach, 155, 161, 162, 168-169
    cognitive-behavioral therapy, 169-174
    drug therapy, 156-157, 158
    family interaction, 157
    family participation, 157-158
    family problem solving effectiveness, 158-161
    family problem solving logic, 155-156
    family problem solving training, 156-161, 200-203
    integration of, 156-157
    mental health, 155-156, 161-174, 179-180
    Metropolitan Area Child Study, 178
    parent education, 171-172, 180-182
    parent management training (PMT), 172-174
    Preparing for the Drug Free Years, 177
    prevention programs, 174-180
    primary prevention, 175-176, 177-178
    problem solving skills training (PSST), 172-174
    resistance to, 167
    role play, 170-171
    schizophrenia, 179-180
    secondary prevention, 176, 178
    strategic family therapy, 59-64, 67-68, 162
    success rates, 167-168, 172, 175, 180, 182
    Systematic Training for Effective Parenting, 181
    tertiary prevention, 176, 178-180
Twenty-minute problem solving, 137-138, 143, 144, 151

Uncertainty absorption, 98-99
Unfair rule structure, 113-114

Unmet needs, 152-155, 159, 169

Validation ritual, 125
Verbal behavior coding, 138, 146-147

Video-conferences, 204-205
Videotapes, 198-203

Williams, Tennessee, 4-6

About the Author

Sam Vuchinich is Associate Professor in the Department of Human Development and Family Sciences at Oregon State University. He was born in Pennsylvania and earned degrees at Indiana University (B.A. in Sociology) and the in University of Michigan (Ph.D. Sociology) with specialization in social psychology. He has published widely in family studies, developmental psychology, and related fields. Much of his work has focused on family conflict, the development of antisocial behavior, parent-child relations, and conflict resolution.